London Borough of Tower Hamlets

91000008055393

Dr Rosly ... ...e of the leading practitioners and trainers in interpersonal psychotherapy for adults and adolescents (IPT/IPT-A) in the UK, and Chair of IPTUK, the professional body for IPT and IPT-A therapists across the UK and Ireland. She is Deputy Director of Children and Young People's IAPT at University College London, which is part of a national programme to transform mental health services for young people by giving them access to evidence-based therapies and ensuring that they have a strong voice in how mental health services are organised and delivered. She is the IPT and IPT-A lead at the Anna Freud Centre, an internationally respected charity in which children and their families are supported to build on their own strengths to achieve their goals in life.

D1586784

WITHDRAWN

Also by Roslyn Law

Defeating Depression

Defeating Teenage Depression

Roslyn Law

ROBINSON

ROBINSON
First published in Great Britain in 2016 by Robinson

3 5 7 9 10 8 6 4 2

Copyright © Roslyn Law, 2016

The moral right of the author has been asserted.

All rights reserved.
No part of this publication may be reproduced, stored in a
retrieval system, or transmitted, in any form, or by any means,
without the prior permission in writing of the publisher, nor be
otherwise circulated in any form of binding or cover other than
that in which it is published and without a similar condition
including this condition being imposed on the
subsequent purchaser.

A CIP catalogue record for this book
is available from the British Library.

ISBN 978-1-47212-025-0

Typeset in Gentium by Initial Typesetting Services, Edinburgh
Printed and bound in Great Britain by CPI Group (UK) Ltd, Croydon CR0 4YY

Papers used by Robinson are from well-managed forests and
other responsible sources

MIX
Paper from
responsible sources
FSC® C104740

Robinson
An imprint of
Little, Brown Book Group
Carmelite House
50 Victoria Embankment
London EC4Y 0DZ

An Hachette UK Company
www.hachette.co.uk

www.littlebrown.co.uk

To Joanna, Michael, Mairi, Ciara,
Matthew and Chloe

Acknowledgements

Returning to my roots in working with young people has been an inspiring and challenging opportunity in recent years. I am very grateful to Peter Fuggle for the invitation to start this journey and to so many colleagues who have contributed to my re-education. Particular thanks to David Trickey who has challenged and inspired throughout. The therapists who have attended IPT-A practitioner and supervisor training courses have taught me a huge amount and I am very grateful for what they have contributed while they have been learning this approach. In particular, I would like to thank Bob Pritchard for his generous and thoughtful comments on the book, chapter by chapter, as it was being written. Thanks are also due to the young advisors at the Anna Freud Centre, Helena Miles, Ben Lejac, Rashaun Pacquette-Simpson, Alysha Buttress and Fran Dunn, who acted as my first editors, reading the book before it was submitted. Their comments gave me confidence and guidance for which I am very grateful. As ever my greatest thanks are to the young people and families who have shared their stories and difficulties and who have had the courage to ask for help.

Contents

Important note

Many of the templates and examples used in this
book can also be found online at
www.overcoming.co.uk

Chapter 1

How can other people help?

In this chapter you will learn about:

- Why it is important to involve other people when you use this book
- Why recovering from depression is a team effort and finding your team will be the first step away from depression and towards feeling better
- How IPT-A helps you to manage the problems that are often difficult for young people with depression

  ◊ Adjusting to unwelcome change
  ◊ Not getting on with someone who is important to you
  ◊ Learning to live with someone close to you dying
  ◊ Struggling to make or keep relationships going

In this chapter you will be asked to:

- Watch a short animation film about depression
- Make an IPT-A team list
- Watch a short animation film about depression with

1

> your IPT-A team or ask them to watch it to learn about how to help you
> - Start to think about how the common problems that are often difficult for young people with depression feature in your life

If you are reading this book you're probably not feeling great. You might be feeling sad, irritable and tired a lot of the time, and it's probably difficult to keep your mind on anything for long or see the point in doing things, even the things you used to enjoy. So it is quite something to suggest you read a book in order to feel better! Why do I think it might help?

The ideas I am going to describe to you in this book are based on a therapy called Interpersonal Therapy for Adolescents – IPT-A. An American psychologist, Laura Mufson, and her colleagues developed this treatment and they have used it to help lots of young people with depression. IPT-A focuses on sorting out the difficulties with other people that are so important for many young people with depression. That is why it is called *Interpersonal* – it is about what goes on between people. Research has shown that this approach is very effective in helping young people find a way out of depression and into better relationships. This book is going to walk you through how to use IPT-A and get the help you need.

What is depression?

Depression is a word most people know, but it is used in lots of different ways, which can be confusing. For now, here is a quick summary of the difficulties that lots of young people who have depression describe.

The main problems, sometimes called symptoms, relate to how you are feeling – feeling sad or irritable or not being interested in much a lot of the time – but depression also has an impact on how your body works, how clearly you think and how you feel about yourself and other people. You might notice that you are tired a lot or forgetful, perhaps you feel bad about yourself, even if you don't really know why, and think other people are a pain to be around. You might feel hopeless and wonder what the point is to anything.

Important things to remember about depression are that:

- It is an illness
- It is not your fault and
- It can be treated

If you find it difficult to concentrate when you are reading you might find it easier to watch a short animation that has been made to describe what it is like living with depression. The film, 'I had a black dog, his name was depression' was made by the World Health Organization and you can find it here:

www.youtube.com/watch?v=XiCrniLQGYc

3

Why is it a good idea to involve other people?

The world you live in is suddenly getting more complicated and might seem confusing at times. As an adolescent you are somehow meant to find a way to make sense of all the changes going on inside and around you and you are trying your best. What other people think, what you have to do to get on with them, and what you do when you don't get on with them are big issues when you are growing up. Lots of young people find these things difficult, even overwhelming at times, and this can make them vulnerable to becoming depressed. Once they are depressed the complex world of relationships with other people can seem even more confusing. With problems stacking up like this, it can be difficult to know what to do. IPT-A understands that the problem can run both ways – depression can set off problems with other people and not getting on with other people can be part of the reason you feel depressed.

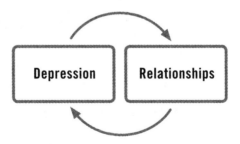

IPT-A looks at the day-to-day difficulties you are experiencing and helps you to sort out the inevitable problems with other people that develop when you are depressed. The basic aim is to help you to understand how depression and problems with other people are connected and to disentangle them. IPT-A deliberately focuses on what will be realistic and useful for you to try right now.

Using support from the people around you

There are some things that it will be useful for you to know so that the rest of this book makes sense to you. This isn't just opinion; it's what years of research has shown us.

- Depression is weakened when you have support from other people
- Talking to other people can help you to make sense of your-self *and* can help other people to understand you and give you more of the kind of support you need, when you need it
- Using support from other people isn't only useful now, it is an important skill that will protect and help you throughout your life

Depression does its best to persuade you that these things aren't true. It tells you that you will be better off on your own. That's why you want to spend so much time alone in your bedroom – you really do think it will help. You really are trying your best when you do the things depression tells you to do. The problem is that depression gives very bad advice. It knows that it is stronger when you are alone than when the people around you are supporting you, so it really doesn't want you to work that out. But, the secret is out!

Janine

Janine doesn't want to go to school. She can't get her head off her pillow because she stayed up until 3am trying to catch up on her homework – again. She went over the same question what felt like a hundred times and just couldn't get her mind to focus. She meant to concentrate but she got tempted to look at Facebook – just a quick look – to see what her friends were up to. An hour later she was still looking, even though it just made her feel worse because they were all having fun and she wasn't included.

She hasn't been going to school much recently because she doesn't want to stand out as the one who isn't keeping up. She thought it wouldn't make a difference but now there is even more to catch up on and it seems more impossible than ever. She thinks it is really unfair that, even though she is trying her best, she is so tired that anything she does isn't very good, so it all seems like a waste of time. That makes her feel even more anxious and down and her head sinks further into her pillow.

Because she has been missing school she hasn't seen her friends much and she imagines they are all coping much better than she is. She doesn't want to look stupid so she hasn't been answering their text messages and she has noticed that there haven't been so many messages recently. That makes her even more upset because it feels like they have just forgotten her and moved on. A couple of messages have sounded a bit angry and said something about Janine ignoring them. She hasn't known what to say to that so she just deletes the message, but then she feels even more stuck and alone.

When she finally makes it into school – three hours late – she meets one of her friends. At first Janine feels guilty and thinks her friend is going to be angry with her for not answering her messages – she is the friend who hasn't stopped sending texts. Janine is about to make an excuse, any excuse to get away, but before she has a chance her friend starts talking about how worried she is about the exams that are coming up. It's almost as if Janine isn't there, her friend just launches into what is worrying her. Janine is really surprised to hear the things she has been worrying about coming out of someone else's mouth.

After a few minutes Janine decides to take the risk of telling her friend a bit about how bad she has been feeling and is astonished to find that her friend understands some of it – mainly the bit about worrying about exams that her friend is feeling too. Her friend says she has been texting Janine to ask her to meet up so they could study together, because she finds it easier to learn things if she has someone there to talk to. For just a moment Janine feels less alone and that there might be a way to catch up. She likes the idea of having someone to ask about the things she doesn't understand instead of struggling on by herself. She decides to take the chance and agrees to start studying with her friend. For the first time in weeks she notices a smile on her face and some of the weight lifting off her shoulders.

What's the difference between Janine at the start of the story and at the end?

At first Janine's plan is to shut herself away and try to sort things out by herself. That means she has no support, her problems seem just as confusing as ever and she carries on feeling low and having sleepless nights. Depression thrives when you are facing it on your own.

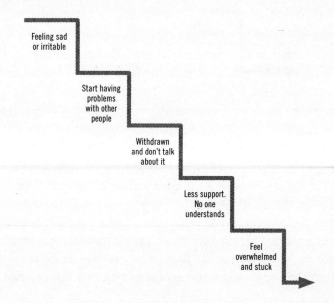

Later in the story, she talks about what is worrying her and discovers that someone understands and this makes it easier to work out what might help. This lifts her mood and makes her feel less alone. Depression struggles to keep going when you face it with the people in your life alongside you.

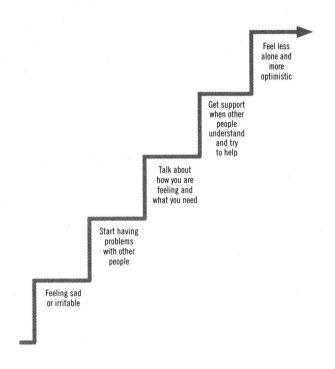

Feel less alone and more optimistic

Get support when other people understand and try to help

Talk about how you are feeling and what you need

Start having problems with other people

Feeling sad or irritable

This is why IPT-A is not a private therapy and you will get the most out of it if other people know what you are doing and are invited to help. This book contains lots of information and exercises to steer you towards feeling better, but most of what will help happens when you put the book down and put the ideas into practice with the people in your life. Recovering from depression is a team effort. This might feel daunting, but getting your team on side is the biggest step you can take away from depression and towards feeling better.

Finding your team

The members of your team should be the people you trust, who you can spend time with and feel able to talk with about your feelings. You might find it difficult to imagine who they are right now, especially if you don't want to be around other people. Depression is good at making you feel that way. That's OK, lots of people have to work out who is going to be on their team. You won't be forced to tell anyone on your team anything you do not feel ready to discuss, but it is useful to bear in mind that gentle encouragement when you are facing things that are difficult can be very helpful – in fact, research has shown that talking to other people improves mental health generally, not just when people are depressed.

Your IPT-A team are the people who will support and encourage you in the coming weeks. Your team might include your parents or carers, friends, other family members, a helpful teacher or your IPT-A therapist. The size of your team is up to you. You might feel more comfortable sharing what you are doing with just one or two other people, or you might want to tap into the different kinds of support available from a wider range of people. Just like on any other team it is a good idea if the people on the team contribute different things – you are unlikely to win the match if everyone is a striker and no one is playing in goal!

Your team can help you in a number of ways:

- **Company**: It's good to have someone to do things with, especially as it is going to be important for you to try to do things that you used to enjoy, because we know that helps to beat depression.

- **Understanding**: Feeling understood by another person is good for everyone and can be one of the best ways to understand yourself better. Each of the chapters in this book is broken up with a series of questions that help to develop your understanding. These will be most useful if you discuss them with the people on your team.

- **Practical help**: Some team members might know relatively little about what is troubling you but can still offer practical help that will really contribute to you feeling better. Young people often have to rely on the people around them for a lot of the practical things that make life possible, e.g. having a safe home, getting to and from places, having money, and it really helps to know who you can rely on.

- **Tracking progress:** It can be very helpful to have someone who knows what you are trying to achieve and who helps you to review your progress regularly. This might highlight successes that you hadn't noticed, help you to refocus if you get distracted and help you to think through the inevitable setbacks that will interrupt your progress at times.

Getting your team on side as soon as possible will help you to make the most of the ideas and information you are about to read. Talking to your team about what you read in this book will be very helpful. The questions below will help you to think about the people it might be useful to include. Don't worry if you can't answer all of them right now. The questions are designed to start you thinking about who could help and we will revisit this many more times in the chapters that follow. But do make sure you come back to these questions – IPT-A is much more effective when you use it with other people's support.

Exercise 1.1: Getting your team together

A word of warning before you read these questions – depression will whisper and then shout in your ear that no one is interested in you or cares about you. That is what depression does. But remember depression gives very bad advice. Take another deep breath and try hard to think about these questions. If it helps, imagine how you would have answered them six months before you started feeling depressed. It is amazing who and what depression can make us forget without us even noticing. Now, let's think about your team.

- Who would you like to be interested in how you are feeling?
- Who is interested in you feeling better and could help you to do that?
- Who do you talk to about how you are feeling?
- If you aren't talking to anyone right now, who have you talked to about how you are feeling in the past?
- Who would be willing to listen, even if you haven't tried talking to them yet?
- Who do you find it easiest to spend time with?
- Who comforts you when you are feeling sad or irritable?
- Who encourages you when you are finding things difficult?
- Who comes up with good ideas when you can't think what to do?
- Who would be interested in knowing about what you are trying to do with this book and would want to help?

Who did you think of when you answered those questions? Could you tell any of them that you are using this book to help you to feel better? To help you to do that, Appendices 1 and 2 have information for family and friends to read. Appendix 1 has information about IPT-A and Appendix 2 explains depression and suggests ways the people around you could help you to feel better. Ask the people who you would like to be on your team to read those pages. You might find it helpful to read them too.

 If it would be easier to watch a short film about how your team can help, you and each of the people on your team could look at another short animation film made by the World Health Organization, for people who live with someone with depression. It is called, 'Living with a black dog' and you will find it here:

www.youtube.com/watch?v=2VRRx7Mtep8

 Watching the film together can be a good way to start talking about how you have been feeling and the ideas in the film and in this book you think are helpful.

When you have some ideas about who could be on your team, create a team list and keep it somewhere easy to find, e.g. make a special team contact list on your phone. Add pictures, names, telephone numbers and email addresses to make it easy for you to contact the people on your team whenever you need them. The nursery rhyme, 'head, shoulders, knees and toes', is a simple reminder of who is good to have on your team:

Head – someone to help me to think about things

Shoulders – someone to lean on and a shoulder to cry on when I need it

Knees – someone to help me to do things and have fun with

Toes – someone to encourage me and give me a push when I need it

Eyes – someone to look out for me

Ears – someone to listen to me

Mouth – someone to talk to

Nose – someone to sniff out problems and help me to solve them

Try to include at least one person for each job, if you can, and add a note to remind you how each team member can help, e.g. listens to me, is good to spend time with, has good ideas. Remember you can add to this list later.

What kinds of problems can IPT-A help?

Depression typically doesn't just appear out of nowhere, and so IPT-A will help you to think about what you are going through in context – that is, in terms of what's going on with other people, to help you to make sense of how you are feeling. IPT-A is organised around four main themes, which capture common problems for many young people with depression. Often you will recognise more than one theme in your life, maybe two or three. That's really not unusual. Our lives are complicated. However it is important not to take on too much at once when you are depressed, and working on one problem often indirectly helps other areas of your life too. You will look at your depression and relationships very closely in the chapters that follow, and this will help you to work out which problems and relationships provide the most important backdrop to your story. This is at the heart of IPT-A – understanding the connections between depression and your relationships. The points at which symptoms and relationship difficulties overlap will become the focus for the rest of your IPT-A.

The four IPT-A themes are:

Adjusting to important change you are unhappy about

Examples including families splitting up, breaking up with a boyfriend or girlfriend, changing schools and adjusting to a physical health problem.

Not getting on with someone who is important in your life

Examples include fights with parents, friends or the person you are dating. It can also include not talking to someone close to you, like a brother or sister.

When someone close to you dies

Examples include a parent or grandparent or friend dying.

When it is difficult to make or keep friends

Examples include not having many friends, finding it difficult to talk to other people or falling out with people again and again.

Exercise 1.2: Organising your story

Do any of these difficulties feature in your life? Can you see any ways in which these problems contribute to how you have been feeling recently? You probably notice that some of the problems they describe overlap with others. Don't feel under pressure to pick one theme; we will spend time in the following chapters working out which difficulty will be most useful for you to focus on. For now, just notice if you can see anything of your own experience in the four themes. Talking it over with someone in your team might help you to think about this. If you can, show them the list and ask if they have any ideas about what has been affecting you.

Use the bubble diagram below to organise your story. You will find a copy online. Note down anything that has been happening in your life that fits with one of the themes. We will come back to this in each chapter to help you build up your story.

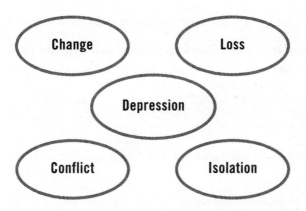

Knowing more about depression and how it differs from the typical highs and lows of being a teenager is important to understand – so this is where we will start in the next chapter.

Summary

- IPT-A is not a private therapy. It works with what goes on between people.
- IPT-A will help you to learn to disentangle depression and what is happening in your relationships with other people – relationships of all sorts, distant or close, fleeting

or long-standing. By positively tackling problems with other people, you can improve your depression and your relationships at the same time.

- IPT-A focuses on four interpersonal themes: change, conflict, loss and isolation.

Chapter 2

Understanding your depression

 In this chapter you will learn about:

- The symptoms and relationship problems that are common when someone is depressed
- How becoming an expert in your own depression can help you to interrupt the cycle of symptoms and increase your chances of feeling better sooner
- How talking to someone else about how you feel, sharing your successes and having support through setbacks increases your chances even more
- How the relationship skills you develop now can protect you against depression for the rest of your life
- The help that is available for young people: www.mycamhschoices.org

 In this chapter you will be asked to:

- Watch three films of young people describing their

> real experience of living with and recovering from depression
> - Colour in the symptom wall to describe your experience of depression and discuss what you can with your IPT-A team
> - Identify ways to give yourself a break and ask for help
> - Add your symptoms of depression to your bubble diagram

Nothing in life is to be feared, it is only to be understood. Now is the time to understand more, so that we may fear less.

Marie Curie, Nobel Prize-winning physicist

What is depression?

Feeling low or in a bad mood is something we all experience from time to time – it is totally normal and might be because your football team lost or someone let you down or all kinds of other reasons. We use lots of different words to describe these feelings – sad, unhappy, empty, fed up, irritated and sometimes depressed. This kind of depressed mood is typically unpleasant and doesn't last very long. With time or when the situation changes the emotional temperature goes up or down and you feel different. Most of the time this kind of mood doesn't seriously interfere with how you manage and you still go to school, see friends and do the things you normally do. Feeling low sometimes is just part of everyday life.

Occasionally, however, these feelings are more serious and you don't bounce back within hours or days. This type of low or irritable mood hangs around and it feels stronger than the passing sadness I described a moment ago. It is more difficult to change this kind of mood and it lasts even when your situation changes. When a low or irritable mood stays around for more than a few days it might mean there is a more serious problem, which is likely to have a greater impact on your life. You might start to notice that other things in life change too. Maybe you feel less interested in seeing your friends, or have difficulty sleeping. The longer the depressed mood lasts, the more likely it is that other difficulties will start to develop.

Leticia

Leticia is fourteen and lives with her mum and her little brother, Omar, who is seven. Her little brother needs lots of attention because he finds it really hard to sit still or concentrate on anything. Leticia feels guilty when she gets annoyed with him because her mum says he can't help it, but sometimes it is hard to remember that when he is being so annoying. Leticia is used to her little brother getting more attention from her mum than she does, and, until recently, she could always rely on dad to make up for that. Dad doesn't live with Leticia, he moved out when she was eight, about a year after her brother was born. Dad and his new wife had a baby six months ago and that means Leticia sees much less of him. She has been feeling lonely and scared, although she doesn't really understand why. She has been crying a lot and is irritable almost all of the time. It feels like everything and everyone annoys her. She doesn't like being away from home and spends a lot of time in her bedroom – she would stay there all the time if she could. This causes fights with mum because Leticia doesn't want to go to school but mum forces her to and that makes her even more irritable. Leticia doesn't want to go out with her friends because she doesn't want to be away from home if she doesn't have to be, but she worries that her friends will be annoyed with her so she doesn't reply to their text messages anymore because it is easier to ignore them than to have to try to explain. She hasn't been able to sleep properly for weeks, even though she is exhausted during the day. Schoolwork just seems impossible because she is too tired to concentrate or remember things. It makes no sense to her – she feels like she could fall asleep all day but then at night she is wide awake. She usually ends up looking at pictures of her dad's new family when he posts them online and this makes her feel worse and she worries dad won't want to see her anymore.

Entering adolescence can turn your world upside down and depression makes that much more confusing and difficult. Feeling depressed can be even worse when the people around you don't seem to know how to help or what to say. They might seem, and feel, as overwhelmed by what is going on as you feel inside. The world and the relationships you have with the people around you are more complex than they have ever been at any time in your life, and some people think that having to cope with so many changes and new demands during adolescence might explain why depression is more common at this age.

This seems to be happening for Leticia. She has had to cope with the change from being in one family to being in a separated family to now being part of two different families. All of this happened at the same time as her body is changing, she is more sensitive about her relationships than she has ever been before and her mind is clogged up with new thoughts and ideas and worries. She feels confused about who she is and where she fits in. The person she could rely on in the past, her dad, isn't around for her in the way he used to be and the person who has least time, her mum, is now the one she needs the most. She hasn't felt able to tell anyone how she is feeling and so no one has been able to reassure or help her and she is worn out by trying to cope with it all on her own.

This is the kind of situation in which depression can flourish. It is also the kind of situation in which IPT-A can help.

When problems start to cluster together, like sleeping too much, losing your appetite, not being able to concentrate and nothing seeming much fun anymore, it is possible that feeling down has become 'depression'. This is a well-recognised illness that often improves with time and can improve even more quickly with the right treatment. Typically, this kind of depression affects:

- How you manage day to day
- How you feel about yourself and other people
- How clearly you can think
- How much energy you have
- How hopeful you feel

If you think you are depressed it is important to talk about it to one of your IPT-A team and to consider talking to a professional, such as a therapist or your GP, who is trained to help. There is a lot that can be done to help with depression. This book will provide some of the help you need, but it is always more useful if you involve other people too. This website – www.docready.org – can help you prepare for going to see a GP for the first time to make sure you get the most out of your appointment. Ask your parent or carer to look at it with you to help you plan what to say and what to ask.

What do we know about depression?

A lot is known about depression and understanding how it

works can help you understand more about what's going on for you at the moment. The rest of this chapter sets out information about depression when it gets stuck. But don't worry – you are not expected to learn all of these details! Becoming expert in your own depression is not going to be like studying for an exam. Read through as much as you can manage and think about whether the things I describe match your own experience. You might find it easier to do this one section at a time: so you can use this chapter as a reference, something to dip into when you want to think about one part of the picture more closely. You can jump forward to the later chapters even if you have not read everything in this one, and then come back to it when you want a little more information. Lots of the information will be repeated in future chapters, so there will be plenty of opportunity to become familiar with the characteristics of depression as they are described here.

 In another short film, three young people describe their real experiences of living with depression and how therapy helped. You can find the film here:

www.bbc.co.uk/education/clips/zxqcd2p

This film and those I suggested in the previous chapter offer a good starting place for talking to the people on your team about how you are feeling – especially if you find it difficult to find the right words to describe what it is like. Let someone else do some of the talking for you and then you might find it easier to talk about what it was like to hear things you are living with described by someone else who has been through the same.

Exercise 2.1

Watch this film and ask the people on your team to watch it too – ideally watch it together – and talk about it afterwards:

- How many of the experiences described by the three young people do you recognise?
- Are there parts of your depression that they didn't mention?
- Can you tell your team about your experience and how they can help you?

Symptoms of depression

Depression has two signature symptoms – the things that really tell you that it is depression – as well as a number of other symptoms that are common but vary in the way different people experience them. Depression can be quite different from person to person. The table overleaf describes the common symptoms of depression.

The signature symptoms of depression are:

- Sadness or feeling low and irritable most or all of the time
- Feeling things aren't much fun anymore, even the things that you normally enjoy

Feeling sad or irritable Nothing is interesting or fun			
Problems sleeping	Can't remember things	Feeling guilty or to blame all the time	Problems at home
Eating too much or not enough	Can't concentrate	Feeling bad about myself	Problems at school
Feeling restless or wound up	Can't make up my mind	Feeling hopeless	Problems with friends and family
Feeling tired		Want to die	

Other common symptoms are:

- Disturbed sleep compared with your usual pattern. This might be difficulty in getting off to sleep, waking up through the night or early in the morning and not being able to get back to sleep
- Changes in your appetite. This often means having no appetite and losing weight without trying to, but for some people it might be the opposite and involves eating too much and gaining weight
- Feeling tired a lot of the time or having little energy, regardless of what you've been doing
- Feeling on edge or wound up, or the opposite, slowing down and finding it difficult to get moving or get started on anything
- Problems concentrating, feeling forgetfulness and finding it difficult to make up your mind. This might make it difficult at school or to follow what people are saying

- Feeling worthless or guilty about lots of things, even when you haven't done anything wrong
- Thinking about death and dying more often. For some people thoughts such as 'Life's not worth living' or 'I don't care if I don't wake up' appear in their minds more often. For a much smaller number of people this might develop into a plan to harm themselves

Several additional symptoms are also commonly described, and these are included in Exercise 2.2 below.

Symptoms alone aren't enough to be sure that depression is the main problem. How long the symptoms last and the impact they have on your life are also important. Depression is the most likely explanation if:

- You experience both of the signature symptoms and three or more of the other symptoms described above *and*
- Your symptoms upset you and interfere with how you manage day to day, such as making it harder to cope with schoolwork and getting on with your family or friendships; *and*
- Your symptoms trouble you most of the time, on most days and have lasted for at least two weeks; *and*
- Your symptoms are not a side effect of taking medication, or using drugs or alcohol or another physical condition

Some young people have fewer symptoms, perhaps just two or three of those we have looked at, but they last for a long time. That is called Persistent Depressive Disorder because a small number of symptoms persist over a long time. Sometimes young people fluctuate between the two – having more symptoms some of the time and not so many at others but never quite getting back to feeling entirely well over a couple of years. This is called Chronic Major Depressive Disorder because the recovery that typically happens within a few months of symptoms starting doesn't happen naturally. In both cases the young person will need treatment to help him or her to feel better rather than simply waiting for things to improve with time.

Depression is complex.

- Some symptoms are clear for anyone to see, such as appearing sad and tearful, looking exhausted, or losing weight
- Some symptoms are subtler and only become obvious because of their consequences, for example, struggling at school because you can't concentrate
- Others symptoms might be invisible to anyone other than the person who has them, such as feeling worthless or guilty

Because depression is a complex disorder and can affect people in so many different ways, it's important that if you think you might be depressed, you talk to someone close to you and ask them to go with you to see your doctor and have a proper assessment and diagnosis – that will confirm whether the problems you are experiencing are best described by calling them depression. The information in this section, and Exercise 2.2, will be useful in preparing to ask for the support you need. Follow the link to this website to find lots of information about what is available when young people ask for help with the difficulties they are experiencing www.mycamhschoices.org. It is not your fault that you are depressed, and the symptoms and effects described above make it obvious that depression is a very difficult condition to live with.

What is depression like for you?

You might have noticed that these descriptions focus on the problems that are common when someone has depression. However, personal experiences of depression differ from young person to young person and can change over time. Looking at the list of common symptoms above, you can see that one young person could be worked up, not eating and exhausted, while another might struggle to get going, go back to bed several times a day and eat to take their mind off their sadness. Both could be diagnosed with depression.

Alongside knowing about common experiences of depression, it is important to identify the specifics of *your personal experience*. Exercise 2.2 will help you pinpoint how depression is affecting *your* life.

Exercise 2.2: Identifying your symptoms of depression

This exercise works best if you use colours to describe your experiences, a bit like a traffic light system. This makes the picture of your experience of depression much easier to see. Use red, yellow and green highlighter pens to show how difficult each symptom is for you. The red marks the symptoms that bother you most, yellow marks those that bother you some of the time and green marks those that don't bother you much or at all. You might want to use more than one colour for some of the symptoms, e.g. half yellow and half green, if your experience is quite changeable. A completed example is available to look at online.

Go through the list in the symptom wall below and pick out the symptoms that you have noticed in yourself during <u>the last two weeks</u>. If you have noticed any other symptoms that are not on the list write them in the blank bricks at the bottom of the wall. Remember this is about you, so feel free to personalise the wall as much as you want. There aren't any right or wrong answers, only your answers. The more you can think about and describe how depression feels to you, the better chance you will have of understanding and changing it.

Feel sad	Feel tired a lot	Can't get to sleep	Not eating
Nothing is fun anymore	Wish I was dead	Feel guilty and blame myself for things	Problems with friends
Can't think clearly	Don't want to see people	Wake up early and can't get back to sleep	Feel bored
Problems at home	Sleep too much	Feel irritable	Feel restless and on edge
Feel bad about myself	Can't get going	Eat too much	Difficulties at school
Wake up during the night	Feel hopeless	Forgetful	Feel I have let other people down

If you don't have coloured highlighter pens, draw a circle around the symptoms that trouble you most or most often, <u>underline those that trouble you a bit or sometimes</u> and leave the symptoms that don't bother you very much unmarked. Sometimes you might not be sure how to mark some of the items described. That's OK, leave those items blank this time and you can add them later if you start to notice a change.

A completed example might look like this:

Feeling sad	Feel tired a lot	Can't get to sleep	Not eating
Nothing is fun anymore	Wish I was dead	Feel guilty and blame myself for things	Problems with friends
Can't think clearly	Don't want to see people	Wake up early and can't get back to sleep	Feel bored
Problems at home	Sleep too much	Feel irritable	Feel restless and on edge
Feeling bad about myself	Can't get going	Eat too much	Difficulties at school
Wake up during the night	Feel hopeless	Forgetful	Feel I have let other people down
Scratch my arms	Cry a lot		

Questions to talk about with your team:

- What did it feel like to fill in the symptom wall?
- What did you learn about your depression?
- Have any of the symptoms changed over time?
- Did anything surprise you about your answers e.g. more mixed than you expected or are there some green boxes that show there are things that you are still managing OK?
- Which situations or people came to mind when you thought about your symptoms?

- **Does that give you any clues about which of the IPT-A themes – change, conflict, loss and isolation – might be most relevant for you?**

Use the symptom wall to help you to talk to your IPT-A team about your experience of depression. Remember the depression handout in Appendix 2 and short films described earlier that will be helpful for your team to look at to help them to understand depression.

How to use the symptom grid in the weeks ahead:

- **Fill in a new blank wall chart once a week, while you are using this book, to help you to track your progress.** A blank copy is available in Appendix 3 and online. Just doing that increases the likelihood of you feeling better sooner. As you start to feel better you will start to see bricks in the wall that had been coloured in with red turn yellow and green, or circles and lines disappearing from the page.
- **Talk to someone on your team about how you are doing – that will increase the chances of feeling better even more.** Remember they can celebrate your successes with you, maybe even some you don't notice, and help you through setbacks. Recovery doesn't usually happen all at once, and trying again when it doesn't work first time is a really important part of breaking the hold depression can have on you.
- **Use the wall chart to become an expert in your own depression.** Your expertise will develop with practice; you will get much better at noticing when depression is creeping in and getting in the way of doing what you want. Knowing it is there and how it is affecting you is the first step to banishing depression from your life. It is understandable that you will want depression to go away as quickly as possible and you might hope and expect depression to follow a steady course

of improvement when you start working on it. For most people getting better is a mixture of staying steady, occasionally sliding backwards and being helped along a few steps at a time.

What do we know about depression?

If you agree that depression is a useful way to think about what is happening in your life it is helpful to know a bit more about it. Some of the frequently asked questions are answered below.

Who gets depression?
Depression can affect anyone, no matter what age, gender, intelligence or background. It is more common if someone else in your family has depression too.

How often does it happen?
About 2–4 per cent of children and around 4–8 per cent of teenagers have depression. Teenage girls are twice as likely to get a diagnosis of depression as teenage boys.

**What's the difference between being
sad and depressed?**
Depression is more than being sad. It changes your mood,
making you low or irritable a lot of the time, but it also changes
how you feel in your body, making you tired and slowing you down.
It makes it harder to concentrate or feel interested and you might
feel guilty or hopeless about your future or ever feeling better.
When you are sad you can feel better if something good
happens. This is harder to do when you are depressed.

What causes depression?
There is no single cause and often a mixture of things
contribute, such as stressful situations like bullying, big changes
like families splitting up, being isolated and not having someone to
talk to or losing someone you care about when they die. Being
neglected or treated badly when you were a young child increases
the chances of depression, as does being physically unwell.
Depression also runs in families so some people are vulnerable to
depression because of the family they were born into or grew up in.
Some people explain depression in terms of a chemical
imbalance in your brain that causes the symptoms.

How long will it last and will it come back?
Fifty per cent of young people recover within three to twelve months and 90 per cent within two years. Treatment can reduce the length of time a young person is depressed. Depression comes back within five years for 70 per cent of young people, but the chances of another episode of depression are reduced if it is treated effectively the first time it happens and if treatment is started quickly when symptoms return.

Is it dangerous?
Thinking about death and dying is a frightening part of depression for around one in five adolescents. For many young people with depression this is a way of wishing the bad feelings would stop and does not lead to harming themselves. Around 6 per cent of adolescents make a suicide plan but only half of that number act on it and many of them will not succeed in completing their plan. Girls are twice as likely as boys to make a suicide attempt but boys are more likely to complete the plan. Some young people act impulsively without a plan, especially if they are very anxious or using drugs including alcohol, which make behaviour less predictable. **It is very important to tell someone and get help if you feel this way. It doesn't mean you are going mad or are going to hurt yourself, but it does mean you need some extra support.**

If you are troubled by thoughts of dying or life not being worth living, there is help available twenty-four hours a day. You should contact your GP or Childline (call 0800 1111 or contact online at www.childline.org.uk) or go to your local A&E department. People who are trained to talk about these difficult feelings can offer immediate support and help you to think about the longer-term options for managing depression.

Which problems often go with depression?
We have already highlighted that problems in relationships with other people are very common when you are depressed. Up to 60 per cent of young people also have symptoms of other problems such as anxiety, behaviour problems (being aggressive or violent), deliberate self-harm (such as cutting or burning), and substance misuse problems. It can sometimes be difficult to tell which problem comes first, e.g. lashing out when you feel frustrated and sad or drinking alcohol to take away bad feeling. Treating depression is likely to help and can make it easier to manage other problems, but sometimes the other problems need special treatment too.

What will help?
Lots of young people recover within a few months without any treatment. However for some young people it takes longer and needs treatment for depression to improve. Talking therapies, like IPT-A, Cognitive Behavioural Therapy (CBT) or Family Therapy, and anti-depressant medication have all been shown to be helpful and speed up recovery.

Why is this important to know?

Untreated depression in adolescence increases the risk of:

- Misusing drugs, including alcohol
- Having difficulty making and keeping close relationships
- Underachieving in school
- Deliberately self-harming
- Being depressed as an adult

Identifying depression and doing all you can, with the help of the people around you, is therefore very important for the quality of your life now and for your future.

 In these two films two young people talk about the difficulties they faced with self-harm and feeling suicidal when they were depressed. They both got help when they talked to someone and you can do the same if depression affects you in this way. You can find the films here:

www.bbc.co.uk/education/clips/zhjgkqt

www.bbc.co.uk/education/clips/zn7cd2p

Remember depression is treatable, even when you feel really bad and can't think of any other solution than to hurt yourself, and it is important that you tell someone how you feel. IPT-A can help when you are feeling this way but you should use it with an IPT-A therapist who is trained to understand and help you to cope with how you feel without damaging your body.

An IPT-A therapist can help you to build your skills and resilience to overcome the problems depression creates in your life.

Many young people will not know that what they are experiencing is depression. Depression often goes unnoticed, and only about half of all people with depression are diagnosed by their GPs. Why might depression be overlooked?

- Thinking it is normal to feel this way
- Believing you are being weak or lazy
- Being told you are just a typical teenager
- Depression in boys might be especially vulnerable to being missed because boys are more likely than girls to act out their distress and problems in their behaviour and conceal the distress they feel inside
- Confusing the symptoms of depression with another physical illness and missing the emotional impact
- Substance misuse can conceal the distress someone is feeling inside

The risks of blaming yourself or being misunderstood in these ways are all good reasons for becoming your own expert. When you know what depression looks like and feels like you can talk about it and ask for the help you need, when you need it.

Becoming an expert and starting your own recovery

IPT-A takes a 'no blame' approach. Depression is real but it's not your fault that you are depressed, and blaming yourself or feeling blamed by others won't help you to get better – in fact, it will probably make you feel worse! However, 'no blame' is not the same as 'no consequences' and it is likely that you are experiencing difficulties in a number of areas of your life, including with family and friends and at school.

Three very important points to remember:

- It is important to get you well as quickly as possible
- It is just as much in other people's interests for you to be well as it is in your own
- *It is entirely reasonable to ask other people to help you to feel better*

These are really important points to emphasise. Lots of young people who have depression know that help is available but struggle to ask for it. You might worry about what people will think of you or that you will seem like a nuisance. That's another example of the bad advice depression gives you – 'keep quiet, suffer on your own'. Don't listen! Letting other people know how you are feeling and letting them help you when it is hard to help yourself is one of the best things you can do to start to feel better. You already started to do this when you thought about the people who could be on your team.

 If you haven't watched the film with **3 young people** talking about their depression, watch it now and you will hear how important talking to other people was in helping them to feel better.

You can find the film here:

www.bbc.co.uk/education/clips/zxqcd2p

Exercise 2.3: Giving yourself a break and asking for help

Now let's start to get that team working for you. Try to answer the following questions:

- Who could you ask for help?
- Could you ask anyone on your team for help?
- What could you ask them to do for you?
- What do you need to keep doing because it helps you to feel better, even if it is only for some of the time?
- What could you stop doing, just until you felt better, because it is especially difficult or draining for you just now?

The people who come to mind when you answer these questions are the people it would be useful to talk to about your depression. The things that you thought of changing are your own personal examples of 'anti-depressant activity', which we will think more about in the next section. In Appendices 1 and 2 you will find information to share with the people in your life. The information explains about depression and the valuable role the people in your life can play in supporting you to feel better. Read over this information yourself and pass copies on to them. This is homework for your parent or carer and your team. Get them working!

Give yourself a break and have some fun

An important part of feeling better is deliberately searching out the 'anti-depressant activities' that you can do – those are the things you enjoy doing and that lift your mood, however briefly.

One of the most characteristic signs of depression, as you now know, is having less interest in people and doing things, and enjoying the things you do and the people you see much less than normal. Depression whispers bad advice in your ear and in no time you are doing less and not seeing anyone. It's no wonder life seems boring if you deliberately cut out all the things you used to enjoy. It seems obvious when you think about it like that.

So the weird thing is you have to start doing things and being around other people *before* you feel like it in order *to* feel like it. It is tempting to try to tackle this the other way round, that is, to say: 'When I feel better I'll do more, see more people, try new things.' Unfortunately, depression doesn't work like that – it's *through* doing more, seeing more people and trying new things that you will start to feel better.

I admit, this doesn't sound like a great plan at first glance! But, what you are doing is giving yourself the *chance* of feeling better, a spark of interest, a hint of fun. Admittedly at first this might be little more than a spark – like a camera flash that briefly lights up a space and lets you glimpse what is there before the darkness returns. Gradually you will start to find that, instead of just a single flash, you might have a cluster of flashes that keep the light on for a little longer. You might be able to string some of these together, or start to regain a sense of control over making the flash light up. Depression is good at robbing you of both your sense of control and your sense of hope, and it's understandable that after a while you stop trying, but those people and activities that you once enjoyed are the things that could turn that around. IPT-A is about creating those opportunities again and asking your team to help you do that.

It is a bit like waiting for a bus. If you want to catch a bus you go to the bus stop because you know the bus will pass there. You might have to wait a while but it will come past eventually. Doing the things you used to enjoy is like standing at the pleasure bus stop. You might have to wait a while but it is where you are most likely to catch an opportunity to have fun.

What can you start doing right now?

- Say yes when your friend asks you to do something
- Make plans to see a friend
- Eat more healthily to give your brain the fuel it needs
- Go for a run or a walk
- Read a book you really like
- Play your favourite music and dance to it
- Watch your favourite film
- Watch YouTube videos that make you laugh
- Laugh for no reason

Exercise 2.4

Write the main symptoms of depression that are troubling you in the centre circle of your bubble diagram. You will find a copy in the online folder.

Summary

- Depression is a recognised and treatable illness that is more common as young people leave childhood and enter adolescence
- Depression is more than just feeling sad. It disrupts how you feel, how you think, how your body works and what you do at school, at home and with your friends
- Many people experience depression more than once, and it is often a condition to manage rather than cure. The ideas and ways of managing depression that you learn now can help you for the rest of your life
- Difficulties in relationships, or the lack of them, can contribute to depression. Sorting out those problems can protect you against depression
- Tracking symptoms on the grid each week (using the form in Appendix 3) will help to develop your expertise in managing your depression
- IPT-A takes a 'no blame' approach towards thinking about depression
- Understanding and accepting depression is the first step in recovery
- Working towards recovery is a priority
- Recovery is a team effort

Chapter 3

It's all in your head . . . and that's a good thing

 In this chapter you will learn about:

- How your brain works and how it changes during adolescence
- How the things you do shape the way your brain grows
- How changes in your brain affect your sleep and what you can do about it
- Why adolescence is the best time to learn about relationships
- Why adolescents take risks and when this is great and when it is dangerous

 In this chapter you will be asked to:

- Watch a video about the mysterious workings of the adolescent brain
- Watch a video about why we sleep
- Watch a video about how adolescents make decisions and why you take risks

- Watch a film about young people who experienced and recovered from addiction
- Watch a film about young people talking about their experience of binge drinking
- Watch a film about adolescent brain development with your parents or carers

This chapter is all about how beautiful, amazing and wonderful your brain is right now. As an adolescent you are brimming over with potential and possibility, and a big part of that is because your brain is doing such fantastic things. People used to think that an adolescent brain was a not very good version of an adult brain. Now we know better. Your brain is astonishing, wired up differently to adults' brains and still developing.

First of all let's cover the basic things you need to know to understand how brilliant your brain is. There is a lot going on in there.

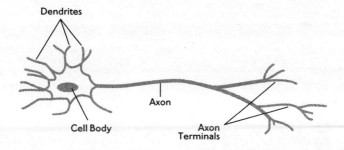

Every human brain has around 86 billion neurons, sometimes called nerve cells. A neuron is a cell that processes and transmits information by passing tiny electrical currents. The current travels from the cell body along its axon, which is a bit like the tail, and then these signals leap across tiny gaps at the axon terminals (called synapses) – a bit like bus terminals only much, much smaller! The signals are picked up in the dendrites of neighbouring neurons – the dendrites are the branches reaching out from the cell body that receive messages from other neurons. You can see it all in the picture on page 43.

A hundred billion neurons might seem a lot, and of course it is, but unlike other cells neurons don't divide to make new cells, because they are designed to last a lifetime. However, only some of them will, and your adolescent years are vital in deciding which neurons make the journey through life with you. Neurons are sociable cells – each neuron is connected to up to around 10,000 other neurons and the more they 'talk' to each other the more likely it is that that neuron will stay active and talk to the neurons around it for the rest of your life. It is a bit like having your own social network in your head.

When we are born we already have almost all the neurons we need – a baby has about 95 per cent of the neurons it will ever have – but we don't yet have a well-developed system of connections between them. So when a neuron fires in a baby there aren't many places for the signal to go. That's why babies can't do very much when they are born. But have you noticed how quickly a baby learns? That is because new connections are growing between the neurons all the time, helping the baby to learn and remember, wiring it up to its body and the world. Each time the baby does something new, dendrites and synapses are created, and every time the baby repeats that thing – smiling at mum, reaching out to grab something, taking those first wobbly steps – the connections get stronger. Important messages move around the brain more easily when they have been practised because each repetition strengthens and multiplies the connections. During adolescence there is another major surge and then loss of connections going on inside your brain, this time deciding which of those connections will serve you for the rest of your life.

Making connections

The brain is made up of white and grey matter. The grey matter, which forms the thin, wrinkled outer layer that is wrapped around the brain (the cortex), contains the neurons and dendrites and processes information (the brainy bit). The white matter is made up of the connections between the different parts of the brain, the long axons running between neurons. Scientists have measured these connections and found that the total length of axons in the human brain is 176,000 km – that's long enough to wrap around the earth's equator four and a half times! No wonder it looks wrinkled squashed up there inside your head.

Mirror Neuron

Our brains don't only learn from what we do but also from watching what other people do. This is the job of mirror neurons. Your brain is so keen to learn it starts practising while you watch someone do something you haven't tried yet. The mirror neurons in your brain fire up in exactly the places they would be needed if you were doing the thing yourself, making it a little easier when you try. We used to think this was only true for physical actions but we now know it applies to feelings and sensations and is a building block for empathy and imagining someone else's experience. This makes the environment you live in very important. If you see good examples you learn from them. However, if you see bad examples you are just as likely to learn from them too.

45

Imagine what a child will learn if he is comforted and soothed when he is upset rather than being smacked and told to be quiet. His brain will learn what to expect and how to behave towards other people and the way he was treated will provide a template in his brain circuitry for how he will behave towards other people in the same situation.

 Watch this film to learn more about the neurons that shaped civilisation here:

www.ted.com/talks/vs_ramachandran_the_
neurons_that_shaped_civilization?language=en

Grey matter grows rapidly when you are around eleven if you are a girl and twelve if you are a boy, thickening the dendrite branches around each neuron. We could say that your brain is getting ready to handle the more complex life you are about to start leading. However not many of the white matter connections are in place across your brain by then and they will continue growing to link up the different parts of your brain until your mid-twenties. They continue to grow for the rest of your life too but at a slower pace. Your brain works best when the grey matter in different regions is well connected by the white matter. This is a big job and is mostly completed over the years of your adolescence, so you don't wake up one morning to find yourself remodelled and ready for the adult world. It takes time and can be a bit bumpy when your brain is still under construction.

Living through this 'work in progress' can be tricky because the remodelling doesn't happen at the same time across your brain. Your brain develops from the inside out and from the bottom up.

It is a bit like having all the parts of a really great entertainment system but not having it wired up yet, so you can turn on the TV but the sound system is either on full volume or muted, the Internet link is slow and you can't find the remote control. The lower part of your brain, called the limbic system, is like the sound system. It processes your experience of emotions like fear, anger, anxiety, disgust and happiness, sensations and gut reactions and is wired up much earlier than the higher parts of your brain that are to do with planning, attention, seeing things from different points of view and judging whether something is appropriate or not. The higher brain is like the missing Internet link and remote control. The higher part of the brain most involved in those activities is called the prefrontal cortex (PFC), and it sits just behind your fore-head. In an adult brain the PFC is very active and well connected and it helps to regulate activity in the limbic system, sometimes motivating and sometime calming it down (volume control and switching channels). In teenagers, the limbic system is much more active and relatively few connections are made to the PFC until the final stages of adolescence, which isn't until your mid-twenties, so in contrast to the full-volume limbic system the PFC operates on a whisper and its messages are often missed.

It's not that adolescents can't make good decisions or have no impulse control, but rather that the ability to use that control *consistently* doesn't develop until later when the PFC is fully wired up. This kind of control is especially shaky when emotions are running high. In emotionally charged situations you might be just as surprised by what you say and do as the people around you. The reward system in your brain, which is especially sensitive to positive signals from your peers, appears to hijack the relatively poorly connected and poorly insulated control centre. That's why sometimes you find it difficult to control how you are feeling and questions like, 'Is this a good idea?' occur to you a long time after you have already done the thing with your friends that looked like it would be fun. Meanwhile the adults around you are wondering, 'What were you thinking?' Your brain is wired up differently, so you sometimes don't see things in the same way. In an adolescent's brain, in the heat of the moment, it is a bit like stamping your foot on the accelerator before you have worked out where the brake pedal and the steering wheel are. The occasional crash is pretty much inevitable but doesn't have to be fatal. The main point is that teenage brains aren't fully wired up yet, often making it more difficult to resist fun even when you know there will be a price to pay, consider different points of view and regulate how you feel. This point is really important.

Use it or lose it

Just before puberty the brain gets really busy and makes lots more connections (dendrites) than you will actually need. Although having lots of connections might seem like a good thing the mass of connections has to be tidied up and organised to be of most use to you – this is called synaptic pruning. Imagine pruning a plant so that the weak stems are cut away to help the stronger ones to grow and you have the idea. The neurons you use most survive and get stronger and those you use least fade away. Before that happens an adolescent's brain has to work harder than an adult's to do things like judging someone else's intentions. It may be because the connections are not very efficiently organised that there is much more widespread brain activity in adolescents' brains than in adults', which have learnt to fast-track. In fact, during synaptic pruning you lose up to 50 per cent of the neurons and synapses you have been so busy making for years. You literally lose about half your brain! Don't worry, this is entirely normal and helps you to become quicker and better at doing the important things you need to do now and in the future, **BUT** that does rely on you doing those things during your teenage years.

This process of selecting some pathways and letting others fade away makes the brain increasingly integrated and efficient, and surviving neural connections become even better at transmitting information because they are wrapped in a fatty coating called myelin. This is like insulation around the connections, protecting them against interference and background noise and allowing nerve impulses to travel around the brain more quickly and efficiently. Think of it like fibre optic broadband replacing dial-up and wire cables. It makes a big difference!

 As interesting as all of this is, it might be easier to follow when you listen to someone talking about it. This Ted Talk on 'The mysterious workings of the adolescent brain' gives a great overview:

www.ted.com/talks/sarah_jayne_blakemore_the_mysterious_workings_of_the_adolescent_brain?language=en

Sleep

Sleep is often a big issue for teenagers, typically not getting enough of it. This can lead to unfair stereotypes of teenagers being lazy and staying in bed all day. I am not saying you don't like to have a long lie-in, but there is a reason for it and it isn't as simple as laziness. Our bodies follow circadian rhythms that tell us when to sleep and when to wake up. This is your body clock, which makes it harder to sleep when the clock is ticking and harder to stay awake when the clock switches off. This clock is reset in adolescence and it is set to sleep for longer. This body clock change is natural, it is giving your brain and body more time to grow, but it can leave you feeling out of sync with the world and if your body clock isn't working, day and night-time start to get confused.

The brain produces a hormone called melatonin to help ease you to sleep, and studies have shown that this is released around two hours later for adolescents than it is for adults and it stays in your system for longer, which is why you want to go to sleep late and struggle so much to wake up in the morning. This hormone doesn't just knock you out, it doesn't work like a sleeping tablet, but if you work with it by having a wind-down routine it can make it easier for you to sleep when it will be of most use to you.

Here comes the problem. Adults need, on average, around seven to eight hours of uninterrupted sleep to function adequately during the day. As a teenager you need closer to nine and a quarter hours of uninterrupted sleep each night. This isn't only a problem because it is unpleasant to drag yourself out of bed when you are still convinced that it isn't time to get up yet (and you are right!). Your brain is doing a lot of work while you are asleep and that is being interrupted too. Brain scientists have shown us that the sleeping brain – far from resting – is getting down to a busy night at work, practising what you did while you were awake. You don't simply need more sleep to get you ready for the day but also for:

- Your brain to grow well (pruning and myelination)
- Your immune system to work to keep you healthy
- Your metabolism to work effectively to prevent unhealthy weight gain
- Memories to be consolidated from the day before and available for the day after and therefore learning to take place
- Managing stress

- Developing cognitive control for paying attention, problem solving, connecting with other people and regulating your emotions

Like I said, your brain is busy while you are asleep! So everything would be OK if most adolescents were tucked up in bed by 10.30pm every night, but obviously they aren't – most of them aren't even sleepy yet. In fact many adolescents describe being much more awake at night than they are in the morning and so the end of the day often extends late into the night and early morning, all the time eating into the nine and a quarter hours of sleep you need. This can be understood to an extent by the change in body clock and late release of melatonin, but routinely staying up until 1 or 2 am or later usually also has a lot to do with the dizzying array of digital stimulation from phones, TVs and computer screens to game consoles that is confusing your brain by telling it to stay awake. Given all that activity into the small hours, it is no wonder that adolescents struggle so much to get out of bed in the morning – it is effectively still the middle of the night.

Much of the work your brain has to do during the night happens when you are in REM (rapid eye movement) sleep, which is when you dream and reorganise the information from the day. If you have fewer hours of this stage of sleep, by staying up late into the night, or being interrupted by, for example, text messages or flashing lights on games consoles it can have some serious and unwanted effects:

- Learning slows down or doesn't happen
- Anxiety increases (more stress hormones are released)
- Depression increases, including an increase in suicidal thoughts
- Risk of physical health problems increases

51

- More likely to gain weight
- Poorer concentration
- Poorer memory
- Feeling overly emotional
- Less able to cope with difficult situations
- Clumsy and more prone to injury
- More sensitive to pain

 If we compare this list with the symptom grid completed in Chapter 2 you can see why not getting enough sleep plays such a big part in depression and how easily it can contribute to having problems with the people around you. This is always an important target for change in treating depression and it can have a huge positive effect when sleep disturbance is reversed. Look at Appendix 4 for ideas on how to improve your sleep and watch this video to understand 'Why do we sleep?' here:

www.ted.com/playlists/223/talks_to_inspire_you_to_go_to

Adults used to think that over time adolescents 'grow out of it', as if adolescence is simply a phase that you go through and you just have to wait it out. Actually it may be more accurate to say that adolescents **grow into it**. Scientists still aren't sure but it may be that instead of your brain catching up with what you need to do as an adult, overcoming a developmental time-lag, actually your brain is shaped by your experiences and it develops in a way that reflects what you do. If that's true then the choices you make and the things you do as an adolescent will determine how easy you will find doing those things as an adult. This gives you an important say in your own future. If you spend your adolescence joining in and making friends, solving problems, being creative, playing sport, playing music, exploring new ideas and perspectives your brain will be wired up to do those things throughout your life. If, on the other hand, you watch hours and hours of TV, spend a lot of time on your own playing on your phone, eat fatty foods and take no exercise your brain will be wired up to do those things for the rest of your life instead. Learning to do the things you didn't do as an adolescent won't be impossible but it will be harder, so this is the time to give yourself a head start. Your really do have a choice in the shape of your brain and those choice are the ones you are making right now – **use it or lose it!**

Your social brain

The parts of your brain that are most important for forming and maintaining relationships are sometimes described as your 'social brain'. Here is a brief summary of some of the things these parts of your brain allow you to do:

- Recognise people
- Consider someone else's perspective
- Feel a range of emotions
- Recognise and interpret social signals
- Create a story to make sense of what you and other people do
- Learn from observing and experience
- Understand someone else's feelings
- Control attention, thinking and feeling
- Judge costs and benefits

It would be far too simplistic to suggest that there are individual parts of your brain that are responsible for each of these activities separately. In fact the process is much more in keeping with its name – the social brain works because different parts of your brain 'speak' to each other. The PFC, which you have already learnt about, is central to many of these conversations. As we know, connections to and from this part of your brain are developing during adolescence, and these connections follow the pathways you use most, so you can see how important the way you behave now will be for the quality of your relationships with other people now and in the future. This is the perfect time to learn and make the social connections you need and your brain is as ready as it will ever be to do that.

Your social brain will also help you to answer the questions you have about who you are, what kind of person you are, what you believe in, how you fit in etc. Many of these questions are very social in their nature even though they might feel like they are all about you. Just as babies discover who they are by seeing themselves reflected in their parents' faces, so adolescence is a time when you will discover yourself by looking at and learning from the people around you.

In order to learn about yourself and create your place in the world you start to move away from the familiar and branch out into the unknown, uncertain and at times unsafe. The necessity of exploring in order to learn helps us to understand the shift from a stable family focus in younger children to an expanding friends focus in adolescents. This is a kind of survival instinct. Human beings are social creatures so being happy and succeeding in life depend at least in part on being able to go out into the world, form relationships and be part of the group. It makes sense, therefore, that what the people around you think of you will be important. An adolescent's inbuilt curiosity is a great incentive to go out and try new things and be open to new ideas and possibilities – exactly the kinds of things it is important to do at this stage in your life and why adolescence is such a creative and exciting time.

Recognising emotions

An important part of becoming socially skilled is being self-aware while also imagining what someone else is thinking and feeling. This is sometimes called mentalising and has been described as seeing yourself from the outside and others from the inside. Imagine yourself being like a film director, switching camera angles and moving inside and between the characters to capture a range of different perspectives (we will come back to this idea in Chapters 8 and 10). This requires imagination and interpretation.

None of us are mind-readers, although we might be tempted to think we are and we have probably all met people who are sure that they are. Have you ever said, 'I know what you are thinking' or had someone say it to you? In reality we can't know how other people see us or really know what it is like to be them but every single day we are asked over and over again to try to guess as best we can. It is the basis of all of our interactions: Does this person understand me? Do I understand him? Does he want to be here with me? Does he think I am stupid? Do I trust him? Are we talking about the same thing? The list goes on and on and runs through our minds more or less explicitly much of the time. When we ask these questions and have an idea of the answers we are mentalising. When we ask the questions but have no idea what the answers are or, even more extreme, when we don't even ask the questions, we are not mentalising. The more we mentalise the better shape our relationships will be in because we will be trying to hold each other in mind – this is the basis of great teamwork. The less we mentalise the greater the risk that we will be overwhelmed when things change, we get into conflict, we lose people and we feel isolated and disconnected from the people around us. One of the core objectives in IPT-A is to help you to mentalise better and more consistently to help you to navigate your way through common relationship problems.

In order to mentalise you have to be able to continue to think when faced with emotional information. As we have already seen, this is a real challenge for some adolescents, especially in emotionally charged situations, such as trying to work out what someone is feeling. When adolescents try to guess what another person is feeling they actually use a different part of their brain to an adult trying to do the same thing. Emotional triggers, like facial expressions and tone of voice, communicate directly to the emotional centre of a teenager's brain, bypassing the reasoning centre on the way. Adults mostly use the thinking part of the brain (PFC) because they are working out how to respond, while adolescents' brains light up in the amygdala, the emotional centre. This is the difference between a gut reaction (which happens quickly and instinctively) and responding (which is slower and more considered).

Interestingly, not only do adolescents use different parts of their brain to read emotions, they also come up with different answers, at least for some feelings! The facial expression for fear is especially vulnerable to being misread, and about half the time it gets mixed up with shock, sadness or confusion by adolescents. This raises the possibility that when adolescents are talking to their parents or teachers, they may be misperceiving or misunderstanding some of the feelings that are being displayed. Importantly they may see anger when there isn't anger, or sadness when there isn't sadness, i.e. threat when there isn't a threat. This information makes it easier to understand the common complaint between adults and adolescents when they talk to each other i.e. the adolescent feeling justified in flaring up when it seems to be for no apparent reason from the adult's point of view. In the adolescent's brain there is a perfectly good reason – he has registered a possible attack by seeing shock and anger in his parent's concerned and worried face and is defending himself. If we hold in mind what is going on in the adult's brain and the adolescent's brain at the same time (mentalising) this kind of miscommunication becomes much easier to understand and hopefully to manage. We will come back to this in Chapters 8, 10 and 12.

Imagine the difference it could make to your life as an adult if you started practising reading emotional cues and interpersonal signals now, when your brain is wide open to learning exactly that kind of thing. Adolescence is the best time to learn how to be around other people and get close to them. Your brain is going to be most forgiving of the mistakes you make and most rewarding of your success now and in the future. We will look at this in more detail in Chapter 8. Surely that isn't an opportunity to miss!

Making decisions and taking risks

The curiosity that characterises healthy adolescence is largely driven by a neurotransmitter called dopamine, which is responsible for many of the good feelings you have. Every time it is released, rewarding you for doing something new or exciting, it makes it more likely that you will do the same thing again because it feels good. During adolescence this reward system works differently than it does in adults and children. When nothing much is happening, levels of dopamine are lower in adolescents, which is why you feel bored, but reward levels when you do something new are much higher than in adults, especially if the things you have been doing involve other people. This means good experiences with friends, like being the one to make everyone laugh, feel better for adolescents, and bad experiences, like being left out, feel worse. This makes adolescents super sensitive to even subtle changes with other people, including just being watched by them, because they provoke intense changes in how you feel, which you don't always feel able to control or think your way around.

This might be why some adolescents take potentially dangerous risks, especially when their friends are around and even when somewhere in the back of their mind they know the likely consequences. This is a really powerful effect and adolescents who take no more risks than adults or children when they are alone take twice as many risks when they know their friends are watching. The thrill of the fun and the threat of being left out are more powerful than knowing there might be a price to pay somewhere down the line. The decision-making part of the brain is effectively anaesthetised by the drive for reward and being a part of the group. Decisions are biased towards excitement rather than safety because the positive high is more compelling and persuasive than possible consequences, which are downplayed. This isn't a thought-through process – that's the point – the thinking-through part of your brain is on a whisper while the feel-good part is on full volume. It is useful to remember that adults and adolescents work on a different scale of reward and incentive and this can make it difficult for you and your parents or carers to understand each other's choices.

This exaggerated and socially inclined reward system in adolescents helps us to understand why you:

*   Try more new things and act impulsively
*   Take more risks
*   Are more influenced by friends

 Watch this video to get an insight into how adolescents make decisions and why you take risks:

www.youtube.com/watch?v=LWUkW4s3XxY

As exciting as all of this can be it can also lead to problems when the time-lag between your ready-to-go limbic system and whispering PFC result in taking dangerous risks. This can go badly wrong for some adolescents who get drawn into taking dangerous risks, very often because they are encouraged to do so by their peers.

Risks of addiction

The downside of learning so well in teenage years is that you are also more vulnerable to the effects of drugs and alcohol than adults. Drugs and alcohol have a greater effect on teens than adults and the effects last longer. This is why, although adults typically drink more than teenagers, teenagers are more likely to binge drink. Some of that is to do with opportunity but it is also to do with the adolescent's reward system. When you like something you REALLY like it and your PFC isn't wired up to set limits on you in the way that it is in adults. This has serious implications and produces some frightening statistics. During adolescence the risk of all of the following significantly increase:

*   Reckless driving resulting in death and injury

- Unprotected sex leading to STDs, including HIV
- Alcohol and drug abuse
- Smoking

The effects of drugs also hang around in an adolescent's brain for longer than they do in adults, which is important to know if you are tempted to chill out with a drink or by using drugs in the days leading up to an exam. The drug will interfere with your learning and memory and will lead to a worse performance *days* later. An even more frightening finding is that drug and alcohol use in adolescence is a strong predictor of drug and alcohol problems as an adult. Remember your brain is primed and keen to learn and will shape itself to do whatever you do now more easily in the future.

 In this short film three young people who developed addictions talk about the impact it had on their lives and how talking to the people in their lives and to professionals helped them to make different decisions:

www.bbc.co.uk/education/clips/zcbhyrd

In this series of four short films four young people describe their real experiences of the consequences of binge drinking: falling out with friends, life at risk, physical assault and sexual assault:

www.bbc.co.uk/programmes/p015dny5

www.bbc.co.uk/programmes/p015dp6c

www.bbc.co.uk/programmes/p015dnkq

www.bbc.co.uk/education/clips/z274wmn

What has all this got to do with IPT-A?

The good news is that adolescence is the perfect time to become an expert and really good at something because your brain is primed to learn through all the super-efficient connections left after synaptic pruning that are now wrapped in myelin. That means that becoming an expert in your own depression is easier for adolescents than adults, and you will practise doing that when you track your symptoms carefully each week with the symptom grid. If you can talk to your team about how you are feeling and ask how they think you are doing you will have a weekly opportunity to build those mentalising connections too.

Similar opportunities will come up in the chapters that follow when you map out your relationships and your story of being depressed. Each time you do that you will be asked to involve other people and to learn from what they have noticed about you. This will help you to understand your own experience more clearly by gathering new information you might not have imagined before and practising holding others in mind while you learn more about yourself.

When you use the other techniques in IPT-A, you will be encouraged to pay attention to what other people are thinking and feeling while also becoming more aware of your own thoughts and feelings to help you with interpersonal problem solving. Because we know that adolescents find this kind of thing difficult to do at times and are more likely to misread facial expressions like fear and to overlook the other person's perspective we will slow this process down and offer step-by-step guidance on how to manage these kinds of situation. IPT-A can't speed up brain development but it can make sure that if you use the ideas in this book you will be laying down just the kind of information superhighways you will need in your brain for successful and satisfying relationships across your life.

By highlighting and explaining predictable problems, IPT-A informs you and the people around you, like your parents and carers, so that together you can understand why problems crop up and what to do about them. You are less likely to end up in an argument or be accused of never thinking about anyone but yourself if you and your parents understand that it genuinely takes your brain longer to imagine another perspective and at times you will need gentle encouragement to do that rather than assuming that it will happen spontaneously. These are great life skills to develop, so this isn't an excuse for not trying, but it is buying you some time while you are making those connections for yourself.

 This film recaps on a lot of the information we have covered in this chapter and also offers some really good advice to parents about how to help adolescents during this amazing time:

www.pbs.org/wgbh/pages/frontline/shows/teen brain/view/

A big concern that has been raised in this chapter is that if you don't do things now that you might need to do later in your life your brain won't have built the information superhighways where you need them. This is especially true for relationship and social skills, which are learnt most easily during your teenage years when those parts of your brain are developing and being wired up. Depression tries hard to stop you doing exactly that kind of really important stuff, like seeing friends, sticking with something when you don't feel like it, asking for help when you need it or having fun and being playful. This doesn't mean you won't be able to learn new things in the future, it is just likely to be harder for you to do and it will take you longer. This can be difficult and confusing to think about, especially if you are feeling low and under-confident. It is important to remember that none of this is your fault – it is all perfectly natural – and you can get the skills back by practising and making sure that the connections that let you do the things that are important to you now and for your future become stronger and quicker. Go back to Exercise 2.3 in Chapter 2 and think about whether there is anything you could add.

Lots of studies have shown us that having other people around to interact with and solve problems with helps our brain to develop. Receiving gentle care from another person – being touched, held and cared for – also improves learning and in some animal studies even led to a longer life! Being in a stimulating environment is very important but even more important is for you to interact with that stimulation – physical and social. Mirror neurons will get you ready by practising in advance but you also have to put practice into action and if you do that with someone else your learning potential is at its greatest.

The instability and pressures of adolescence can be difficult for some adolescents to cope with, which is why difficulties with mental health, like depression, become much more common at this age. Change, conflict, loss and isolation are easy to stumble into during adolescence, for example if you are unsure about your sexuality at a time when the people around you are beginning to experiment in intimate, sexual relationships, leaving you feeling alone and confused. It is important to understand and tackle these problems as quickly as possible to help your brain to develop resilience rather than vulnerability.

Now you are armed with information and support to begin work towards your recovery, it's time to start looking for the central theme of your own story that will provide a focus for you to work on. The next chapter shows you how to set about this by drawing up your own storyboard or timeline.

Summary

- Your brain is growing and developing throughout adolescence and is getting you ready to take your place in the adult world.
- Your brain development will mirror what you do during adolescence so use it or lose it.
- Adolescents needs more sleep than adults because of all the changes going on in your body and in your brain. It is important to protect your sleep time to help the work in progress.
- Adolescents take more risks and try new things as a healthy and normal way to explore the world.
- Adolescents are more vulnerable to taking dangerous risks, especially when in the company of friends, and this can result in higher rates of injury, addiction and death.
- Adolescents are much more sensitive to social encouragement and social exclusion, which makes IPT-A ideally suited to help with the problems some adolescents experience.

Chapter 4

Why stories are so important

In this chapter you will learn about:

- Why stories are important for you and the people around you to help you to make sense of what is happening in your life
- How the IPT-A themes – managing change, conflict, loss and isolation – feature in your own story and how they can help you to recover from depression
- How talking to other people can help you to understand yourself better

In this chapter you will be asked to:

- Start to develop your story and tell it to your IPT-A team
- Draw a timeline of your depression story

Why do I a need a story?

Storytelling is something we are asked to do all the time, even if we don't know it. Think about how many times a day you are asked,

'How was your day?' or 'What have you been up to?' It might not be called a story but that's exactly what it is. When you are feeling well you might go right ahead and tell the story but when you are depressed this is far less likely. You use fewer words, you open up less easily and you keep yourself (and your stories) to yourself. Fewer people get the chance to help you work out what is going on and what to do about it.

However, when you become unwell it is hard to avoid the many demands to tell a story. Family or friends ask for an explanation when they see changes in you. Teachers ask for an explanation when your schoolwork suffers or you stop going to school. Healthcare professionals ask you over and over to tell your story to guide their attempts to help. Perhaps you are using IPT-A with a therapist, and you are trying to understand your story together. Providing these stories is all the more difficult if you are not quite sure what is going on yourself.

IPT-A uses stories to help you and your team to think about what is happening in your life and how to make it better. In IPT-A, you will be telling a particular kind of story, quite possibly one that confuses you at the moment. Because it is a real story of real life, it is likely to be untidy and incomplete. This doesn't matter. The aim is not to create the perfect story, or the right story: it is to create one that does its job – to make something confusing more understandable to you and to the people who are involved in your life.

Ali

Ali thought his story was about breaking up with his girlfriend. He knew he wasn't happy about it but he found it difficult to understand why he was so upset. They had been dating for three months and he had liked Somayya, but it didn't make sense to him that he found it so difficult to feel better after the break-up. When he looked back over the months before the split he began to realise that he had relied much more on her than he normally would because she had been his only friend at his new school. He had moved there six months earlier and had been very lonely for the first three months. Moving to a new school in the middle of the year had been difficult; everyone else in his class seemed to have their own friends and it was difficult to find a place in these established groups. When he thought about this bigger picture Ali began to think about the reason he had had to move school – his mum, who had brought him up on her own until then, had found a new boyfriend and had insisted that she and Ali move to be closer to him. Ali hadn't wanted to move – he liked his old school and had good friends there, but he wanted his mum to be happy and went along with the move without complaining. He began to realise that he had found this bigger change much more difficult to cope with than he had admitted and he had been dealing with all of that on his own for months.

The IPT-A approach understands how complicated life can be. It is exactly because of this complexity that you are encouraged to simplify what you are trying to do. Trying to cope with too many things at once rarely leads to progress. Many people with depression try over and over again to make changes, only to feel overwhelmed by the prospect of all that needs to be done and so sink back into the despondency they felt at the start. Tackling one thing at a time creates much more scope for change.

Imagine trying to disentangle the knot of cables behind your computer or TV. If you lunge in with both hands and pull in all directions the cables are likely to become even more tangled and knotted. If, on the other hand, you take one cable and follow it through the loops and spirals it forms around the others, progress may be slow but the knots will loosen and the cable will eventually come free. What's more, some of the cables you were *not* trying to disentangle will have found their way out of the knot as well, as an indirect result. This is how IPT-A tries to tackle the problems of living – one at a time.

The IPT-A focal areas help to break a complex story into more manageable sections, each one of which will open up options for small but useful changes that make your recovery more likely. This is an opportunity to pinpoint the difficulties that are tripping you up and keeping you depressed, and – most importantly – to plan what to do about it. It can be difficult to decide which direction to go in, but for now simply consider the possibilities. Don't feel under pressure to choose between them at the moment; simply note how they feature in your own story.

In the next section I will explain briefly how IPT-A can help you to resolve your depression and the common problems that go with it – change, conflict, loss and isolation.

Managing change

Life changes all the time. As it does it throws up new challenges, such as when you change school or fall out with friends. These changes – whether wished for or not – can leave you feeling uncertain about how to cope with what is expected of you in the new situation.

If you decide to focus on a big change that has happened in your life you will be helped to:

• Think about what you have had to give up and why that has been difficult for you

- Think more positively about the possibilities and opportunities in your new situation
- Build up your confidence and self-esteem so that you can make the most of those opportunities

In order to do this, you and your team will:

- Talk about your symptoms of depression every week
- Try to understand how your depression and the difficulty you are having in coping with your recent change are linked to each other
- Talk over the positive and negative aspects of what you have given up and the situation you find yourself in now
- Help you to evaluate realistically what you have lost and talk about the feelings you have about that
- Help you to think about your feelings about the way the change happened, if that is important for you
- Help you to discover opportunities in your new role
- Encourage you to develop the social support and new skills that you need in your new role

Ali: managing change

Ali's story is a good example because it involved several changes. The first change he faced was moving house when he didn't want to and leaving friends he was close to and the school he liked going to. After this change Ali was much more isolated. In the past he would have turned to his mum when he felt this way but he felt like he couldn't do that this time because his mum was so happy about moving close to her boyfriend, and because Ali wasn't sure his mum had thought about what it had been like for him. This was another change – his mum was still his mum but she wasn't looking out for Ali in the way she normally did, and Ali felt like he had lost her too. Given how difficult all of this had been on him it was no wonder Ali felt so grateful when someone showed some interest in him and he began to rely on his girlfriend much more than he normally would. When they broke up it didn't just feel like the break-ups he had experienced before when he bounced back as soon as he saw his friends and started hanging out with them again. This time it felt like he had no one to turn to and so this change was much harder to manage.

Can you think of ways IPT-A would help Ali?

- Help him to talk to his mum about how he feels about all of the change
- Remind him of the good friends he still has, even though they live further away
- Support him to get in touch with his friends by texting and phoning
- Help Ali to identify the people he would like to be friends with in his new school and plan how to start to create opportunities to spend time with them

Managing conflict

No relationship is perfect but sometimes, important relationships at home or at school can get stuck in disagreements or arguments, and this can bring your mood down and be upsetting.

If you decide to focus on a relationship that you are finding difficult right now you will be helped to:

- Work out which relationship is most important to focus on
- Understand why you are stuck and not getting on at the moment
- Get a clearer idea about the most important things you disagree about and what each of you wants from the relationship

- Learn from other relationships that are going better
- Learn better ways to talk and listen to each other so you can understand each other better and sort out differences more easily

In order to do this, you and your team will:

- Talk about your symptoms of depression every week
- Try to understand how your depression and not getting on in the relationship you are focusing on are linked to each other
- Talk through arguments or times when it has been difficult to say what you really feel or when you don't think you have understood each other very well
- Learn ways to put your point across and understand the other person's point of view more clearly

Suzanna

Suzanna doesn't want to go home because it will mean another fight with her dad. He doesn't have a clue what it is like to be a teenage girl and he will hit the roof when he sees that she has had a tattoo done on her wrist. Suzanna doesn't see why it is a big deal, she can wear long sleeves if she wants to cover it up, not that she wants to cover it up. He is so old-fashioned and thinks he should have a say over everything she does. She is sixteen years old and will be seventeen in four months' time! All he does is go on about what it was like when he was her age and how he would never have spoken to his parent like that. No wonder, Gran and Grandpa are lovely – why would anyone want to fight with them? She can't wait to be able to move out and live her life the way she wants to live it, but she isn't going to university for another eighteen months. It feels like forever.

Can you think of ways IPT-A would help Suzanna?

- Encourage Suzanna and her father to read about teenage brain development and understand how she is experimenting with expressing herself
- Help Suzanna and her father to imagine themselves into each other's shoes so that her dad can see the world through his teenage daughter's eyes and Suzanna can understand the concerns of a teenager's parent
- Help Suzanna and her dad to describe what upsets them more clearly and listen more carefully to help them to work out the problems between them together
- Talk to Gran and Grandpa about what it was like when dad was younger – find out how he pushed the limits and how they helped him. They might have some good ideas
- Spending time with Gran and Grandpa might also remind Suzanna about some of the good things in her family before she rushes to throw them all away

Managing grief and loss

It is natural to feel sad when someone close to you dies. Sometimes, however, it can be so difficult to adjust to life without that person that you may want to put your life on hold and feel unable to carry on with your normal routines with the people who are still around.

If you decide to focus on an important bereavement you will be helped to:

- Talk about the person you have lost and how you feel about them not being here any more
- Use support from the people around you to adjust after losing someone who was important in your life

- Consider how you can still do some of the things that were part of the relationship you lost with the people who are in your life now
- Reconnect with people and routines that you may have given up recently

In order to do this, you and your team will:

- Talk about your symptoms of depression every week
- Try to understand how your depression and missing the person who died are linked to each other
- Talk about what it was like when the person was around
- Talk about what it was like when they died and who was around to help you then
- Make a safe place for you to let out the feelings that you may have been trying to hold inside
- Help you to pick up the routines you used to enjoy and to see the people who are still available to be part of your life now

James

James' dad died in an accident a year ago. Everyone was so shocked that they don't know what to say. James finds it really difficult to talk about it with his friends and he doesn't want to talk to his mum because she gets so upset and that makes him feel even worse. So he doesn't say anything about it or about his dad, but that makes James miss him even more because it is just like he never existed. He remembers the good times he had with his dad and tries really hard not to think about anything else, but that is hard to do. Sometimes he dreams about him and that throws him for the whole day. James can't be bothered seeing any of his friends. He can't imagine they will understand how he feels and he isn't interested in the things they talk about anymore.

They all seem so unimportant and trivial and James gets really worked up and angry when they make a fuss over such stupid things. He knows they aren't trying to annoy him but he just can't seem to help feeling angry at everything and everyone all the time.

Can you think how IPT-A would help James?

- Help James to talk about his dad with someone he trusts and remember the good things and the painful parts of his life
- Help James and his mum to understand how important it is that they can talk about his father to each other, even if they do get upset
- Help James not to be afraid of upset feelings and to learn how to soothe difficult feelings without bottling them up inside
- Help James gradually to start to spend more time with his friends and to make room for the fun and silly things that are still so important in life and the things he enjoyed when his father was alive

Managing isolation

Sometimes relationships are difficult because of what is missing, for example not having enough people around or not feeling as close to others as you would like. Not having someone to turn to for company or support can be very stressful and can leave you feeling alone and overwhelmed by the demands of life.

If you decide to focus on not having the kind of relationships you want you will be helped to:

- Start to connect with other people and feel less isolated
- Learn to prevent or manage problems that have repeated in your relationships

- Make the most of your existing relationships
- Start to make the kind of relationships that you want and bring new people into your life

In order to do this, you and your team will:

- Talk about your symptoms of depression every week
- Try to understand how your depression and not having the kind of relationships you want are linked to each other
- Talk about the important relationships you have had and think about what was good and what was difficult about them
- Try to understand why certain problems seem to come up over and again with different people and how to avoid those problems in the future
- Talk about what you notice in your relationships with each other that could help you to understand the problems you have with other people
- Help you to find ways to start connecting with other people to make the most of the people around you and to add to the people who are in your life

Selina

Selina has always felt like an outsider. When she and her family arrived in the UK she didn't speak any English and it took months before she could have a conversation with anyone without blushing and feeling embarrassed by her accent, which sounded so strong compared to everyone else. The bullying didn't start until a few years later. By then she had developed a physical condition that made her feel tired a lot and caused a rash on her face and hands, and she was picked on for looking different. Selina made a couple of friends in primary school and that really helped but they went to a different secondary school to her and she felt like she was entirely on her own again. She was scared that the bullying would start again and when she worried her rash got worse and she felt even more tired. She tried to stay out of everyone's way but that was hard work too and she wished she just didn't have to go to school at all.

Can you think about how IPT-A would help Selina?

- Help Selina to remember that she did have good friends at primary school and to think about how she made those friends and the things they did together
- Help Selina to think about the things she enjoys doing and look for opportunities to do them in her life now
- Help Selina to develop simple scripts that can get her through the awkward first conversation with someone new so that she can be less isolated
- Encourage Selina to find ways to calm herself when she starts to feel anxious so that she doesn't have to hide away and her rash doesn't flare up

Now let's think some more about your story.

Exercise 4.1: Thinking about your own story

- What do you think your depression story is about?
- Has your story involved any big changes, not getting on with someone, someone dying, or feeling on the outside of things?
- Tell someone on your team as much of your story as you can and spend some time thinking together about whether any of the IPT-A focal areas fit your story

When did it start?

All stories have a beginning, a middle and an end, although very often they aren't told in that order. We often start in the middle, especially if that is when things heat up, but missing the beginning of the story, which gives it context, can create a lot of confusion.

To help you to organise your story we will create a timeline of the period you have been feeling depressed. Your timeline will include things like:

- What happened
- Who was involved
- Where you were
- What made it so difficult at the time
- What has happened since then

It will help you to understand how the pieces of the puzzle fit together and it will also help you to tell other people about it more clearly. Depression usually doesn't come out of nowhere, so understanding what was going on at the time you became depressed is really important for deciding what to do about it.

Let's look at an example before you try your own. This is Gemma's story. As a first step in creating her timeline Gemma draws a graph to describe what has been happening in her life and how she has been feeling. A blank copy is available for you to use in Appendix 5 and online.

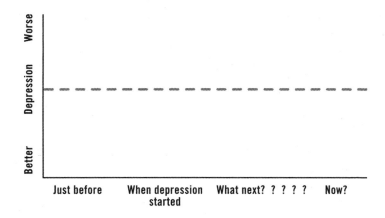

Then she adds a list of all of the important things that have happened in her life since just before she started feeling depressed until now:

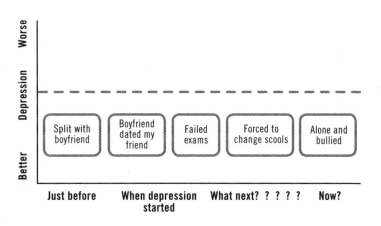

We can see that Gemma's timeline describes a lot happening. The story starts with splitting up with her boyfriend, followed by her boyfriend starting to date one of her friends. After that she failed her exams and then had to change schools and in her new school she felt alone and was bullied. Clearly she has been having a difficult time but we don't know enough to make sense of her story because we don't yet know if any of the events are connected, or how these events relate to Gemma's experience of depression, if at all.

Next Gemma drew a line to show how strong her symptoms of depression were during that time. You will see on the left-hand side of the timeline depression is described as being worse if it is marked high on the timeline and better if it is marked low. A dotted line runs across the middle of the picture. This is to help us to distinguish between times when Gemma was feeling OK or maybe a bit sad (below the line), and times when she had more of the symptoms of depression (above the line).

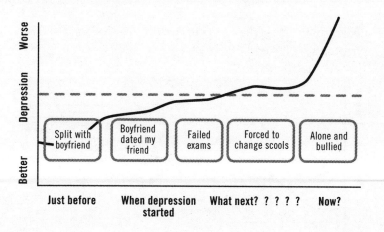

When Gemma adds a description of her depression it is easy to see the gradual increase in symptoms over the story. Gemma then thinks about how the events she is describing are linked to her symptoms of depression. She thinks about whether each event should sit above or below the dotted line.

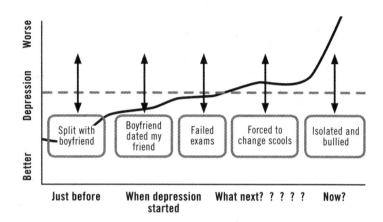

Gemma then moves the events to describe how the story and her symptoms are linked.

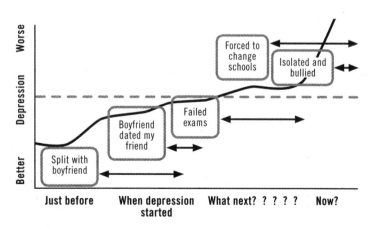

This is really helpful in understanding her story. We can see that she felt quite sad after she split up with her boyfriend but not depressed. This got a bit worse when her ex-boyfriend started dating one of her friends soon after the split. She was upset and angry with both of them and this made it difficult for her to concentrate and study for her exams. She still didn't think she was depressed then so the story stays below the dotted line. However, when she then failed her exams, because she hadn't been able to prepare for them properly, she felt worse. It was at this point her parents insisted that she changed schools because they wanted Gemma to get better exam results. Gemma was very unhappy about this change because the new school was very competitive and she had to do a lot of extra homework and studying. This is when she thought she became depressed and so the story moves above the dotted line. Gemma was unhappy in her new school because she had no friends there and she felt picked on by the students who teased her about failing her exams and didn't try to help her to settle in.

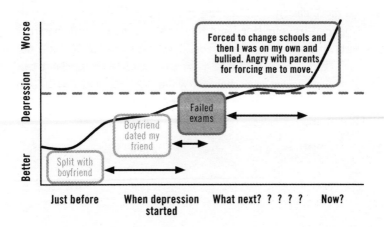

In the final version of Gemma's timeline we can see that the things that upset her at the start of her story – splitting up with her boyfriend and falling out with her friend – haven't continued to be important. Her friend apologised for upsetting her and neither of them see her ex-boyfriend any more. Although she passed her exams when she sat them again she is still unhappy in her new school and is angry with her parents for forcing her to move. This doesn't quite tell us which focus will be best for Gemma – working on the change of school or working on the conflict with her parents – but it has helped to clarify which options she could consider.

Now it is time to draw a timeline for your own story. Blank copies of the timeline diagram are available online or if you prefer you could use a really big sheet of paper and be creative in drawing all the detail you want. Before you get started it will be handy to have some sticky notes and pens ready. Ask someone on your team to help you, especially someone who knew you at the time you are describing. Building your story together can really help you both to understand what was going on for you more clearly. You can use sticky notes to describe what has happened in your story and move them around until the story starts to become clearer to you. Don't worry if you are still not sure which focus will be best for you, we will think about this more in the next two chapters when we look at the people in your story and organising your story, making a choice about the focal area.

Exercise 4.2: Sketching out the timeline of your story

- Draw out your own timeline of feeling depressed recently. Examples and a blank template are available online to help you. Add all the details that seem relevant to you, as you understand it so far
- Use the questions below to help you to decide what to include
- When did you first notice yourself becoming depressed recently, e.g. 'last summer', 'February last year'? If it is easier ask yourself, when did you last feel really well?
- What was going on in your life at the time and just before?
- What has happened since then?
- Use the IPT-A focal areas as a guide
- Talk to your team – can they suggest anything else to add?

Change

Having to adapt to change and to adjust how you organise what you do and who you see from day to day is a common feature of life, but sometimes the nature of the change can unsettle you rather than push you on to something new and exciting.

Around the time you became depressed:

- Was anything changing in your family or with your friends?
- Did your day-to-day routine change?
- Did the people in your life change?
- Did anyone change in what they expected from you or did you change in what you expected from them?
- Did a relationship start or stop?

- Did anything at school change – changing class groups or moving to sixth-form college?
- Did someone close to you experience a change in their life that had an impact on you? For instance, did one of your parents lose their job, or someone become ill, or your parent's new partner move into your family home?

Conflict

Think about the relationships you had when you started to feel depressed.

- Were any of them going through a tough patch?
- Were you feeling less close to anyone or enjoying their company less than normal?
- Were you arguing with anyone more often or feeling frustrated or disappointed with anyone?
- Were the disagreements sorted out or are they still a problem?
- Did anyone have different ideas to your own about how your relationship should be?

Loss

Many people experience something very similar to depression when someone important in their life dies, such as a parent or a friend. That is not to say that everyone who is bereaved becomes depressed, but it is a common human reaction to feel very sad at those times and for life to feel messed up as a result. Most people describe gradually learning to live with the loss they feel, even though it is still sad. If this gradual progress doesn't happen it might suggest that the person has become stuck and depression has started to develop.

- Did anyone close to you die around the time your depression started?
- Or was there an anniversary of a significant bereavement at that time?
- Did you start to miss someone who wasn't there more than you had done before?
- Did anything happen in your life that made the absence of the person you miss more obvious?

Isolation

Being socially isolated can make you more vulnerable to becoming depressed. Sometimes people live with isolation for a long time, and find it difficult to imagine anything else. The fourth area in IPT-A is a bit different from the other three we have just looked at. It helps you with difficulties in making and keeping relationships going and so may not involve a specific event, although this kind of difficulty can become more obvious when you are facing change, conflict or loss and feel more isolated than you usually do. Often your isolation becomes more apparent when something else changes, for example, when someone you relied on is no longer around, or if you suddenly have to be around more people than normal and find that overwhelming, e.g. when starting a new school and having to get to know new classmates. Finding relationships difficult is unlikely to feel new but it may have become a bigger problem recently and made your depression worse.

- Have you noticed not having relationships becoming more of a problem?
- Have you had to be around other people when you don't feel confident or comfortable with them?
- Has making friends always felt difficult?

- Is it confusing when you try to work out if someone is your friend?
- Do you find yourself on the edges of social groups but not getting what you want from them?
- Do you have enough support to see you through an unusually tough time, or would this stretch your friendships too far?

Now that you have thought about your story, add your notes to your timeline. It may be easiest to start by adding them in the order they happened. If you have difficulty remembering the order of events, move the notes around until you think it matches what happened. Think about whether the events overlapped with each other, clustered together or made other parts of the story seem worse. For example, splitting up with her boyfriend felt bad for Gemma but it felt much worse when he started dating her friend immediately afterwards. If events overlapped you can cluster the notes together to remind yourself how much was happening at the same time.

Once you're happy that you've got the events in order, think about them in relation to how depressed you were at the time. Draw a line to describe how your depression developed, marking the line higher for more depressed and lower for less depressed. If some events were clearly linked to being depressed, place the notes above the dotted line. If other events were not related to your depression, place them below the dotted line.

When you have completed your timeline, think about what it tells you about your depression right now. Does it suggest what it might be useful to focus on to help you find your way out of this episode? You don't have to be sure about this yet. In fact, it is helpful to try to keep an open mind and consider as many possibilities as you can. This is another reason why it is a good idea to involve someone else in putting together your timeline. They might be able to see or imagine links that have not occurred to you, and that may open up other options for ways out of the depression you are experiencing.

If, in the past, you have been depressed or had times that felt similar to now, even if they weren't so bad, make a note of them on your timeline too.

- When you think about times that you have been depressed or very sad or irritable in the past, can you see any similarities with the difficulties you are experiencing now, for example, were things changing or had you fallen out with someone?
- What helped in the past? Was it talking to someone, sorting out the problem, medication? It is very helpful to remind yourself about what has helped in the past, because it might be of use to you again now.
- Are you still using any of the things that helped in the past, such as talking to someone or taking anti-depressant medication?
- Is there anything you could do to make those ways of helping yourself even more useful, e.g. talking more often or having your medication reviewed?
- If you're finding it difficult to do the things that help for yourself at the moment, is there anyone who could help you to do them? What would you need to do to get this help and to start using the things that you know have been helpful to you in the past?

Exercise 4.3

On your timeline you wrote down all the events and relationships that had an impact around the time you became depressed and that are still having an impact on you now. You have been thinking about whether they involved a change, or a disagreement with someone (conflict), or bereavement (loss), or becoming more isolated. Look back at your timeline now, and add any events that still affect how you feel into the relevant bubbles in the diagram you have been working on. Sometimes the same event might appear in more than one bubble, for example if you were excluded from school (change) and you have been fighting more with your parents since that happened (conflict). In that case, add it to both bubbles. Adding to this diagram after you have read each chapter will help you to build the layers of your story.

Now look at the issues in the outer bubbles below, and for each one that you think contributes to your depression, draw a line if you can see a connection between what was happening and your symptoms of depression. You can use thicker lines for the issues that you think make the biggest contribution to your depression and finer lines for the things that didn't bother you so much.

I have used Gemma's story to provide an example.

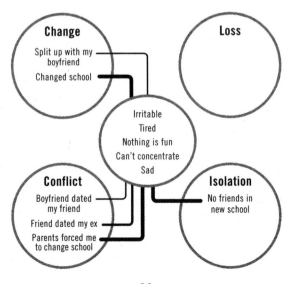

Which focus do you think would help Gemma? The conflict bubble has most items, but the thickest lines all relate to changing school. This change has led to more conflict with her parents and feeling more isolated in a new school without her friends. The diagram helps us to identify which is the headline story for Gemma but we still need a bit more information before we can decide which focus will be most useful to her. The next chapter will help to fill in any remaining gaps.

I hope you will be starting to see by now some of the ways in which your relationships with the people around you may be intertwined with the story of your depression – and how some of those people can help you recover. In the next chapter we will look at your current relationships more closely when we set about making an 'inventory' of them: what in IPT-A we call your own 'interpersonal inventory'.

Summary

- Creating your story helps you and the people around you to understand your difficulties.
- The timeline looks at the overlap between what's happening in your life and your depression.
- The timeline helps you to distinguish between your current problems and problems you have already solved.
- The timeline looks at how the main IPT-A themes of change, conflict, loss and isolation feature in your story.
- These themes relate to common difficulties in relationships, especially when you are depressed.
- Choosing a focus helps you to do what you can now, with what you have, where you are.

- It is exactly because our lives are complex that simplifying your focus is a good idea.
- A focus gives you a place to start. It does not try to tell the whole story.

Chapter 5

Your interpersonal inventory

 In this chapter you will learn about:

- Drawing an inventory of the people who help you and the people you have difficulties with
- Identifying the different kinds of support people can offer to you
- Understanding how change, loss, conflict and isolation have featured in your relationships

 In this chapter you will be asked to:

- Draw your relationship network

The characters in your story

By now you should have built up a good picture of what depression feels like for you and the important things that have been going on in your life. Now it is time to think a bit more about the people who are in your story.

The interpersonal inventory lists all the relationships that have an impact on you and how you feel, whether that is good or not so good. It will include:

- The people who support you, how well you use that support and how that has changed since you have been depressed
- The people you don't get on with so well and the part they play in your depression
- The changes, conflict and gaps in your interpersonal world
- How all of that fits into your plan to overcome your depression

As with everything else in IPT-A, it is really helpful to involve someone else in putting together this list. Describing your relationships to someone else will help you to think about them more clearly. Ask one of your IPT-A team to help you make this list.

Getting an overview

Let's start by drawing a map of the important people in your life – the ones who will help us to understand your depression and what to do about it. There are lots of ways you could do this – feel free to be creative. Here are a couple of examples:

Your interpersonal inventory

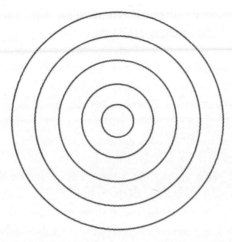

This is a closeness circle. With it, you are at the centre and you add people to show how close you feel you are to them. The people you feel closest to are added close to the centre of the circle and you move to the outer circles for the people you feel less close to.

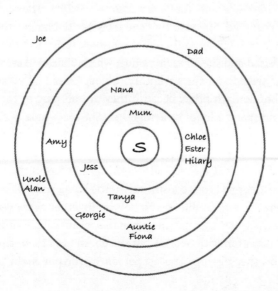

The diagram shows Sharon's relationships mapped out in this way. It's her 'relationship world' that is being described, so she is in the centre of the picture. Working out from the centre, the first circle is where Sharon put her closest relationships. The people who go in this circle are typically the people you are most emotionally involved with and often who you spend most time with. Placing a relationship close to the centre of the diagram *doesn't* mean that the relationship is perfect – there might be things that are tricky about these relationships, too – but they generally hold a significant place in your life. Sharon has identified her mum as the person she is closest to, so she is in the circle next to Sharon. No one else is in that circle, which suggests Sharon sees this relationship as being different to all of her other relationships. Sharon said that her mum is the person she is most likely to talk to when she has a problem. In contrast Sharon put her dad in the circle furthest away. Her dad works a lot so she doesn't see him very much. He looks after her in practical ways but she doesn't feel close to him. Jess and Tanya are Sharon's sisters. They are four and six years old. She says that she likes her sisters but they are too young to help her, although sometimes Tanya can tell when Sharon is sad and she gives her a hug, which Sharon likes. Sharon put four friends on the inventory. Chloe, Ester and Hilary are placed beside each other because they are all part of the same group and spend a lot of time together. She feels equally close to all three friends. Amy is another friend, who Sharon used to be closer to but she moved away. They still keep in touch but it isn't the same since Amy moved and Sharon doesn't feel as close to her anymore. Georgie is her cousin and Auntie Fiona and Uncle Alan's daughter. The two families go on holiday together every year and they see them at Christmas and when they visit Nana. Sharon likes them and has fun with Georgie but she doesn't tell them anything about how she is feeling. The last person Sharon put on the picture is Joe. They used to go out with each other but they split up five months ago. Sharon doesn't want to be his friend anymore but still sees him because they have friends in common. He is added to the diagram because Sharon says seeing him winds her up.

Another way of creating your inventory is to draw a spider diagram, like the one below. Each additional relationship is added in a new bubble. There is a lot of flexibility with this type of diagram, e.g. the people you feel close to can be added nearer the centre of the diagram and other people further out; family members or friends might cluster together, especially if you tend to see them together. You could use different shapes for family (Sharon used circles) and friends (Sharon used diamonds) or you could use pictures. Sharon also used a symbol to show she didn't want to be Joe's friend and used broken lines to show when a relationship wasn't as strong as it used to be.

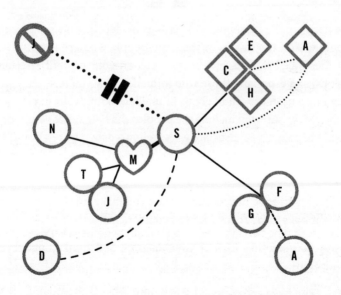

Whichever style of diagram you choose, aim to collect all of the information on a single page to help you to get an overview of what your current relationships – your interpersonal world – look like. When you draw up your own inventory, it's a good idea to begin by putting all of the people you want to think about on your diagram, and then go over the questions that are suggested later in the chapter for each person in turn. That's because the overview itself might already tell you something quite important.

How will you draw your relationships?

Exercise 5.1: Creating your inventory

A copy of the closeness circles is provided in Appendix 6 and online. Add the names of the main people who are in your life, as described for Sharon above. Focus on your current relationships, and especially those who influence how you feel. They will be more useful to think about in understanding your depression now. Make sure you include the people who help to lift your mood *and* the people you associate with feeling worse. The relationships included are likely to range from intimate to distant, and from happy to troublesome.

Involve someone in your team when you make this picture – they might have ideas about who you could include.

Now take another look at your diagram and think about these questions:

- Who have you included, e.g. family, friends, classmates, etc.?

- Are any groups missing – e.g. people you share an interest with, such as sports, music etc.; or people you used to be close to but haven't seen so much recently?
- Does this list include the people you come into contact with as part of your daily routine, e.g. people you live with, who you spend time with during the day, in the evenings or at weekends?
- Have you spent time with anyone in the last month that is not on the list?

Add anyone else these questions brings into your mind. The aim isn't to make a 'final' or 'correct' version, but one that is a good snapshot of your current relationships. You can always add people later if someone pops into your head.

Taking a closer look

Exercise 5.2: Beginning to explore your relationships

Now think about each person, one at a time, and try to answer the questions below about everyone on your diagram. Share what you feel comfortable to with the person who is helping you with this task.

- **When and how did the relationship start? What is its story?**
- **Is this a relationship you chose and still choose to be in?**
- **Has this relationship adjusted as your needs have changed?**
- **Has the relationship stayed strong through good and difficult times?**

- **What difficulties have you faced in this relationship and how have you come through them?**
- **How has this relationship featured in the story of your depression recently?**
- **How could this relationship contribute to your recovery?**

When you have answered these questions for everyone, consider:

- What strengths your answers reveal within your network – for example, adaptable relationships that you have chosen to be in and that have lasted over time
- What vulnerabilities your answers highlight – for example, an inflexible network, or one that has been forced on you, or one where the people change rapidly and unpredictably

The questions set out below in Exercises 5.3 and 5.4 will guide you in filling out the sketch you have just made for each of your relationships. Think about the questions for each relationship in turn, and try to use them as guides to prompt you, rather than just as a checklist. Add stories about the relationships to bring the inventory to life. This will help you to be specific and include details rather than noting only general patterns, which often miss out some of the more interesting and useful information.

The questions ask you to consider several different aspects of each relationship, more than you can easily hold in your mind at once. So it's a good idea to take simple notes about each relationship as you consider each set of questions. A summary table is provided below, after the questions, to help you to gather this information together. This will help you to summarise your thinking and may help you to pick out patterns that repeat across your relationships. This will also be useful to you later when you are monitoring your progress. It is likely that you will have much more to say about many of your relationships than you have space to record in the summary table. Write your full notes in your notebook and use the table to summarise your responses, as in Jakob's example on pp. 107–111. The summary chart also includes space for you to summarise your thoughts on how each of the four key themes of IPT-A – change, conflict, loss and isolation – may be connected with your relationships. We'll look at these connections, through another set of question prompts, in the next section of the chapter.

For now, let's start with the practicalities.

Exercise 5.3: Reviewing your inventory (1): contact and routines

Ask yourself, for each person in your inventory:

- How often are you in contact with each other? How happy are you with this amount of contact? What change would you make to this, if any, to make it better? How do you think the other person feels about the amount of time you spend together?
- Is your contact face to face, by telephone or online, through text messaging or a mixture? Are you happy with this type of contact? What change would you make to this, if any, to make it better? How do you think the other person feels about the type of contact you have?
- How would you describe the time you spend together and what you do together?
- Does one of you take main responsibility for staying in contact, e.g. getting in touch, suggesting things to do, or is

this shared between you? Are you happy with the balance of responsibility for keeping the relationship going? What change would you make to this, if any, to make it better? How do you think the other person feels about the way your time together is organised?

- Has the routine between you changed since you have been depressed? If so, in what ways has the relationship changed? What change, if any, would you like to see in this relationship? How do you think the other person feels about the changes, if there have been any?

Exercise 5.4: Reviewing your inventory (2): help and support

Now think a little more about letting other people know how you feel.

- Does this person know that you have been feeling depressed? If yes, how did they find out and how have they responded to this information? If not, what has stopped you sharing this with them? Do you think they might suspect even if you haven't told them? Are you happy with how much this person knows about your depression? What change would you make to this, if any, to make it better? How do you think the person feels about you being depressed?
- Is this someone you would normally be able to speak to about your feelings or when something is troubling you? If yes, when was the last time you did that, and did you find it help-ful? Has this changed since you have been feeling depressed? If so, how has it changed? How do you think the other person feels about being asked for this support?
- Is this someone you can go to for practical help or advice that

might not relate to how you are feeling, e.g. to give you a lift somewhere? If yes, when was the last time you did this, and was it helpful? Has this changed since you have been feeling depressed? If so, how has it changed? How do you think the other person feels about being asked for this support?

- Would you describe this as a flexible relationship – one that can adjust to a change in circumstances for either of you – or does it tend to stick to a set routine that is difficult to change? Has this changed since you have been feeling depressed? If so, how has it changed? What change would you make to this, if any, to make it better? How do you think the other person feels about your routine together?

- Do you think this is a two-way relationship with give-and-take on both sides? If not, how would you describe the balance in this relationship? In healthy relationships it is common for each person to be interested and involved in the other's life. This does not need to be a perfect balance, but most relationships work best if you both make a contribution and are satisfied with the balance that exists. To evaluate this in your relationships, look back over the previous questions and ask them in the opposite direction, i.e. does the person talk to you about their worries or come to you for practical help, etc.? Has this balance changed since you have been feeling depressed? If so, how has it changed? What change would you make to this, if any, to make it better? How do you think the other person feels about the balance in your relationship?

Here's the chart for your summary notes. A copy is also available online.

Person's name					
Your relationship with the person					
How much contact do you have?					
Does the person know about your depression?					
Can you speak to the person about your feelings?					

Your interpersonal inventory

Do you see each other socially?					
Can you ask the person for practical help and advice?					
Is this a flexible relation-ship?					
How would you describe the give-and-take in this relation-ship?					

Are you satisfied with this relation-ship?				
Has this relationship changed since you've been depressed?				
Has this relation-ship been affected by a change?				
Has there been conflict in this relation-ship?				

Has this relation-ship been affected by someone dying?				
Is it difficult to get what you want from this relation-ship?				
Will this person be in your IPT-A team?				
How will this rela-tionship feature in your plan?				

This inventory can also help to clarify the relevance of each of the IPT-A themes – conflict, change, loss and isolation – to your relationships. Again, use the questions in Exercise 5.5 as prompts to help you.

Exercise 5.5: Reviewing your inventory (3): interpersonal themes

Consider how each theme features in your inventory:

- Are any of your relationships going through or influenced by a change? What kind of change? Is this welcome or unwelcome? Are you managing to adapt or finding this a struggle? Highlight any relationships that are going through a change that contributes to your depression.
- Is there anyone you are not getting on with? What is the problem between you about? Are you working together to sort out the problem or stuck in the middle of a dispute with little idea of how to resolve it? Highlight any relationships that are in trouble or conflict and which contribute to your depression.
- Are any relationships missing because of bereavement? Have any of your current relationships changed significantly following bereavement? Has the bereavement overlapped with the period when you have been depressed? Highlight any lost or changed relationships that contribute to your depression.
- Have you found it difficult to think of people to include in your inventory? Is this because there are only a few people in your life just now or because the relationships you have do not feel very important? How would you like this to be different? Would you like more people, closer relationships with some people or other changes? Highlight in your notebook any current relationships that you would like to develop.

Your interpersonal inventory

When you have filled in the summary table, check if there are any obvious gaps in your inventory, e.g. no one you can really talk to, or not much give-and-take in most relationships. This is usually easier to see when you have filled out the table – for example, when a blank row stands out. You might notice a lot of notes are added for one relationship and not so many for everyone else, which hints at relying heavily on one person but asking less of everyone else. This might put that one relationship under strain and could make you vulnerable if the relationship changed in any way or the person wasn't around for some reason. Involving other people a little more could help to make you less vulnerable.

Jakob's interpersonal inventory

Person's name	Frank	Peter	Stephanie	Joanne	Mark
Your relationship with the person	Dad	Friend	Friend	Mum	Brother
How much contact do you have?	2 / week	Most days	1-2 / week	Daily	1/ every few months

Does the person know about your depression?	No	No	Yes	Yes	No
Can you speak to the person about your feelings?	No	No	Yes	Some-times	No
Do you see each other socially?	Some-times	Yes	Yes	No	Some-times
Can you ask the person for practical help and advice?	Yes	Yes	Yes	Yes	No
Is this a flexible relation-ship?	Some-times	Yes	Yes	Yes	No

Your interpersonal inventory

How would you describe the give-and-take in this relationship?	Take more than give	About the same	Take more than give	Take more than give	Give more than take
Are you satisfied with this relationship?	Not as good as it used to be	Yes	Yes	Yes	Mostly
Has this relationship changed since you've been depressed?	See less often when depressed	See less often when depressed	See less often when depressed	See more often when depressed	No difference
What are your goals in the future for this relationship?	Do more together	Keep it as it is	Talk a bit more	Keep it as it is	Do more together

Has there been a change in this relation-ship?	Moved out two years ago	No	Closer now	Mum is upset more of the time	Moved out when he went to University
Has there been conflict in this relation-ship?	More than there used to be	No	No	Some-times	No more than normal
Has bereave-ment affected this relation-ship?	No	No	No	No	No
Is it difficult to get what you want from this relation-ship?	Not so close since he left home	No	No	No	Have never really been close
Will this person be in your IPT team?	Maybe	Yes	Yes	Yes	No

How will this relationship feature in your plan?	Possibly a focus because of the big change	Steady support and company	A relationship to work on making closer	A good relationship to make more use of	Won't feature significantly

Exercise 5.6: reviewing your inventory (4): overview

- What have you discovered about your network?
- Have you been surprised by any of your responses? In what way?
- What ideas has this exercise given you about the changes you could make to improve your depression?
- Talk this over with someone on your team

Exercise 5.7

In your interpersonal inventory, you reviewed all of your current relationships. Many of the people in your inventory will have been involved in or affected by the events from your timeline. Write the names of the people who are most closely involved with each event in the appropriate bubble.

Let's follow Gemma's story to illustrate.

111

This diagram helps us to understand the different ways Gemma's relationships have been affected by changing schools. She is angry with her mum and stepdad for forcing her to change, she misses her friends from her old school and she feels lonely at her new school. Each part of the problem needs a different solution but they are all part of a change of role that Gemma is unhappy about. This information confirms that change would be the best focus for Gemma to use.

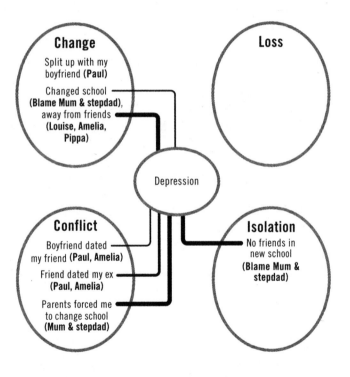

Over the past few chapters you have taken a close look in turn at your symptoms of depression, at the events in your story (through your timeline), and at the relationships in your life (through your interpersonal inventory). Together, your timeline and inventory create the interpersonal context of your depression. Equipped with this information, you are now in a good position to select a focus to work on. This is what we shall be looking at in the next chapter.

Summary

- A useful interpersonal inventory covers supportive relationships, troublesome relationships, persistent themes and plans for change.
- Your relationship inventory is a current snapshot and will develop and change in the weeks ahead.
- Creating your relationship inventory is an opportunity to discover more about your relationships as well as describing what you already know.
- Creating your relationship inventory will reveal the many ways other people can contribute to your recovery.

Chapter 6

Finding your story and selecting a focus

 In this chapter you will be asked to:

- Distinguish between background difficulties and your main focus in IPT-A
- Organise your story to make it clearer to you and to other people

Over the last few chapters we have been trying to identify the main problems for you to focus on in order to feel better. The focus you choose will relate to one of the four themes you have already been looking at, as summarised in the chart below. It can feel tricky to choose between the themes, to decide what should take centre stage and what will remain in the background, at least for now.

Important change that you are unhappy about	Not getting on with someone in your life
When someone close to you dies	When it is hard to make or keep friends

By now you will have created lots of diagrams and noted down ideas and thoughts about what is going on in your life. This should have built up a good picture of how depression affects you, the main things that have had an impact on you recently and the relationships that have featured in your depression story. You might feel confident that you know what your depression is about – or you might feel a bit nervous about trying to choose between several different problems. Feeling undecided about which problem to tackle first doesn't mean you can't use IPT-A. It is exactly *because* there are so many different issues pulling you in different directions that narrowing your focus and working out some simple and realistic goals will be helpful.

Deciding which focus will be most useful for you typically involves making a choice between options. It is not about finding the 'right answer', because there might be several storylines running at once. It is about deciding what will be useful to focus on *right now* in order to get things moving again, to get you unstuck. Your choice should be guided by:

- Relevance to your depression
- Overlap with the time that you have been feeling depressed
- Potential for change in that area
- Support available to you in making this kind of change

A useful focus will be highly relevant to your depression, will have been troublesome most of the time when you have been depressed, will have scope to change and will be something other people can help you to manage.

Look over your bubble diagram, timeline and inventory and then use the questions below to help you to think though the options for how to use IPT-A. Remember you can dip into more than one focal area if a mix of ideas will be helpful, but having a main focus makes it easier to manage.

Exercise 6.1: Distinguishing between focus and context

1. **Was the difficulty around when I first started feeling depressed?**
    (**Yes**: consider as possible focus   **No**: consider as context)

    Let's go back to Gemma's story as an example. By the end of her timeline it looked as though changing school might be the thing to focus on. That didn't happen until a few months into her story but her sad feelings got worse and began to look like depression around the time she changed school and was being ignored and bullied. That means it could be a useful focus for Gemma.

    Another option is the split with her boyfriend. That happened at the very beginning of her story. Even though she was upset about it, she wasn't feeling depressed after the split. That makes it less likely to be a useful focus but it is important to remember that her upset about the break-up was happening in the background if we are going to understand the rest of her story. A final option is conflict with her parents. Gemma was angry with them for making her move schools and has been fighting with them since. That could be another angle on the same story and it would be helpful to look at what choosing that focus would involve to decide between conflict and change. They often overlap and bits of both might be used.

    - **How would you answer this question in your story?**

2. **Does the difficulty affect how depressed I feel now?**
    (**Yes**: consider as possible focus   **No**: consider as context)

    Gemma is still angry and upset about being at her new school and sad about missing her friends. She hasn't made friends at her new school and is being bullied by some of her classmates.

She is still very angry with her parents for forcing her to change school. Again all of this suggests that the change of school or conflict with her parents could be useful ways to focus her IPT-A.

Gemma hasn't continued to be upset about the break-up with her boyfriend or him dating her friend. She doesn't see her ex-boyfriend now and she has made up with her friend, so this is in the past for her. Again that suggests those changes and conflicts give context to her story but they are unlikely to be the focus.

- **How would you answer this question in your story?**

3. **Has this difficulty always been a problem, but was something I could cope with a bit better before I was depressed?** (**No**: consider as possible focus   **Yes**: consider as context)

Fitting in at school hasn't always been a problem for Gemma. She liked her old school and had good friends there. This suggests Gemma hasn't always felt isolated and can make friends but is having difficulty doing that in her new school.

Gemma dated a couple of boys before her recent break-up and coped well when they stopped seeing each other. Managing changes hasn't always been a problem for her.

Gemma has always felt pressure from her parents to do well at school and she coped with this well until exams overlapped with her feeling upset and struggling to concentrate. None of the current problems appear to have been long-standing difficulties for Gemma, which makes isolation seem less likely to be a useful focus. This also suggests that Gemma is angry with her parents specifically about making her change school rather than about lots of things. They didn't fight before this change happened so that might push change ahead of conflict as a useful main focus.

- **How would you answer this question in your story?**

4. **Is there reason to think that this event/relationship could improve?**
   (**Yes:** consider as possible focus   **No:** consider as context)

Gemma has done well at school and made friends in the past so it is clear that she can do both of those things. This gives reason to be hopeful that with some help she could start to do this again at her new school.

Gemma no longer sees her boyfriend and is not interested in trying to improve that relationship.

Gemma and her friend have already patched up their friendship and are getting along well again. Gemma managed that situation without needing any extra help.

Gemma had a better relationship with her parents before she was forced to move school. She is angry with them but would like to get back to the kind of relationship they used to have, although she isn't sure how to do that in this situation. Her parents feel the same way and are worried about how down she has been since changing school. It would be useful for Gemma and her parents to have some help and new ideas to solve this part of the problem.

- **How would you answer this question in your story?**

5. **Do I have the support I need to make a change in this kind of event/relationship?**
   (**Yes:** consider as possible focus   **No:** consider as context)

Gemma's parents would like to help her to feel better, and her friends from her old school miss seeing her and are keen to remain friends and see her after school and at weekends. Gemma has also got support from one of the teachers at her new school who is sympathetic to how difficult the change of schools has been for her. All of this suggests that Gemma could have an IPT-A team who will support her to improve her experience around this difficult change.

- **How would you answer this question in your story?**

Exercise 6.2: Telling your story

You can tell your story in whatever way you feel comfortable. The questions and diagram below are two ways that could help you to summarise the main points. Feel free to make changes so that it feels like your story. Remember, this is only the story *so far*. It isn't finished, and it doesn't have to be tidy and perfect. It is simply a way to get started, and you will add to this story step by step as you continue through the remaining chapters.

Important information to include in your story:

- **I know I am depressed because** . . . (describe what depression is like for you)

- **It all started when** . . . (describe what was happening when you started feeling depressed)

- **The other things that were going on around then that made it easier/more difficult for me were** . . . (describe the context)

- **What keeps the problem going now** . . . (describe the main problem you have identified)

119

- **The things and people I have going for me and that will help me to feel better are** ... (describe the good things about you and the people around you)

- **I am going to focus on** ... (name your focus) **to help me to feel better**

A blank copy of this diagram is available in Appendix 7 and in the online folder.

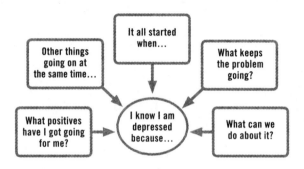

Gemma's diagram might look like the one opposite:

Do you and your team agree on the most useful focus for you? If opinions differ, talk over your different points of view. Ultimately *you* decide which focus you would like to take, but it is useful to think about different perspectives before making your final decision. This can trigger ideas that wouldn't have crossed your mind otherwise. If you still feel unsure, take some time to read through the individual chapters on each focus (Chapters 9–12) to give you a better idea of what each one involves before you make your decision.

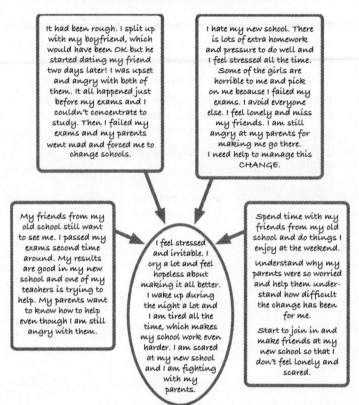

It had been rough. I split up with my boyfriend, which would have been OK but he started dating my friend two days later! I was upset and angry with both of them. It all happened just before my exams and I couldn't concentrate to study. Then I failed my exams and my parents went mad and forced me to change schools.

I hate my new school. There is lots of extra homework and pressure to do well and I feel stressed all the time. Some of the girls are horrible to me and pick on me because I failed my exams. I avoid everyone else. I feel lonely and miss my friends. I am still angry at my parents for making me go there. I need help to manage this CHANGE.

My friends from my old school still want to see me. I passed my exams second time around. My results are good in my new school and one of my teachers is trying to help. My parents want to know how to help even though I am still angry with them.

I feel stressed and irritable. I cry a lot and feel hopeless about making it all better. I wake up during the night a lot and I am tired all the time, which makes my school work even harder. I am scared at my new school and I am fighting with my parents.

Spend time with my friends from my old school and do things I enjoy at the weekend.

Understand why my parents were so worried and help them understand how difficult the change has been for me.

Start to join in and make friends at my new school so that I don't feel lonely and scared.

Now that you have chosen a theme as your most useful focus, at least initially, we can move on in the next chapter to consider your goals – and, most importantly, to see how you can set goals that are *achievable*.

Summary

- **Finding your story and choosing a focus involves a deliberate choice between different options.**

- The focus of your story doesn't try to cover the whole story but rather aims to highlight the area most useful for you to concentrate on.
- Your story will guide you towards one of the main interpersonal themes – conflict, change, loss and isolation – as your most useful focus at this time.
- Your focus will explicitly link your current depression and current interpersonal difficulties.
- Your story will highlight how other people can contribute to your recovery.

Chapter 7

Setting goals and making the changes you want

In this chapter you will learn about:

- Finding goals that will help you to reduce your symptoms and improve your relationships
- Breaking goals down into individual steps
- The importance of tracking your progress and celebrating your successes
- The importance of asking other people to help you to work towards your goals

In this chapter you will be asked to:

- Think about how IPT-A ideas could help you
- Identify your goal buddies
- Identify goals to reduce your symptoms of depression, improve the support available to you and improve your interpersonal problem-solving skills

- Identify milestones when you and your goal buddies will celebrate the progress you make
- Plan how you are going to celebrate your successes

Setting achievable goals

You have done a lot of work over the last few chapters to understand the nature of your difficulties and what makes them tricky to sort out. The personal story you have developed is a great starting place to help you imagine how you could begin to feel better.

Once you have a focus it is very useful to think about how you would like that situation to be different and how, with the help of the people around you, you can make that happen.

You might already have a clear idea of how you would like things to be different and what you would like the ideas in this book to help you to do. That's great – talk to your team about it and get started. However you might still be working that out. Your ideas about what you want to achieve might be a little more vague and being specific can be a real challenge. At first you might find it easier to say what you don't want, e.g. 'I don't want to argue all the time' or 'I don't want to be in a bad mood all the time'. In this chapter we will think about the ways you can turn those 'don't wants' on their head and work out what your 'I want . . .' and 'I can . . .' ideas will look like.

Involving other people in working out what your goals will look like can really help. Remember when we have to organise our ideas enough to describe a problem to someone else we often end up understanding it more clearly ourselves. The same is true of goals. Your team can help you to break down goals that feel too big to tackle into manageable chunks. Your IPT-A team can also become your 'goal buddies', helping you to stay on track and keep going at a pace that you can manage.

Crossing the stepping stones

It is helpful to think of goals as being like stepping stones. Even when the ultimate goal is quite clear there are usually steps that you have to take to get there – by crossing stepping stones one at a time. Rather than only aiming for a distant finishing line that you have to cross, every step is valuable in itself and part of getting better. Individual steps could be your short- or medium-term goals, some of which will also lead to long-term goals. Not every goal has to be completely achieved to be helpful. Sometimes simply moving towards a goal, even though it is still out of reach, can be very useful. **Imagining how things could be better is an 'anti-depressant activity' in itself**, and it is likely you will see the effect of your efforts towards a goal long before it is actually achieved.

IPT-A has two main goals for all the young people that use it:

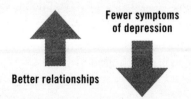

Fewer symptoms of depression

Better relationships

Will any of your goals focus on symptoms that are troubling you? For example:

- Follow the sleep advice in Appendix 4

- Do one thing you used to enjoy with friends each week to help you to start enjoying yourself again
- Go for a walk or a run to boost your energy
- What can you and your team think of for you?

Will any of your goals focus on the people around you? For example:

- Tell someone you trust about depression
- Ask someone to join you when you go for a walk or a run
- Learn when to walk away from unhelpful discussions
- What can you and your team think of for you?

In Chapter 4 we looked at some of the ways IPT-A approaches common problems in relationships when you are feeling depressed. Look at those examples again, this time holding your own story in mind, and think about how the ideas apply to you.

Managing change

- Understand what you have had to give up and why that has been difficult for you
- Think more positively about the possibilities and opportunities in your new situation
- Build up your confidence and self-esteem so that you can make the most of those opportunities
- Look for opportunities to use support from other people to help you in your new situation

Managing conflict

- Understand why you and the person you are having problems with are not getting on at the moment

- Get a clearer idea about the most important things you and the other person disagree about and what each of you wants from the relationship
- Learn from other relationships that are going better
- Learn better ways to talk and listen so you can understand each other better and sort out differences more easily

Managing loss

- Talk about the person you have lost and how you feel about them not being here anymore
- Use support from the people around you to adjust after losing someone who was important in your life
- Consider how you can do some of the things that were part of the relationship you lost with the people who are in your life now
- Reconnect with people and routines that you have given up recently

Managing isolation

- Start to connect with other people and feel less isolated
- Learn to prevent or manage problems that have repeated in your relationships
- Make the most of your existing relationships
- Start to make the kind of relationships that you want and bring new people into your life

Exercise 7.1: Thinking about how IPT-A could help

- How do these IPT-A ideas fit with your story?
- Is there anything that you need to be able to do to make your situation easier, e.g. talking about how you feel, considering another point of view before making a decision, spending more time with friends?
- What difference would it make to your situation if using those ideas worked?
- Does that give you any ideas about goals that would be useful for you to work towards?

Talk this over with someone in your team and ask if they have any ideas.

Some useful tips for goals

- Describe each goal in a single sentence. If it takes more than that then the goal is probably more complicated than is helpful
- Be specific not general, e.g. 'I will see my friends at least once a week' rather than 'I want to do more'
- When you have decided on your goal write it down. This will help you to remember it
- Don't aim for more than three goals – it can get confusing if you have too many goals at the same time. If you have more than three goals in mind start by working on the top three. If you make good progress on those goals and want to move on

to a new one when you are ready, that's great, but try not to overwhelm yourself by attempting to do too much at once. It could prevent you from making all the progress you can

- Describe your goals to someone else. This will test if the goal is clear and the other person might be able to help when they know what you are trying to do. Ask your IPT-A team to help
- Focus on what you are going to do, not what other people need to do, e.g. rather than, 'I want my parents to listen to me' try, 'I want to communicate clearly in a way that is easy to understand'
- Some people find it helpful to set SMART goals – **S**pecific, **M**easurable, **A**chievable, **R**elevant, **T**imely. This can be a good way to check how well thought through the goal is:

  ◊ Specific – can I describe it in a single sentence?
  ◊ Measurable – will I be able to measure my progress?
  ◊ Achievable – is it a realistic goal for me?
  ◊ Relevant – does it relate to the main focus I have chosen?
  ◊ Timely – is it possible in the time I have given myself?

Tracking progress

One of the most common reasons for not achieving your goals is forgetting all about them after you have set them. That is why it is a good idea to write them down and to tell someone else about them.

It is also very helpful to track the progress you are making towards the goals you set. Often recognising your progress is just as important as achieving the goal itself. Many of the things we aim for remain 'works in progress'. Getting the ball rolling in the right direction is the big achievement.

One useful way to track your progress is by regularly rating it out of ten. Try to do this every week or two and keep a note of each new rating on a graph or by colouring in an image of a stepping stone leading to your goal. A zero rating means you haven't made any progress towards a goal yet and ten means you have completely achieved your goal. This will make sure you don't miss any small successes – there are lots of reasons to celebrate long before you get to ten. Sometimes you won't even want to get to ten and making a smaller change will be enough for you to feel better. Tracking when change is happening and when it slows down will also help to signal if you start to drift off focus or if the things you are trying aren't as helpful as you hoped. If that happens you can ask for help and some new ideas to work through setbacks and to help you to continue to work towards your goal.

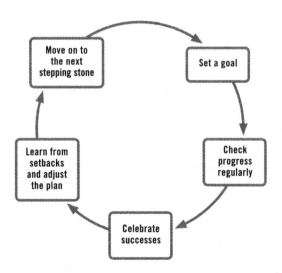

Keeping a visual record of your progress can be a very good way of keeping yourself motivated. You might draw the stepping stones you are going to try to cross on the way to your goal or you could make a graph that measures how much progress you have made since you started. On the graph below zero means no progress has been made towards the goal and ten means the goal has been completely achieved. A score of five would mean good progress is being made towards the goals and you are halfway there. The arrows show the progress made between the first rating, marked by the white bar on the left, and the most recent rating, marked by the end of the grey line.

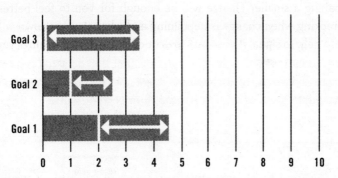

Goal 1 was initially rated 2 and is now rated at 4.5

Goal 2 was initially rated at 1 and is now at 2.5

Goal 3 was initially rated at 0 and is now at 3.5

Exercise 7.2

- Identify your goal buddies
- Identify one each of a symptom-focused goal, a support-focused goal and a skills-focused goal that relate to your chosen interpersonal difficulty and depression, e.g. sleep better (symptom-focused), meet my friend at least once a week (support-focused) and learn ways to soothe difficult feelings that don't involve hurting myself (skills-focused)

- Talk to your goal buddies about what they can do to help you to achieve your goals
- Identify the milestones when you will reward yourself for making progress and decide what that reward will be, e.g. when I have moved up two points or steps I will go to the cinema. Ask your buddies to help you to monitor your progress and to join in the celebration with you
- Start working towards your first goal

Whichever focus and goals you have chosen it is likely that knowing how you and the people around you feel and being able to talk about that will help. This can be difficult to do when you are depressed, so the next chapter is devoted to helping you see how you might be able to develop these all-important skills.

Summary

- **Talking to other people can help you to think of useful goals.**
- **When you decide on a goal write it down and tell other people about it to make sure you don't forget.**
- **Ask other people to help you work towards your goals.**
- **It's helpful to break your goals into short-, medium- and long-term goals rather than aiming for a finishing line in the distance.**
- **Using SMART goals can help to clarify what you are going to do, how you are going to do it, when you are going to do it and how you will know when you get there.**
- **Monitor your progress regularly.**
- **Each step on the way towards your goals is important and should be celebrated.**

Chapter 8

Interpersonal problem solving

 In this chapter you will learn about:

- Developing your self-awareness by tracking both your symptoms and your progress towards your goals each week
- The importance of talking about your feelings
- Ways of making your communication more effective
- The value of practising with your team before you try it for real

 In this chapter you and your team will be asked to:

- Fill in the symptom wall chart and discuss how you feel
- Discuss your progress towards your goals
- Try out different ways to identify feelings and talk about them
- Make a recovery playlist and use songs and lyrics to help you talk about how you feel

- Practise changing emphasis to change the meaning of what you say
- Watch two videos about how easy it is to misunderstand text messages
- Practise reading facial expressions in films and TV programmes and compare your answers
- Practise making people smile by smiling at them first
- Practise using your body to communicate
- Watch a video on how your body language shapes who you are
- Identify strengths and weakness in your own communication style
- Practise understanding how arguments develop and how to change course

Using IPT-A is a good way to improve your interpersonal problem-solving skills – that is, sorting out the problems you have with the people around you. If you can sort out the problems you have with other people you are less likely to feel depressed. The relationship–depression cycle I described in Chapter 1 works in reverse and having better relationships leads to feeling better rather than poor relationships pulling your mood down.

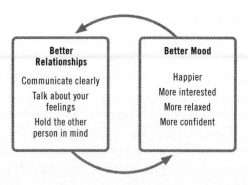

Healthy relationships rely on each person compromising at times and looking after their own needs while holding the other person's thoughts and feelings in mind. That is quite complicated and to do it you have to have *self-awareness* (knowing what you think and feel and want) and *other awareness* (imagining what other people think and feel and want). When these are combined you will be better at understanding misunderstandings, and at seeing yourself from the outside and others from the inside (go back to Chapter 3 for a reminder on mentalising on page 55).

IPT-A will teach you lots of ways to improve your self-awareness and other awareness, that will help with sorting out problems with other people and improve your symptoms of depression. Many of the techniques are useful when you are dealing with change, conflict, loss or isolation and in this chapter we will look at the techniques that are useful whichever kind of relationship problems are troubling you. This chapter is longer than the others because the ideas are useful for all kinds of relationship problems. Don't put yourself under pressure to read it all at once or even as a whole chapter. Use the headings and exercises to guide you to the sections that will be of most interest and use to you. This can be a useful reference chapter to come back to time and time again as you read through the rest of the book.

Self-awareness

Talking about depression

In Chapter 2 you looked at lots of information about depression and when you filled in the symptom wall chart you created your own depression signature – a picture of how depression looks in your life. This is a very good example of self- awareness – you paid attention to ways depression has changed your day-to-day experience and learnt about the ways each of the symptoms contributes to the problems you have been having.

When you ask yourself, 'How has my depression been?' and fill in the symptom grid each week you are maintaining your self-awareness and updating the picture of depression that you hold in mind. By doing this you will see the positive changes as your symptoms improve and you will carefully tune in to any problems that are stuck and need more attention.

You can make even more of this self-awareness by asking someone else, like your parent or carer or someone on your team, what they think depression is like for you. Ask the person you have chosen to tell you how your depression looks to them to fill in the symptom wall chart using red, yellow and green pens every three or four weeks. Look at both of your symptom charts alongside each other to compare your responses and discuss the following questions:

- Which symptoms trouble me that my team member doesn't know about? (Those are the symptoms your team member marks as less of a problem than you do)
- Which symptoms is my team member worried about that I

don't think are such a problem? (Those are the symptoms your team member marks as more of a problem than you do)

* What changes have I noticed in my depression? Has my team member noticed those changes too?
* How has my team member's view of my depression changed? Can I see what they see?

Joyti

Joyti is getting good at rating her symptoms. She has been using the symptom grid for six weeks and has been pleased to see two of the boxes she coloured in red the first time she filled it in – waking up in the middle of the night and not being able to concentrate – switched to amber over the last two weeks. She is thinking a bit more clearly and finds it easier to get started on things so she has started to rate them as green too. The page looks more optimistic with more green and less red and she finds that really helpful. Despite all of this progress, she still feels bad about herself and that she has been a problem for her mum and dad. She knows now, in her head, that depression is an illness but she is finding it difficult to feel it in her heart – that is lagging behind. She still feels guilty and that she has let other people down a lot of the time and so they are still reds for her. Joyti's mum is on her team and has been very proud of the effort she is making to feel better. She has noticed that she looks less tired and is seeing her friends more than she did a few weeks ago. She is so pleased about this that she assumes Joyti is feeling better inside in the same way that she appears to on the outside. She is very surprised when she sees the difference between her own colour ratings and Joyti's when they compare symptom charts. Joyti's mum hadn't realised how fragile Joyti still feels inside and how much responsibility Joyti is carrying around for everyone else's feelings. When they talk about it Joyti's mum tries to reassure her that she loves her and wants to help her to feel better. She can see that her enthusiasm might have felt like pressure for Joyti to get better more quickly than she feels able to and this had the opposite effect than she intended. They decide to watch the videos about depression again to remind both of them how difficult it can feel and how to be patient with each other as Joyti starts to turn things around. The videos of other young people who have felt the same way and have come out of it help Joyti to believe that things will get better and remind her mum how painful it can feel when depression takes hold.

Reviewing your goals

Recovering from depression and improving your relationship problems will look different for each person. Sometimes you will capture the changes that are happening for you more quickly or accurately by tracking progress towards your goals. As I said in Chapter 2, recovery from depression often involves doing things before you feel like it, so you might notice that even though the symptoms are still troubling you, they don't interfere with your life so much and you can do more of the things that you want to do.

When you rate your progress towards your goals every week or two you are also maintaining your self-awareness. Rating your goals will highlight positive changes that might not be captured on the symptom grid and will highlight areas where you might need some more help or fresh ideas.

Asking other people, like the people on your team, about the progress they can see you making towards your goals can help in just the same way as asking about your symptoms. This is also a very good way of making sure that they are holding your goals in mind and thinking about the ways they can help you to achieve them. When you have both rated your goals compare your responses and discuss the questions in the following exercise.

Exercise 8.1 : Comparing your goals rating
with your teams'

- What progress have I made that my team member doesn't know about? (The goals your team member scores lower than you do)
- What progress has my team member noticed that I hadn't? (The goals your team member scores higher than you do)
- Does my team member know which goals I am finding difficult to achieve? How can they help?

Kamal

Kamal hasn't been at school for three months. He gets nervous and starts to feel sick if he has to go out and so he almost never does. He set a goal of going back to school next term but it seemed like a big leap from where he is now and he isn't sure he is going to even get close to doing it. When he set his goal he planned to gradually get used to going out again by going to places he knows well and staying for slightly longer each time. He used to play football for a local team and one of his short-term goals was to go and watch the team play on Saturday mornings. This would also mean he would see some of his friends again but he wouldn't have to talk to them for too long because they would be playing in the match – so it seemed like a good place to start. Kamal's dad said he would go with him to the match because he used to watch the games when Kamal played in the team. They have gone to two games so far but Kamal found it harder to do than he expected. He quite enjoyed watching the game and seeing his friends once he got there but he

139

was very nervous on the way and left as quickly as he could after the game was finished. He doesn't think his dad really understands how difficult it is for him because he has been busy for the last two weekends and says he thinks Kamal can go on his own from now on. This difference showed up really clearly when they rated Kamal's goals – Kamal rated going out to familiar places at 4/10 and his dad rated it at 9/10 because he assumed that if Kamal had done it a couple of times he could do it whenever he wanted. Comparing scores made it easier for Kamal to explain that he is worried that the progress he has made will disappear if he doesn't have his dad's support to keep going out of the house and beat the anxiety that is mixed in with his depression. Kamal's dad realises that he has mistaken doing something once or twice for being able to do it all the time and that Kamal needs to practise doing the things that will help him more often to give his confidence time to build up again. Kamal has done really well to start to make change but needs to cross smaller stepping stones to make the change stick.

Understanding your feelings

Lots of research has shown that understanding and managing your feelings contributes to:

- Better mental health
- More successful relationships
- Greater satisfaction in life

Developing your emotional awareness (noticing what you and other people feel) and communication skills (being able to say what you want to clearly and listening carefully) are therefore going to be really useful to you in recovering from depression and sorting out relationship problems.

Symptoms of depression help us to understand when something is going wrong and knowing about them makes it more likely that you will get the treatment you need, because you know when to ask for help. However, you will also have lots of feelings – like being excited, surprised, angry, disappointed or ashamed – that aren't symptoms of being ill and are a normal and useful part of life. Unlike symptoms, which we would always like there to be fewer of, there might be lots of different ways in which you would like your feelings to change, e.g. you might want to feel happy more of the time or to be able to feel excited and silly about things again. You might want to be able to express angry feelings that you have been keeping buried deep inside yourself or to let someone know when you feel let down by them so that they won't do the same thing again. It is important to make this distinction between symptoms and feelings, even though it can be difficult to do sometimes. Having feelings doesn't mean you are ill or need treatment. You might need help to recognise, control or talk about your feelings but it isn't a good idea to try to get rid of them. Knowing and talking about your own feelings and being able to recognise and understand feelings in other people are great and unique things about being a human being and can be a key to making your relationships better.

Sensations, thoughts and feelings

Being aware of what you are feeling is the first step towards feeling better. This involves registering that something has changed inside you and accurately identifying which emotion or emotions are involved. At a basic level this means that you know when what you are experiencing is an emotion, and can distinguish it from a physical sensation (e.g. heart racing) or a thought (e.g. I am stupid). Our feelings, sensations and thoughts often get mixed

141

up, and when this happens you can get confused about what you feel.

Let's look more closely at the examples I've just mentioned to understand the difference. When your heart races – that is, your heart rate increases – you feel a physical sensation in your chest. This might happen for a number of reasons, e.g. you are about to ask a question in class, you have just had an argument or you have been running. In each case the *physical sensation* will be the same, reflecting the physical reality that your heart is beating more quickly. You might be thinking 'I feel stupid because I don't understand', 'I am mad that you said that to me' or 'I am really pleased that I cut two minutes off my best running time'. The *feelings* that go with the sensation and thoughts are very likely to be different in each example. You might feel *anxious* about speaking up in class or *angry* about the argument and you might feel *proud* to have improved your running time. Anxiety, anger and pride are the range of *feelings* potentially associated with the same physical sensation and a range of different thoughts.

Stefan

When Stefan tries to describe how he feels when he has down days he says, 'I can't be bothered'. He might be describing having no interest or perhaps no energy, but it isn't very clear because his feelings are confused with his thought that he 'can't be bothered'. It has become such a habit for Stefan to describe how he 'feels' in this way that he has nothing else to offer himself or his friends by way of explanation when he backs out of plans at the last minute time and time again. Given this is all the information he has to go on, he often goes back to bed for the rest of the day and his friends are left feeling confused and upset by his apparent lack of interest. As Stefan learns to distinguish between his thoughts and feelings he realises that when he thinks he can't be bothered he sometimes feels sad that his boyfriend hasn't called when he said he would, sometimes disappointed that his friend hasn't noticed that he is upset, and sometimes anxious that everyone will get fed up with him and won't want to see him anymore. By distinguishing how he feels from what he thinks and naming individual feelings (sadness, disappointment, anxiety, etc.), he begins to understand more clearly what triggers his feelings and can explain them to the people who are involved and who can help him.

What am I feeling? What are you feeling?

Talking about feelings that are painful, unwanted or that you have only just become aware of is difficult to do. It is also difficult when you notice these kinds of feelings in other people. Many of the feelings that are part of depression are unpleasant, and in trying to tune out or distract yourself from them you might have switched off awareness of other feelings too. Trying to hold back painful feelings is an exhausting part of depression, and recovery involves re-learning how to pay attention to the subtle emotional changes that happen from moment to moment.

In order to recognise and understand what you are feeling you have to be able to tolerate the experience of the feeling in your body for long enough for it to register and become clear to you. Our high-speed world does a great job of stopping you from taking this time and makes it easy for you to become a mystery to yourself and to the people around you. You might feel afraid to slow down and let feelings come through or worry that you will be overwhelmed or damaged in some way if it feels too painful. This is where other people can be very important and can hold you up when you find this difficult to do for yourself. In order to think and wonder about yourself and the people around you and to understand what you and they feel you have to be able to step into each other's 'mental shoes'. Being able to tolerate difficult feelings without overreacting when you are with someone you trust is the basis of the best human relationships.

Try to think of your feelings as messages to yourself. Your body and mind are trying to tell you something and they will keep trying to deliver the message until you hear it. If you ignore the message and bounce it back the redelivery loop will repeat. If you can be brave, slow down and take time to understand the message there will be less need to deliver it again and so the feeling will lose strength and will make room for other experiences. Other people may be able to read the messages that you are afraid to receive and help you to understand them and cope with them.

Naming your feelings

It is helpful to be able to describe what you are feeling or think someone else is feeling. In order to name your feelings, you must be aware they are happening and have an *emotional vocabulary* – a selection of words that you can use to describe different emotional states. Your vocabulary might cover just a few basic feelings or might be more fully developed, allowing you to make subtle distinctions in the quality or strength of the feelings you describe. When you are depressed you often find it easier to think of words for negative feelings than positive feelings. This can mean that your positive feeling vocabulary gets neglected and underused. Enjoyable feelings get edited out of your world. It is useful if your emotional vocabulary describes both the:

• **Type** of feeling, e.g. happy or sad, and
• **Strength** of feeling, e.g. content/ecstatic or glum/miserable.

How well developed is your emotional vocabulary?

Each column in the table below describes a different emotion, e.g. anger, sadness, happiness etc. The words in each column relate to the feeling described at the top of the column. The words in each shaded section describe different strengths of that feeling, e.g. feeling furious, annoyed and grouchy are all examples of angry feelings at different intensities. Read through the words in the table below and highlight any that you feel comfortable using to describe those feelings in yourself. If you have other words that you prefer to use add them in the empty box under each pair of suggested words. You will find a copy of the tables online.

	Anger	Sadness	Happiness	Fear	Shame	Disgust
Strong	Furious	Depressed	Ecstatic	Terrified	Humiliated	Repulsed
	Outraged	Miserable	Overjoyed	Petrified	Mortified	Detest
Moderate	Irritated	Unhappy	Happy	Frightened	Unworthy	Disgusted
	Annoyed	Sad	Delighted	Scared	Guilty	Loathe
Mild	Grouchy	Gloomy	Glad	Anxious	Regretful	Dislike
	Frustrated	Subdued	Content	Worried	Embarrassed	Disapprove

Exercise 8.2: Talking about feelings with your team

Questions to discuss with your IPT-A team:

- Do you recognise when you are feeling the emotions named in the table above?
- Do you recognise them when someone else is feeling them?
- Do you use all of the words that are suggested or stick to a few basic descriptions?
- Do you skirt around naming your feelings by saying you are 'fine', 'OK', 'just the same', 'whatever'?
- What impact does *not* naming your feelings have on how well you understand yourself and how well other people understand you?
- How would a better emotional vocabulary help with understanding misunderstandings?
- Who would like to know how you are feeling and whose feelings would you like to understand? Maybe looking at the table together could be a first step.
- Discuss your answers with someone on your team. How well do you understand each other's feelings?

Music as a fast track to feelings

One of the main reasons we listen to music is because it makes us feel things – sometimes happy, sometimes sad, sometimes energetic and sometimes nostalgic. This is so powerful that music can amplify what we see – if we see a happy image it looks *happier* if we are listening to happy music, if we see a sad image it looks *sadder* if we are listening to sad music.

Music has this effect because the movement, emotion and reward centres in your brain are much more active when you are listening to music. Music stimulates your emotional brain in a similar way to facial expressions. The similarity between these responses is probably because they are both seen as socially significant information they communicate in some way, and you know how social your brain is.

Music helps us to be social in lots of ways, so is a great way of getting you more involved with other people again and making the kinds of connections that are really useful to have in your brain:

- It brings you into contact with other people when you listen to music together, e.g. at a concert or at a party
- It invites you to imagine someone else's intention, e.g. what do the lyrics mean?
- It invites you to imagine someone else's feelings, e.g. when they are playing or when they are listening
- It communicates stories, feelings, memories
- If you play music it requires co-ordination and co-operation with other musicians
- If you dance with other people to the music it requires co-ordination and co-operation too (although occasionally standing on someone's toes can be forgiven!)
- It connects you with other people who like the same music and gives you a sense of belonging

So let's take this step by step. Music stimulates your motor centre and so it makes you want to move – how often do you start nodding your head or perhaps even dancing when you hear music? This is important because depression makes you less likely to move. Music might trick your brain into getting going when depression is trying to do the opposite.

147

Music also triggers feelings that match the quality of the music – happy feelings with happy music and sad feelings with sad music. Think about your own playlists – have you got playlists that always get you fired up and ready to go and others that let you wallow in a melancholy mood? They work because they have triggered your emotional brain. Once the emotional has been triggered you start to display physical signs of that emotional state, e.g. you smile or dance to happy or high-energy music. That smile or dance move then feeds back into your system and reinforces the happy feeling. Once again music can trick you into an emotional state that you might find quite difficult to achieve at the moment. Unfortunately it isn't powerful enough to switch your mood out of depression simply by pressing play but using music to motivate and move you can start the ball rolling and could be one of the techniques you can use to start moving in the right direction.

Finally, music doesn't only simulate these feelings and behaviours; it also triggers the part of your brain that rewards you, by sending out good feelings and dampening down stress, which makes you more likely to want to do the same thing again. Do you listen to music you like over and over? Each time you listen you make it more likely that you will do it again.

So how can all of this help your depression? We don't yet have evidence that music is powerful enough to cure depression but it might help you to do the things that will help:

- If you find it difficult to get started or to make progress towards one of your goals, listen to some happy, energising music before you try. If you have to go out, do it with some music playing in your ears to get you moving when depression tries to be a weight holding you down.
- Think about the music you listen to. Do you use it to change your mood or to keep an existing mood going? Sometimes

sad or angry music can help you to tolerate the feelings long enough to start to think about how you feel. If you find it difficult to let your emotions come through, music might help you to connect with feelings you have tried to push down. Remember it is important to think and talk about the feeling when you have connected with it rather than just repeating it. Listening to sad or angry music over and over will trigger those feelings time and time again too, which isn't an antidepressant activity.

- In just the same way, music can also help you to connect to feelings that might seem out of reach at the moment, e.g. happiness or excitement. Listening to music that lifts your mood, makes you laugh or want to dance can be a great way to reintroduce feelings that have been pushed out of your day-to-day experience by depression.

- Often music isn't only about how it sounds but also what it says. Song lyrics can capture how you are feeling in ways that you might find difficult to say for yourself. Have you ever had the experience of listening to a song and thinking it was written about you? If someone captures part of your story borrow their words until you can find your own. Play the song to your IPT-A team and tell them why it says something about how you feel right now.

Exercise 8.3: Making a recovery playlist

- Make a playlist of music that helps to get you moving, dancing and into the day. Listen to it when you have difficulty getting going, e.g. before going to school in the morning, when you are doing exercise

- Make a playlist that lifts your mood and brings back good memories. Tell your team about the good memories that this music triggers
- If sad music or lyrics capture how you are feeling, play a sad song to someone in your team and explain what it expresses about your feelings. Remember music can be really useful if it helps you and the people around you to understand what is going on for you and how you feel but it doesn't help to listen to sad music over and over on your own. Switch it off or switch playlist

When is a good time to talk about feelings?

Knowing what you are feeling and how strongly is helpful in deciding when is a good time to talk about your feelings. We know that sometimes decisions get hijacked by your emotional brain but there are lots of other times when you will be able to stay calm enough to make good decisions (typically when your friends aren't there cheering you on to do something they think is hilarious that will have your parents holding their heads in their hands!). When you get more practised at making calm decisions about what to do and when to do it you will be able to catch feelings as they build up and this will signal to you when it might be time to cool things down or walk away for a while.

That is not to say that you should always avoid difficult or emotionally charged situations. Sometimes the situation will be fun and you will enjoy how it feels. There will also be conversations that you might feel awkward about but are important to have, and they might be necessary to sort out your difficulties. Knowing when to have those conversations – when you are calm enough to talk and the other person is calm enough to listen – can make a big difference in how successful they are.

Continuing an argument when you are angry and want to have the last word is very tempting, but is rarely a good idea. Similarly, having an important discussion when you can't be bothered to make any of the points that are important to you because you feel so depressed is unlikely to get you very far. The trick is to find a window of opportunity when communication is helped by your self-awareness, but not overwhelmed by it.

The emotional thermometer below is a good way to track when it is a good time to talk about how you are feeling. When you have cut off from your feelings you may find it difficult to get to the heart of important conversations. On the other hand, if feelings are running very high and your limbic system is in charge you might find it very difficult to think and express yourself clearly. If your feelings are somewhere in between you are more likely to be able to think about them and talk about them in a helpful way. Developing your self-awareness to recognise the tipping point between too hot and too cold will greatly improve how clearly you can talk about how you feel and this will make it easier for other people to understand what you are going through.

Reading emotional cues in your friends and family will also help you to decide when to have an important conversation and when to wait. Judging when another person is calm enough to listen to what you have to say is just as important as taking your own emotional temperature.

This kind of self-awareness will help you to understand your own feelings and turn the volume up or down when you need to talk about your feelings without getting caught up in them. If you can do that for yourself you will be much better at doing it when other people are emotional too – your PFC will be able to soothe your limbic system when it responds to a call-out from someone else's emotional brain.

Rachel

Rachel can hear her mum's voice in the distance telling her to get out of bed. She ignores it because she knows it can't be time to get up yet, it feels like she has only just gone to sleep. In fact, she is sort of right because she didn't sleep again last night so she's only been asleep for three hours when it is time to get up. Suddenly Rachel remembers an argument she had with one of her friends yesterday and she is convinced she can't face school today so she wriggles further down under her duvet and pulls the pillow over her head. She knows she overreacted with her friend and she is way too embarrassed to face her so she just can't go in, that's all there is to it. Suddenly her mum bursts in the door and screams at her to get up, it is the fourth time she has told her and she is going to be late for work because Rachel is holding her up. Rachel feels overwhelmed and like she just can't cope and screams at her mum that she hates her and couldn't care less about her stupid job. Rachel's mum screams back at her that she is selfish and ungrateful and then they both start to cry. Neither of them is able to think or say what they really feel so they take their upset feelings out on each other and Rachel ends up locking herself in the toilet and her mum storms out but feels angry and guilty for the rest of the day.

That evening when Rachel hears her mum's key in the door she wonders if it is all about to kick off again. Her mum is wondering the same on the other side of the door.

- **Why did they both get so upset?**

    ◊ Rachel is very tired and isn't thinking clearly
    ◊ Rachel's mum is feeling stressed and isn't thinking clearly
    ◊ Rachel is feeling embarrassed about the way she behaved with her friend and her emotional brain is determined to make her avoid facing another socially threatening situation
    ◊ Rachel's mum doesn't understand how difficult it is for Rachel to wake up in the morning and takes it personally, as if Rachel is deliberately ignoring her
    ◊ Neither of them is able to imagine what it is like in each other's 'mental shoes'

- **What could have helped them to avoid this situation?**

  ◊ Rachel could have followed the suggestions on how to sleep better in Appendix 4

  ◊ Rachel's mum could have read Chapter 3 to help her understand how tired Rachel feels and how difficult it is for her to wake up

  ◊ Rachel could have told her mum about the fight at school before she went to bed and her mum would understand how difficult it is for Rachel to face her friend again today

  ◊ Rachel and her mum could have talked about how difficult it is for Rachel to control her feelings about falling out with her friends right now and mum could have helped Rachel to plan how to approach her friend the following day or encouraged her to call to apologise and make up that night

- **What would it take to make the next conversation better?**

  ◊ Both try to stay calm

  ◊ Both apologise for the fight in the morning and agree that they don't want to fight again now

  ◊ Tell each other how they feel and why they got so upset that morning

  ◊ Listen to what each other has to say

  ◊ Agree to work on the things they can to avoid the same thing happening again (see suggestions above)

Painful feelings

A final advantage of this kind of self-awareness is that it will help you to think and talk about feelings that are normally ignored or overlooked. These might include painful feelings that are buried deep inside you and that you haven't felt it was safe or acceptable to talk about.

Uncomfortable feelings are often dismissed as 'unacceptable' or 'bad'. However, keeping these feelings inside often takes a lot of energy and rather than quietening them down it can make them fight back against being ignored. The effort this demands contributes to feeling tired and ashamed, which are so common in depression. While it's quite understandable that you don't want to feel bad all of the time, it isn't possible to block your emotions indefinitely, and attempting to hold them back often creates additional problems as well as concealing what the feeling might usefully tell you.

Ali

In Chapter 4 you read about Ali, who didn't tell his mum how he felt about moving house and leaving his school and friends. He worried about upsetting his mum and didn't tell her that he was afraid that she had forgotten about him because she was so happy with her new partner. Keeping these feelings to himself made Ali more vulnerable to becoming depressed. By telling his mum that he felt lonely, afraid and let down Ali helped his mum to understand how difficult this move had been for him. Ali's mum realised that she hadn't spent as much time with him as she normally would and this had made a big change more difficult for Ali. She apologised for not noticing this sooner and although she did feel sad when she realised what had happened, she was also glad that Ali had told her because now she understood much more clearly what she could do to help her son.

Trying to ignore unwanted feelings is a bit like ignoring open documents on your desktop even when you aren't using them. They clutter up the screen and pop up unexpectedly when the cursor brushes against the file. You can end up spending a lot more time than you would like minimising them or finding what you were looking for behind the clutter. If, instead, you take some time to read through the document and understand what it is about you will have a much better idea about what to do with it. You might need some of the information so it will be useful to file it somewhere that you can find it when you need it or you can throw the parts you don't need away and free up some space. The same is true of your feelings, and talking about them with other people is a helpful way of deciding what is useful to save and what you can let go.

Feelings aren't facts, and they don't make you a better or worse person. They are simply a response at a moment in time and will inevitably change as time passes. This is just as true of uncomfortable feelings as it is of positive feelings, such as happiness and compassion, which can seem all too fleeting in depression. It is the nature of your emotions to change with time. Noticing and accepting your own and other people's feelings, rather than reacting and judging them, can help to bypass the guilt and self-blame that makes depression worse.

Feeling better

Doing what you enjoy, or used to enjoy, is also part of recovering from depression. Admittedly, this is difficult when you don't want to do things or see people. But the catch is that cutting out the things that used to feel good keeps depression going. Searching out 'anti-depressant activities' and company will create the possibility of pleasure and will begin to loosen the grip depression has on your life. Cutting them out plays into depression's hands by limiting your options. This is the difference between standing at the bus stop or in the middle of a field when you are waiting for the 'pleasure bus' to arrive. It can take time for positive feelings to come back, but this process can be helped along by making a deliberate effort, that is, looking for enjoyable experiences rather than waiting for them to find you. It is a way of acting yourself into a different feeling rather than waiting to feel your way into a different way of acting. This is likely to start in small ways – like using your interpersonal inventory to identify the people who lift your mood and deliberately spending time in their company. Here's a reminder of some of the suggestions you considered in Chapter 2. Have you been doing them?

- Say yes when your friend asks you to do something
- Make plans to see a friend
- Go for a run or a walk. Even better do it with someone else
- Read a book you really like
- Play your favourite music and dance to it
- Watch your favourite film. Ask someone to watch it with you
- Watch YouTube videos that make you laugh. Share them with friends
- Laugh for no reason

Keep going with the anti-depressant activities you have already started and try to add one more each week to create as many opportunities for feeling better as you can.

Other awareness

Why is communication important?

You might have noticed that it is much more difficult to think things through and express yourself clearly in the heat of the moment.

That is because the emotional part of your brain is having more influence than the reasoning part of your brain in those situations. Your social brain, which controls many of the functions you need to communicate well – planning, making good decisions, judging appropriateness and holding the other person's perspective in mind – gets overwhelmed and temporarily goes offline. This means you are less likely to **respond** (deliberate and planned) and more likely to **react** (impulsive and automatic). This can be contagious – it is difficult to stay calm when someone is very emotional – and your emotional brain might provoke the other person's emotional brain to fire up too. The chances of any useful communication happening at that point rapidly fall through the floor. This kind of emotional hypersensitivity can put you at a disadvantage because it gets in the way of making your point and listening to what other people have to say. It is important to remember:

- Communication is a process, not an event
- Communication isn't something you can do on your own – it is a two-way process
- Communication involves *sharing* information. Sometimes you are *giving* information and sometimes you are *receiving* it. You swap back and forth between these roles when you are communicating
- You could say something clearly, but if the other person isn't listening the communication won't work. Similarly, you might be listening closely, but if the message is not clear the communication may break down
- The best communication happens when you attend to what is going on in your mind and the other person's mind at the same time

You communicate in lots of different ways and your success relies on choosing the best way to get your message across and being sufficiently aware of the people you want to communicate with to be able to adapt your style of communication to hold their attention. Misunderstanding can occur at any stage of the communication process. Effective communication involves minimising potential misunderstandings and overcoming any barriers to communication at each stage. It is more useful to think of good communication working on a feedback loop with opportunities to adjust and fine-tune what you are doing rather than as a one-shot deal, like an exam, where all you can do is give it your best shot and hope it works out.

Forms of communication

- What you say **(verbal communication)**
- How you say it **(paraverbal communication)**
- What you do while you are saying it **(non-verbal communication)**

When the verbal and non-verbal parts of a message are saying the same thing they reinforce each other and it is likely that the message will get across. For example, if you say you are pleased to see your friend in a bright and cheerful voice, smile broadly and open your arms to hug her, all parts of the message are saying the same thing and so your friend is likely to believe you. However, if the individual parts of the message contradict each other the communication begins to break down and it is less clear what the message really means. This can create tension and confusion. For instance, suppose you say you are pleased to see your friend but sound bored and don't look at her. What would she think? Would she believe your words, how you sound or how you look? Confusing, isn't it?

The individual parts of a message aren't very reliable on their own and, in fact, can be quite misleading. It is important to consider the overall consistency of the messages you send and receive and be prepared to ask questions if something is unclear.

Written communication

How many text messages or online posts do you send or receive in a day? How many face-to-face conversations do you have in a day? I would be willing to bet that the first number is higher than the second. They are all examples of communication but in our digital world a lot less communication is spoken and a lot more is in brief, coded, written messages. Sending text messages and posting online are the most common ways many people communicate. That can be a problem. Have you ever found yourself in an unexpected disagreement after a text message was misunderstood? Perhaps you wrote the message in one tone of voice in your head and the person read it in a totally different tone of voice. Texting is fun, easy and everywhere. However, it is almost never a good way to communicate about something complicated, private or emotionally significant. It is important to develop skills in talking as well as typing and now is the time your brain is most open to learning how to do that.

It's not just what you say but how you say it (paraverbal communication)

Paraverbal communication describes the ways your voice gives clues to the feelings and attitudes that are behind the words you use. These include your tone of voice, emphasis and the flow of your speech. Have you ever rushed over your words when you are not quite sure what you are talking about or slowed down and said something much more deliberately when you really want to get a point across? Then you've got the idea.

You can pick up these clues even when the person who is speaking isn't talking to you. Imagine you're sitting on a bus and you over-hear a conversation from a few seats away but you can't make out the words. Would you be able to tell if someone was excited or start-ing an argument? What clues would you tune into – a high, quick and playful tone versus a loud, harsh and aggressive one? How you sound says a lot, especially when there is emotion in the message.

Exercise 8.4: How meaning changes with emphasis

Look at the following sequence of sentences. The written words remain the same, but the stress changes – and as it does, it changes the meaning of the sentence. Read each sentence aloud, each time stressing the word in bold italics.

_**I**_ did not say you were to blame.

I did _**not**_ say you were to blame.

I did not _**say**_ you were to blame.

I did not say _**you**_ were to blame.

I did not say you _**were**_ to blame.

I did not say you were to _**blame.**_

•   Try to identify the different meaning in each sentence

- Then ask someone else to do the same and see if you both understand each example in the same way
- Discuss any differences you notice
- Does misplaced emphasis ever cause problems in your communication?

As I already mentioned, the paraverbal element is missing in most examples of written communication, which makes them more vulnerable to misinterpretation, especially if it is in a very brief form like text messaging. Capital letters, emojis or exclamation marks etc. are sometimes used to try to create emphasis but this is rarely a reliable method to communicate something subtle or complex. Relying almost exclusively on written communication in texts, online posts and emails cuts out all of the gestures, expressions, tone of voice and eye contact that we rely on to understand face-to-face communication and can put you at a disadvantage when you are forced into more direct contact without having built up the skills and awareness to read the situation. Remember your brain learns from what you do so it is really important to have this face-to-face time to make the connections in your brain that you are going to need.

Exercise 8.5: The dangers of text messaging!

These videos show just how easy it is to misinterpret text messages if you don't text tone deaf:

www.youtube.com/watch?v=e6qlMcMa6SY

www.youtube.com/watch?v=y-iN_fPuykg

What you do while you are saying it (non-verbal communication)

Non-verbal cues like eye contact, gestures, facial expressions and posture impact on the quality of your relationships – they can encourage and reinforce or close things down and confuse. Non-verbal signals can reveal your own – and help you to read others' – unspoken feelings and underlying messages. They can help to create trust and show understanding and interest. If used well, non-verbal communication can improve your communication and relationships, but if it's used poorly, your relationships may suffer through a lack of understanding and trust.

Non-verbal communication is likely to increase when you feel emotional. Have you ever told someone you are fine when there is a frown on your face? This kind of mixed message can be very difficult to understand.

Eye contact

We often rely on eye contact to work out what is happening with another person. This convention is so powerful that breaking contact for just a few seconds too long can feel very uncomfortable or lead to the conversation drying up (the opposite is true in some Eastern cultures). In a similar way, too much eye contact can quickly start to feel intrusive or threatening. Adolescents, especially girls, are very sensitive to this kind of signal and react much more strongly than children or adults to feeling excluded. The emotional centre in your brain is primed to react to any sign of being excluded and so even subtle changes can provoke feelings of distress and anxiety. This makes sense because we are made to be social and operate in groups. Any sign that you are being pushed out of the group is a social threat. Adolescence is exactly the time when you are working out where you fit in the social group outside of your family so it is understandable that you would be especially sensitive to the signs around this.

When someone is depressed they often make less eye contact than normal and this can contribute to them feeling alone and to other people feeling shut out. Sometimes this is deliberate and used as a way to keep other people at a distance – have you ever pulled your hoodie down low so that someone can't see your face? At other times this is because you can't find the confidence to lift your face and meet someone's eye. Whatever the reason this can be very effective at stopping communication in its tracks and it means that there is less information to work with and a gaze-avoidant adolescent might miss the encouraging cues that could help him or her to feel less alone.

- Has your eye contact changed since you have been depressed?
- What effect has that had on your communication?

Reading facial expressions

This is a feature of communication that the person listening has much more access to, and perhaps awareness of, than the person speaking. We all look at people's faces for hints as to what they are feeling. This information guides how we respond. However, you'll remember from Chapter 3 that an adolescent is more likely to misread these cues than an adult and will respond from the emotional centre of the brain rather than the reasoning centre. You don't decide to do this – it is just a consequence of limited circuitry between those two brain regions right now. In particular, you are more likely to read an anxious or fearful expression as sadness or shock. It's not difficult to imagine how this can go badly wrong in conversations between worried parents and defensive teenagers who firmly believe they are being attacked or judged.

This highlights that it is important not only to know what different feelings are called but also what they look like. One way of putting a face to a feeling is to use a cartoon image, like an emoji or a smiley face. How often do you use this kind of image when you send text messages? This is one of the most commonly used ways of expressing your feelings. If you go back to the emotional vocabulary table on page 145 can you find an image that matches each of the feelings described?

Exercise 8.6: Reading facial expressions

Knowing the names of different feelings and even recognising playful images of those feelings are important steps in knowing about how you and other people feel. Reading changing or subtle emotions on someone else's face or imagining how you look to someone else when you have a whirl of emotions spinning around inside you is a bit more complicated. If you find this difficult to do in real conversations, practise reading facial expressions by watching a TV programme or film with the sound turned down. Identify as many emotions as you can over five minutes and then watch the same clip again with the sound on and rate your accuracy. Ask someone on your team to do the same and compare notes on how you interpret what you see. Check out whether you agree more often with your friends than your parents. This could be a good way to start talking about how the different ways your brains are wired up create problems when you try to talk to each other.

Try a quick experiment – the next time you walk down the street look each person you pass in the eye and smile. Then count how many people smile back. I promise you will be pleasantly surprised. (In the next section I will give you a link to a talk that encourages you to 'fake it till you make it' with your body language – you might find the experiment easier after you watch that!)

Posture

Adolescence is a period of marked physical and social change. Your body is changing rapidly and it can be difficult to keep up with and co-ordinate stretching limbs and muscles. The late development of the part of the brain involved in balance, co-ordination and movement – the cerebellum – goes some way to explaining the physical clumsiness that characterises some adolescents. Physical activity is important for this part of your brain to develop so doing things like sports and dancing improves your co-ordination. We now understand that the cerebellum also plays a role in decision making and social skill and this not quite complete control along with self-consciousness about a new and unfamiliar body may help us to understand the social clumsiness that can characterise this period too. As your brain develops it learns to smooth out all of the internal dialogue necessary to move more gracefully through the complicated social world of adolescence rather than lurching from one thing to the next. Until this happens it is more difficult for adolescents to consistently use postural body language to communicate clearly. It is not surprising that when you don't feel entirely comfortable or in control of your own body you will feel self-conscious and might want to cover up or conceal the changes that are happening. The problem is that that can give out mixed and confusing signals to the people around you who are wondering what to make of this slouching or awkward figure.

Body language is another way of communicating how you feel inside, e.g. turning towards someone you like and away from someone you don't. You might notice a difference in the way you approach a conversation with your parents or carers and with your friends. You are on the brink of becoming independent and don't want that to be threatened in any way so you might turn away and avoid eye contact when you are talking to your parents because you don't want them to have control over you. This can end up with a weird kind of mixed message when you keep your head down, turn away and shrug off any display of affection while asking for money at the same time! It makes sense when you think of it as a way of communicating the mixed feelings of dependence and independence you have inside. The obvious problem is that when someone feels shut out by your body language they might be less likely to listen to what you say or respond to your request – like giving you money. With your friends on the other hand you are probably much more likely to face them and watch their facial expression really carefully and give 'approach' signals because staying in with them is a big priority right now. You don't want to miss any signals so they have your full attention. Again it makes sense if you think about what is going on inside you but it is not surprising that the marked contrast can cause problems if parents or people you are not happy with feel shut out and don't know why.

Lou

Lou doesn't feel like she knows what to do with her body. It is changing and she doesn't like it. She wants to fade into the background and for no one to notice her, but her body makes her more noticeable and attracts exactly the attention she doesn't want. She tries to conceal it by wearing big, baggy clothes that have no shape. She wears a hoodie all of the time and pulls the hood up over her head and down over her eyes. If she can't see other people she hopes they won't see her. In class she sits at the back, hood up, earphones in and shut off from the world. It is all just too scary to deal with. Inside she is feeling scared, sad and lonely. She wishes someone could help but she doesn't know how to ask so she sends out signals to 'keep away', which guarantees that the scared, lonely feelings keep going.

Let's go back to the emotional vocabulary table we looked at earlier.

	Anger	Sadness	Happiness	Fear	Shame	Disgust
Strong	Furious	Depressed	Ecstatic	Terrified	Humiliated	Repulsed
	Outraged	Miserable	Overjoyed	Petrified	Mortified	Detest
Moderate	Mad	Unhappy	Happy	Frightened	Unworthy	Disgusted
	Annoyed	Discouraged	Delighted	Scared	Guilty	Loathe
Mild	Irritated	Glum	Glad	Anxious	Regretful	Dislike
	Frustrated	Sad	Content	Worried	Embarrassed	Disapprove

When we looked at this the first time we were thinking about verbal communication, finding the words to describe how you are feeling. Then we added facial expressions. However, what you say and how your face looks aren't the only ways you could let someone know how you are feeling. Your body will do it too.

Exercise 8.7: Using your body to communicate

Ask someone on your team to help you with this exercise. Write each of the words in the emotional vocabulary table on a separate piece of paper and fold each of them up. Take turns to choose a paper, unfold it, and act out the feeling written there. The other person has to guess which feeling is being modelled, and if they can, the strength of that feeling.

If you feel a little embarrassed to do this with someone else start by practising in the mirror and watch what happens to your face, head, hands and shoulders. Notice how large or small you make yourself and how open or closed your body looks as you move through the list.

You will get more out of this exercise if you do it with someone else because it will be a great opportunity to see yourself from the outside and the other person from the inside.

Exercise 8.8: Watch a video on how your body language shapes who you are

www.ted.com/talks/amy_cuddy_your_body_language_
shapes_who_you_are?language=en

This section has looked at the visual clues that are part of communication. The Ted Talk describes how incredibly quickly we make judgements about what we see and how those judgements influence how you think and feel about yourself and other people. Crucially, however, it also describes research that shows how you hold your body can change your mind, your behaviour and ultimately how things work out for you.

As with each of the other tools in your communication repertoire non-verbal communication is most effective when it is used in combination with the other elements, and most vulnerable to being misunderstood when used alone. Non-verbal communication might be used to:

- **repeat** the verbal message, e.g. nodding when saying you agree
- **complement** the verbal message, e.g. a pat on the back when saying well done
- **underline** the verbal message, e.g. holding up your hand when making an important point

But it can also:

- **contradict** the verbal message, e.g. rolling your eyes while saying you agree
- **replace** the verbal message, e.g. slamming a door without saying a thing

In the last two examples the message is less clear. In the first the verbal and non-verbal communications suggest different messages and create confusion, while in the second there is no verbal element, which creates ambiguity. This sort of mismatch is often evident in depression, when the reasoning brain is vulnerable to being ambushed by the emotional brain and the amount of direct communication often decreases. Patterns of ambiguous and contradictory communication fuel depression.

Effective communication relies on a coherent and consistent message being delivered and received through these different routes. When communication is clear the verbal, paraverbal and non-verbal messages will confirm, repeat and reinforce each other. Poor communication involves muddled messages, with conflicting elements pulling the speaker and listener in different directions and creating confusion about what to pay attention to and which part of the message best conveys what the speaker means.

Exercise 8.9: Identifying strengths and weaknesses in communication

Use the information given above about the three types of communication to think about how you communicate, and identify your own communication strengths and weaknesses.

First think of a recent conversation you had that went well and describe it to someone on your team. Try to answer the questions below in your description.

- **Which features of communication do you use well?**
- **How did the other person contribute?**

Now describe a conversation that was less successful, perhaps an argument or a discussion that didn't go anywhere.

- **How did your communication and the other person's communication differ from the successful example?**
- **What would have to change to make this conversation more like the successful example?**

Discuss this with your IPT-A team.

Listening and checking

The give-and-take of communication means that the way we listen is just as important as what we say, how we say it and what we do while we're talking. In just the same way that you can deliberately choose your words and use your body language to back up your message, you can listen actively and check that what you heard is what the person who is speaking intended. In good communication this works both ways. 'Listening and checking' focuses your attention on the person who is speaking and how well you understand them. The aim is to understand what the other person is trying to say and how they feel as clearly as you can. This requires self- and other awareness combined.

Think about the difference between waiting impatiently for the next opportunity to speak and listening carefully to what is being said. When you are just waiting until it is your turn to speak your attention is likely to be on yourself and what you think and want to say. When you are focusing on yourself and not listening to the other person, there is a good chance that your contribution will change the direction of the discussion and risks losing the thread. If you are listening and checking, your attention is on the speaker and what he or she is trying to say. Whether or not you agree with what is being said you are trying to understand the message and your responses are likely to stay focused on the original point. This reinforces that you were listening and trying to understand.

How can you *show* you are listening?

- Face the person who is speaking
- Look interested
- Act interested – maintain good eye contact, nod, lean in, make encouraging noises to show you are paying attention
- Set aside distractions like phones, tablets, TV or computer screens
- Repeat key points that you have heard
- Ask questions about what you have heard
- Don't interrupt unless you don't understand. If you don't understand go back to repeating what you have heard and asking questions
- Hold the other person in mind when you are speaking – take your message to them rather than expecting them to come to you to pick it up
- Check that your words, tone and behaviour are giving the same message

Ways of checking you understood

Use open questions
Open questions invite more information rather than closing the discussion down. Examples of open questions are:

- 'Would you tell me more about that?'
- 'What do you think about what I've been saying?'
- 'What are you upset about?'

In contrast closed questions rarely need more than a 'yes' or 'no' answer and are mostly useful if you need facts or confirmation, e.g. 'Are you picking me up after school?' Closed questions are less helpful for more complicated issues, e.g. 'You don't care what I think, do you?', 'Did you feel sad?'

Say back in your own words what you heard and understood

You can do this during a conversation to keep you both on track or at the end to summarise the main points. If you understood correctly, carry on. If not, try again.

- 'So the deal is, I can go to the party but I've got to be home by midnight. Is that right?'
- 'It sounds like you quite like your new class but you're not sure about the form teacher yet. You're still making up your mind. Is that right?'

Check if you have understood how the other person is feeling

Remember you aren't a mind-reader, none of us is, so it is important to check that you are imagining someone else's feelings accurately.

- 'You look angry to me. Are you?'
- 'How do you feel about what I've said?'

Say when you don't understand

If the message is mixed or you aren't sure you understand what is in the other person's mind it is much better to ask for more information than to try to fill in the gaps on your own. This reveals something useful about what is going on in your mind – i.e. that you don't understand – and asking for more information will reveal more about what is going on in the other person's mind. These questions fine-tune understanding.

- 'What did you mean when you said . . . ?'
- 'Would you give me an example to help me understand what you mean?'
- 'You said you aren't upset but you look like you might cry. How do you feel?'
- 'You told me to be honest but now you say you don't want to listen. I am confused about what you want me to do, can you help me understand?'

This careful style of listening and checking is more difficult to do when you feel depressed or are trying to talk about emotional subjects and at risk of being hijacked by your limbic system. You may have to come back to those conversations more than once before you both understand each other. Remember you will get better at it each time you practise. **In the meantime, it is just as important that the people in your team follow these guidelines as it is that you do.** It is perfectly reasonable that you should borrow your team's PFCs while yours is under construction. Your mirror neurons will be working hard every time you see or hear a good example.

Ask your team to read this chapter and ask them to help you to practise these listening and checking skills to help you to understand each other better.

When communication goes wrong

- **At least one person *doesn't feel heard or understood***
- **At least one person *doesn't want to hear* or *can't understand* what the other is saying**

One of the most powerful ways IPT-A helps with interpersonal problem solving and improving communication is called communication analysis. This involves thinking in detail about occasions when communication goes wrong, e.g. when a conversation becomes an argument or you don't feel understood, and using the ideas we have been thinking about above to understand what happened and how it could go better next time. Remember to be able to think about and understand what other people think, feel and believe we have to be able to imagine ourselves into their mental shoes. Lots of problems in communication happen because one or both people stop imagining what is going on in the other person's mind – we get overwhelmed by our own feelings and wishes and can't hold the other person's feelings and intentions in mind at the same time. This isn't surprising when we know that your emotional brain is on a hair trigger and when it fires up it sends out hormones that send your reasoning, problem-solving mind to sleep temporarily. Thinking about difficult exchanges in this calm and curious way isn't something most people, including adults, can do without practice. It is even harder when you are depressed. Aim to get better at this rather than thinking you should be able to do it perfectly the first time you try. Practice might not make perfect but now you know that with all those extra connections growing in your brain practice will make better. Your team will be invaluable in helping you to do this because you learn so much in the discussion afterwards.

To get into the habit of thinking about conversations in detail, start with examples on TV rather than one of your own. Sometimes even remembering an argument or a disappointing conversation can bring back powerful feelings and this could distract you as you try to learn this technique. By watching clips of other people communicating you will be acting like the director of the scene rather than one of the actors in it. Almost every episode of the soap operas or fly-on-the-wall reality TV shows like *TOWIE* or *MiC* involves an argument, so examples should be easy to find. Lots of clips are also available on YouTube.

Exercise 8.10: Watching an argument unfold

- Watch a scene from a film or TV show in which two people have an argument. Ask one of your IPT-A team to watch the scene with you – you will be comparing notes afterwards
- Immediately after watching, try to remember as much as you can about what was said (verbal communication)
- Say how clearly you think each character communicated
- Summarise what you understood each character's main points were in your own words
- Say how well you think each character understood what the other person was saying and how they were feeling
- If the argument escalated, identify three things that made it worse, e.g. tone of voice, choice of words, physical setting, etc.
- If the argument was sorted out, identify three things that helped, e.g. listening carefully, finding what they agree on, staying calm, etc.
- What do you think would need to change for this conversation to be more successful? Use the suggestions in this chapter to give you ideas
- Discuss what you and your team member noticed in the clip. Did either of you pick up on things the other missed?
- Did anything in the clip remind you of your own communication? Would any of the ideas you thought of help you to understand your own misunderstandings and communicate more clearly?
- Watch a few more clips until you start to feel confident in noticing what is good and not so good in communication. This will give your mirror neurons a good workout before you try this in your own relationships

Most people find this exercise quite tricky to do at first. You will probably remember some details and completely forget others. You might find it easier to remember details about the character you feel sympathetic towards and more difficult with characters you don't like or don't agree with. Remembering complex information in detail like this is a skill and one you will be able to develop with practice. This isn't a memory test: the aim is not to remember absolutely everything but rather to learn how to pick up on features of communication well enough to follow the ebb and flow of a conversation and to identify when and how it goes off track and when and how to bring it back.

You might find this easier to do if your try to map out the storyboard of the exchange. Add a description of what happened or what was said in the filmstrip and then add notes highlighting when something unhelpful (or helpful) happens. Rachel's argument with her mum is briefly illustrated below.

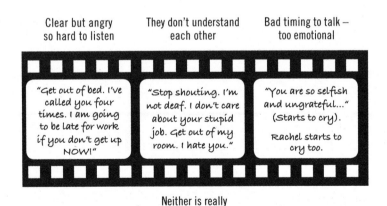

Clear but angry so hard to listen | They don't understand each other | Bad timing to talk – too emotional

"Get out of bed. I've called you four times. I am going to be late for work if you don't get up NOW!"

"Stop shouting. I'm not deaf. I don't care about your stupid job. Get out of my room. I hate you."

"You are so selfish and ungrateful..." (Starts to cry).

Rachel starts to cry too.

Neither is really listening

As the director, how would you want them to play this scene next time?

Exercise 8.11: How your own conversations unfold

When you think you've got the idea start to use the same technique on your own communication. Think back over recent arguments or important conversations and ask yourself the same questions you used in Exercise 8.10, this time with you as the actor/director stepping out of the scene to look at it from behind the camera.

You are piecing together the puzzle of what is happening in your relationships in these exercises and so you might find the prompt sheet below helpful as a guide. A copy is available online and in Appendix 8.

You might start to notice how much you edited out when you thought about arguments in the past or told someone else about them. You might still want to do that – most of us don't show our best side in an argument. Try to be as honest as you can when you think about what took the conversation off track. Try to pinpoint your own contribution and the other person's. The parts that are difficult to look at are often the parts where there is most to learn.

What kinds of things do you notice?

- Not taking into account what was going on before the argument that might have made it more likely, e.g. one or other of you being stressed about something else
- Not remembering a lot of what was actually said
- Mixed messages in verbal and non-verbal communication
- How much wasn't actually said, i.e. things you assumed the other person would know or understand or they assumed you would know or understand?
- How well do you think you were understood?
- How well do you think you understood the other person?

You will inevitably know more about your contribution than the other person's but this is a good way to build up your self- and other awareness. In time you will invite the person you argued with to look through the director's lens with you, and you will try to work out together where your communication tends to go off track. We will come back to that in Chapter 10. For now, though, you are simply learning how to stand back and observe for yourself.

Making good decisions

Making decisions can be difficult. You might not realise when a decision has to be made or you might feel that you have no choice in a lot of things in your life, so making decisions seems irrelevant. Even though you know that you can make good decisions when you have time to think, this ability might seem to disappear when your friends are around and you're pulled in lots of different directions at once, or at least that's probably what the adults around you will say. We already know that in those situations your brain is far more likely to go for the reward than avoid the consequences and so risky, fun and sometimes dangerous options often win out. This might pay off and reveal new and interesting things about the world around you but it can also put you at risk and we looked at some of the serious problems this creates for adolescents in Chapter 3.

IPT-A helps you to:

- Recognise when a decision is necessary
- Learn how to make good decisions
- Involve other people to help you to consider your options
- Revisit decisions when you have to get closer to your goal

Given this is one of the areas that we know can trip you up this is a technique that is of most use when you involve your team. Making good decisions takes practice and your team can help you to think through the options open to you and the possible consequences of each one. Each time you do this your brain will become more efficient at doing this independently.

The first step is to identify when a decision has to be made. Pressure from friends or from the strength of the impulse inside you can mean that you don't notice that a decision was necessary until after it has been made. Finding it difficult to make decisions might make you want to avoid them completely and just go with how you feel. That's understandable but can create unwanted problems that are often easy to avoid.

When you know there is a decision to be made it is also important to think about what the best result would be for you when you make the decision. Often this involves thinking beyond the immediate effect, e.g. you might want to tell someone just what you think of them if you feel angry with them but if you ultimately want to stay friends with that person and don't want them to do the thing that annoyed you again calling them every name you can think of probably won't be your best bet.

There are usually a few different ways that we can achieve what we want so the next step is thinking through all the different options that will help you to achieve your goal. This is where your team can be really useful. When you have thought of all the options you can, ask your team if they can think of any others. It is astonishing how often we miss obvious alternatives when our thinking gets fixed on a certain outcome. Your team may be help you to think more creatively and flexibly, which could open up possibilities you hadn't even considered.

Once you have the options clear in your mind it is important to take some time to think them through and think about what each option has in its favour and what goes against it. This might relate to how easy or difficult it is to do or how popular or unpopular it will be with other people. This will rely on you casting your imagination forward to think about the possible consequences of following each option. Again this should include longer-term and more immediate consequences and should also include consequences from other people's perspectives. Your team can be really helpful when you are trying to think all of this through.

Once you have thought through and evaluated your options, pick the one you think is best and try it out. Take time to evaluate what happens after you've done that. Did it work out as you predicted? Was it better? Was it worse? If this option falls short in helping you to achieve your goal go back through the sequence again and consider ways to improve this by either modifying the first option based on the new information now available to you or trying another option from your original list.

Continue to repeat the cycle until you achieve what you wanted.

Look again at the goal cycle in Chapter 7 for a simple reminder. We will come back to this regularly in the next five chapters.

Using your team to practise

Your IPT-A team offers a great opportunity to try out new ways of saying or doing things before you have to do it for real. Actors have dress rehearsals where they get to mess up, forget their lines, find the best way to steal a scene and polish their performance before going in front of an audience. Why shouldn't you? By talking through and actually practising how you will approach something that is difficult for you, you will understand it more clearly and your brain will have had a trial run so you will be more prepared to do it for real next time.

The questions in this chapter are designed to help you to think about how you express yourself and communicate. With the help of your team you will build up a better picture of what you are doing well and which parts of communication are more difficult for you. Understanding what is going well and what is not going so well is a great start but it is even more useful if you can use that understanding to plan how to approach similar situations differently next time, e.g. how can you make your verbal and non-verbal communication match more closely or how could you say more about your feelings when telling someone why you need their help or how can you show that you are interested in someone by asking open questions to keep a conversation going? Each time you notice a hiccup in your communication turn it on its head and imagine what it would be like to do it differently. For example:

- If your questions and answers close a conversation down

think of some open questions to keep the conversation going:

◊   'That's interesting, tell me a bit more . . . '

- If you are very private and never say anything about your feelings, practise revealing a little more about how you feel to help the other person to understand:

   ◊   'I am not sure what to make of my new teacher, sometimes she is really nice and sometimes she is really strict. I feel a bit confused by her and I get anxious about getting it wrong because I don't know what she wants.'

- If you tend to get defensive when someone criticises you, acknowledging your mistake and how you imagine it made them feel is a great way to cool down a potential argument very quickly:

   ◊   'I am sorry I didn't listen to you properly and checked my phone when you were telling me something important. I can understand why that upset you. Can we try again and you've got my full attention this time?'

- If you hint at what you want without saying it directly think of more direct ways to ask for what you want:

   ◊   'Let me know a couple of days before the gig if you can't come. That will give me time to ask someone else and the ticket won't be wasted.'

Of course we also have to remember that you might be doing a really good job at communicating but the person you are speaking to might be finding it more difficult to do their part. By switching roles when you practise – you play the other person rather than yourself – this might help you to understand what it is like from their point of view and why they might be finding it difficult. This might help you to come up with some new ideas because you have briefly climbed into their mental shoes.

If someone has a stock reply and you aren't sure what to say in response you could ask your team member to use that phrase while you practise different ways of responding. You will find it easier to think in this rehearsal situation than when it happens for real, and will be able to try new approaches that wouldn't otherwise cross your mind.

You can also play around with how you say things to give you new ideas. For example, you could exaggerate and play it really over the top or downplay it and whisper your lines. By working back from these extremes you will have a better idea of how loud, forceful or enthusiastic you need to be to get your point across.

The practice part is very important but so is the discussion afterwards. You can describe how it felt to try different ways of communicating and your team member can give you feedback on how each version sounded to them. Discuss what worked well and what didn't work so well. Remember you are deliberately trying out lots of different options, so feedback isn't about you – this isn't a test of your acting skills. It is far better to hear from someone on you team when something isn't clear or misses the point and then work together to make it better than to get muddled in the real situation and end up feeling let down and misunderstood.

Having a practice run before the real thing is helpful in lots of ways. It involves:

- Saying and doing things that help you to learn about difficult situations and how to manage them differently

- An active kind of practice that creates opportunities for emotional learning
- Accepting that some ideas will work well and some won't work as well as you imagined. This is all useful for learning. The ideas are being tested, not you. You are trying out new ideas to test how well they will work for you in difficult real-life situations

Tips for dress rehearsals:

- Be clear about what you want to practise before you start
- Work out your script before you start but be prepared to stray from it if inspiration strikes
- Swap roles to learn about the problem from both sides
- Talk about it afterwards. This is very important to help you to clarify what you have learnt, confirm your plan and consolidate your learning
- Be creative. Move around, exaggerate and underplay different approaches to help you to imagine new options

Why is it a good idea?

- Each time you do it you practise being in someone else's mental shoes and using your new vocabulary
- You will develop better language and communication skills
- You will start to make sense of difficult real-life situations
- You will explore, investigate and experiment, which is just what an adolescent brain is designed to do
- You will develop social skills through collaboration
- You will learn to be empathic and consider other perspectives
- You will develop self- and other awareness
- You will encourage imagination and creativity, which are the opposite of depression

This chapter has looked at techniques that you can use with all kinds of interpersonal problems. In the next chapter we will start to look at one type of problem in particular – managing unwanted change.

Summary

- Interpersonal problem solving relies on self-awareness and other awareness.
- By tracking your symptoms and goals regularly you are maintaining self-awareness.
- By asking other people to tell you how they think you are doing you are learning to look at yourself from the outside and others from the inside.
- Recognising and talking about your feelings contributes to better mental health and better relationships.
- Good communication says the same thing verbally and non-verbally.
- Your team can help you to learn by talking through situations that you have found difficult and practising new ways of approaching problems next time.

Chapter 9

Change

 In this chapter you will learn about:

- Distinguishing between predictable and unpredictable changes
- Breaking your story down into the beginning, middle and end
- Why we find some change more difficult than others
- How other people can help you to make a change more successfully

 In this chapter you will be asked to:

- Describe the role you have lost
- Distinguish between necessary and unnecessary losses
- Describe the change happening, scene by scene
- Describe the support you had when the change happened and now
- Identify the opportunities available to you now and learn what you need to do to make the most of them

Change

We must be willing to let go of the life we have planned, so as to have the life that is waiting for us.

Joseph Campbell, writer

When you opened this chapter you might have been tempted to say, 'Of course things are changing, I'm an adolescent!' And, of course, you would be right. I have talked a lot about the changes you are going through in previous chapters – changes in your body, changes in your brain, changes in your sense of yourself, friendships and family relationships. Change comes with the territory for adolescents.

These changes are predictable at your age and stage of life. They are normal, healthy and help you to grab the world with both hands. Most young people reading this book will have that in common. For some of you those changes won't cause too many problems. A lot of what is happening to you is new, fun and exciting and you might be ready to take on all the world has to offer. For some of you, adolescence might not be quite so straightforward. You might not feel equipped to cope with the demands that come with being more independent and making new relationships – so all of this change might seem quite daunting. That means for some of you the changes involved in growing up will be the headline story and for others it will be an important backstory to hold in mind.

However, for some of you the changes that you have been thinking about as you read the earlier chapters of this book won't have been to do with the predictable changes associated with growing up – they will have been to do with the unpredictable changes that happen in your relationships e.g. splitting up with your boyfriend or girlfriend, your family or the environment around you e.g. changing school or moving home. These changes are disruptive, undermine your confidence and may make you vulnerable to depression, which undermines your ability to adapt to and meet new demands.

Some of the changes that you have been thinking about might be ones that anyone would find difficult, and sometimes changes we expect to be good can be more difficult than we expect. IPT-A can help with many different types of change, including:

• Falling out with friends
• Splitting up with a boyfriend or girlfriend
• Parents splitting up and families separating
• Two stepfamilies starting to live together
• Changing school
• Moving away to start a new job or course
• Failing a course or losing a job
• Arriving from another country
• Coming out as gay or bisexual
• Becoming a teenage parent
• Having a long-term physical illness or injury
• Recovering from a physical or sexual assault

Depression is not an inevitable consequence of change, predictable or unpredictable, but it is more likely when the change feels like more than you know how to cope with. This might be because of:

• The significance of the change, e.g. your family breaking up or falling out with your best friend
• The extent of the change, e.g. several different parts of your life changing at the same time
• **The unexpected nature of the change,** e.g. a sudden move or end of a close relationship that you didn't anticipate
• The way the change shakes up other relationships and supports, e.g. people you typically rely on aren't around to help you

The strategies in IPT-A will help you to understand how to adjust to big changes, even the ones you really didn't want to happen, to let go of the part of your life that was lost in the change and to make all you can of the new situation you find yourself in. Because IPT-A is especially interested in how change affects and is affected by the people around you we will think about this change in terms of your 'role'. Your role refers to the part you played in the routines and relationships that were typical in the situation that changed. Examples of roles that might have changed include:

- Your role in your family
- Your role in your friendship groups
- Your role as someone's girlfriend or boyfriend
- Your role defined by an activity you were involved in

Let's look at some examples of change to illustrate:

Type of relationship	Role before the change	Change	Role after the change
Family	Son or daughter living with mum and dad	Parents separate	Son or daughter living with one parent and rarely seeing an absent parent
Family	Son or daughter living with one parent	Parent starts a relationship with a new partner	Son or daughter living with a parent, a step-parent and step-siblings

Family	Looked-after child living with a foster family	Placement breaks down	Looked-after child living in temporary care with several foster families for short periods of time
Friendship	Part of a stable friendship group	Fall out with someone in the group and the group takes sides	Left on the outside of the group with some people not talking to you
Friendship	Part of a stable friendship group	Change schools and go to a different school to all of your friends	Alone in a new school not knowing anyone
Romantic relationship	Someone's boyfriend or girlfriend	Boyfriend or girlfriend ends the relationship	Single
Team member	Successful runner	Serious injury stops you running	No longer on the team or able to run. Feel on the outside
Adolescent	Shy child	Peers start to date and go out to parties	Isolated adolescent feeling left behind and overwhelmed

It is not difficult to see why these changes can be difficult to manage. Each example could work out well, but having difficulty adjusting might initially trigger feelings of depression and hopelessness, or feeling depressed makes it more difficult to pick your way through an unfamiliar new situation.

Callum

Callum has been feeling down and irritable for about a year but he has also started to feel tired, unsure of himself and hopeless recently since he moved from his mum's house to go and live with his dad and his dad's new wife. The move was Callum's idea, even though he had never been very close to his dad. About a year ago Mike moved in with Callum's mum. He and Callum did not get on at all. Mike used to be in the army and was very strict. Callum resented someone appearing in his house and trying to take over and he and Mike had a lot of arguments. Callum felt bullied and criticised all the time and didn't know what to do. He felt trapped, upset and angry and gradually spent more and more time in his bedroom to avoid Mike. This also meant he spent much less time with his mum, who he had always been very close to, and he missed her but he also felt angry that she wasn't standing up for him. During one particularly bad argument Callum felt certain that Mike was going to hit him because he was so angry and he called his dad that night and told him he wanted to go and live with him. He didn't tell either of his parents how afraid and upset he was and within two weeks he had moved over an hour away from his mum and his friends, but most importantly, he thought, from Mike.

In Chapter 4 we talked about stories having a beginning, middle and end but quite often not being told in that order. As you try to understand your own change it is helpful to break the story down into chapters to describe how it was, how it changed and how it is now:

- What and who you have lost – your old role

  ◊ This incudes the people you spent time with, the things you did together, the things you enjoyed about this role and the things that were difficult at times

- The way the change happened and what support you had – the process

  ◊ This includes how quickly the change happened, if it was expected and if it was your idea or someone else's

- What and who you find yourself with now – your new role

  ◊ This includes the people you spend time with, the things you do together, the opportunities that the new role offers, the things you do or could enjoy and the things you find difficult at times

Callum

Callum feels torn between missing life with his mum before Mike and feeling awkward and unsure about his life in his dad's house. He liked living with his mum when it was just the two of them. They had a laugh and got on well most of the time. She liked his friends and hardly ever complained when they had band practice in the garage. Callum is hurt that she has made almost no effort to see or speak to him since he left. That makes him think he was right to believe that he was just in the way after Mike moved in. He is just surprised how quickly everything has changed. His dad is a quiet, gentle man but doesn't say much. He is good at fixing things and will give Callum a lift when he needs it, but they have never been very close so Callum feel like a stranger in his dad's house. He stays in his bedroom as much as he did at his mum's. He has also started at sixth form college and doesn't have any friends, and his own friends are now over an hour away, so he almost never sees them either. He doesn't feel like talking to anyone and does his best to keep to himself. He isn't as scared as he was when he lived with mum and Mike, but the sudden move doesn't feel like it has solved all of his problems either and it is lonelier than he expected. He wonders if he did the right thing moving to live with dad.

Sometimes certain parts of the story preoccupy you more than others, e.g. you might spend a lot of time thinking about the good times that you miss, dwelling on the way the change happened or worrying about whether you can make everything work in your new situation. It is useful to take notice of what it is about this change that preoccupies or troubles you most, perhaps bringing your mood down or keeping you awake at night. The significance of each part of the change – giving up something familiar, going through a change you may not have wanted or that didn't turn out as you expected and adjusting to a new situation – will vary from person to person. You might find yourself reacting to each part of the change at different times.

•   Have you found any part of the change that has happened in your life more difficult to cope with than the others?

The exercises in this chapter will guide you through each of the sections of your story. There are questions to discuss with your team for each part. If you find it helpful to create a visual record of your story you could make a storyboard adding details as you complete each section.

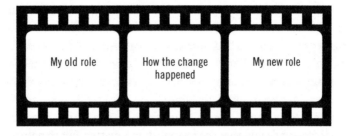

My old role | How the change happened | My new role

Living at home with Mum. Going to school with my friends. Liked being in a band. Saw Dad every few weeks. | Mike moved in and I hated it at home. Wanted to get away so moved to live with Dad. It all happened really quickly. | Living in Dad's house and I feel like a visitor. Don't see Mum or my friends. Lonely at college. Glad I don't see Mike anymore.

Callum's storyboard would start this way. This offers a very basic and simple story. We will need lots more detail and lots more scenes to understand his story properly and to work out how he can come through this change well and recover from the symptoms of depression that have become much worse and that make it much harder for him to adjust.

Understanding what has been lost

We are often selective in what we remember about the past. If you miss something you usually remember what was good about it. If you are happy to be rid of it, you tend to focus on what you didn't like. Neither version is entirely accurate and only looking at one side of the story means you are likely to continue feeling the same way about the change, which is a problem if you are feeling depressed about it. To protect against this kind of misleading memory it is helpful to go over the role you have given up in detail, allowing yourself to think about both the enjoyable and difficult things at the same time. By doing this you start to acknowledge and understand your loss, and free yourself to move on. The aim is not to persuade you that the change didn't matter, but to help you to understand why it mattered so much.

In the exercises you are trying to build a balanced picture that includes both the good and the not-so-good aspects of what has gone. It is important to include the good times. These are the times that you need to mourn, and remembering them will help to make sense of why you feel so sad about letting this role go. However, it is also important to remember what was not so good, so that you have a balanced memory of what you are leaving behind. The picture doesn't have to be perfectly balanced, it may never have been, but it will include the parts you miss and the parts that might be easier to let go.

Exercise 9.1: Thinking over your old role

• **What did you enjoy most about your old role?**

  ◊ Include examples of the things you did, who you spent time with, how you felt when the old routine was in place

- **What has been hardest to give up?**

  ◊ Try to describe this in detail to help you to understand what has been so important about this change

- **What were the difficulties in that role?**

  ◊ Include examples of frustrations, limitations, practical problems, disagreements or difficult relationships that featured in your old role

- **How serious were these problems?**

  ◊ Did you mostly sort out the difficulties or were any of them more serious, perhaps contributing to the change happening?

- **Did anyone help you to manage those problems? If so, who?**

  ◊ Try to remember everyone who helped you by listening to you or doing things for you. Are any of those people still around for you now?

- **Look back over pictures, texts messages or online posts to help you to remember as much as you can about your old routine.**

- **Talk to people who knew you in your old role and ask them what they remember about it – adding another perspective will often help you to think about things more clearly.**

- **Discuss the mix of memories, good and bad, with someone**

on your team and ask them to help you to piece the whole picture together.

Some of these questions might be difficult to answer, especially if you remember the role being mainly good or bad. It might feel tempting to dismiss examples of the other side as not mattering now, but this is an opportunity to consider everything that has been lost in this role change, to give yourself the best chance of moving on.

Callum

Callum misses his mum but he is too angry with her to think about that very much. He used to find it easy to talk to her but they haven't done that for a long time. They stopped doing that after Mike moved in. He used to find it easier to think about things after he had spoken to his mum and he has no one to do that with anymore. He also misses his three friends from school. They used to hang out a lot, played music, went to gigs together and had a laugh. They used to help when he got stressed about Mike complaining and criticising him. They would make him laugh with stories of stupid things their parents said and it didn't feel so bad for a while. The biggest problems started when Mike arrived. Callum resented him and didn't want him to move in. Mike had been OK at first but he didn't know how to handle it when Callum spoke back to him and acted like a tough army guy, putting Callum in his place. Callum hated that and at first it made him talk back more just to wind Mike up. Mum said they were as bad as each other and refused to get involved. Callum hoped Mike would leave and felt backed into a corner when he didn't. He felt worse and worse as the weeks went on – he wasn't sleeping, felt tired all the time and had no interest in anything. It was easier just to stay in his bedroom and avoid everyone than to try and sort it out.

Building bridges between past and present

It may not seem obvious when you are feeling depressed and upset about losing something that was important to you but aspects of the role that you have lost can often be adapted so that some parts of the old routine can be carried forward and remain available to you now. This distinguishes between *necessary* and *unnecessary losses*. Some things are unavoidably lost when a role is given up or taken away, e.g. being really close to a boyfriend or girlfriend when the relationship ends, while other parts of the old routine might continue even when the role disappears, such as continuing to do some of the fun things you used to do with your ex but now doing them with your other friends. When you are depressed it can be difficult to make subtle distinctions, and there is a tendency to imagine everything is lost. For example, changing schools doesn't necessarily mean giving up all the relationships you had with former classmates, but it might mean more planning ahead in order to spend time together outside of school. By looking at the old role you can check whether there is anything from the past that would be useful to take with you to provide a sense of familiarity and continuity in an otherwise unfamiliar situation.

Exercise 9.2: Looking for continuity

- Who would you still like to have in your life following this change? What has to happen for that person to be in your life now, e.g. planning ahead, seeing each other in a different setting?

- What things did you do before the change that you would like to continue after the change, e.g. meeting up with friends after school, talking to a parent who is now absent? What would it take for that to happen, and who can help you?
- What were you good at in the past that is still useful to you now, e.g. good at talking to people, good at organising or good at coming up with ideas? How could you use those skills now?

The guidelines for making good decisions in Chapter 8 might help you to think through some of these questions.

Make a plan on how to reintroduce each of the unnecessary losses you have identified into your life now. Talk to the people on your team if you struggle to imagine ways to do this. Borrowing from other people's imagination is part of the team effort towards your recovery. Put your plan into action and monitor your progress with the people who are supporting you.

Callum

Callum's friends from school made a lot of effort to keep in touch with him and sent text messages and videos of them playing in the band, saying it wasn't the same without him. At first he didn't answer the messages but gradually he started sending ideas for music back to them and they wrote a couple of songs together by sending messages and recordings back and forth. When Callum told his dad about the song he was writing he said he would be happy to drive Callum over to see his friends if he wanted to try the songs out in person. He had noticed that Callum seemed a bit happier after he started playing his guitar again and he thought it might help. Callum expected to feel awkward when he saw his friends again and worried that he'd have nothing to talk about because he hadn't been going out or doing anything, but they had already started playing when he got there so he just joined in like he used to do. After that his dad took him over to see his friends every couple of weeks and when he said they could use his dad's garage to practise his friends started going there when Callum's dad wasn't around to give him a lift.

How did the change happen?

In some cases, it might not be letting go of the past that is the hardest part of the change. The need to change something might have been clear and might even have been your idea, but the way the change happened might be upsetting. Think back to Gemma (see page 77). She wasn't too troubled by splitting up with her boyfriend – letting go of her old role as his girlfriend would have been OK. However, when he started to date her close friend two days later it felt much worse. She felt upset and embarrassed by the way they behaved and this made a manageable change more difficult for her to cope with. Coping with change that is the result of someone else's actions can be complicated: it may leave you feeling powerless, hurt or afraid. It is often more difficult to adjust after this kind of event.

Change can happen in lots of different ways. The predictability and pace of change can make a big difference in how well you adapt. Many young people describe feeling that the change that led to their depression came out of the blue, and this can make it much harder to accept and adjust. Equally a long, slow process might have left you feeling so worn down by the time it was finally over that you have no energy left. The next exercise asks you to think about how your change happened. Include details of the timing, whether it was predictable, how much support you had.

Exercise 9.3: Focusing on the change itself

- Describe the time around the change happening scene by scene. There might have been a single moment when everything changed, or your role might have been transformed over a more gradual process that took days, weeks or months. Try to focus on the time when you finally knew the change was happening, but expand this description as much as you need to give that moment a meaningful context.
- Do you feel responsible for this change or did someone or something else make it happen?
- How do you feel about that, e.g. embarrassed, ashamed, angry, powerless, relieved, grateful?
- How do you think these details affected your ability to adapt or contributed to your depression?
- Share this story with your IPT-A team. They might have questions that help you to add more details.

Callum

This part of the story was difficult for Callum to think about. He didn't like Mike and had felt alone and trapped in his own home. He didn't like thinking about it and tried to push it out of his mind whenever memories popped up, as they did quite often. After he had visited his friends a few times Callum's stepmum suggested that he could visit his mum when he was next there. Callum wasn't keen at first because he hadn't been back to her house for almost three months and had only spoken to her a couple of times. His stepmum asked him to tell her about what had been so difficult at home. This was the first time anyone had asked him and he was surprised to feel relieved when he started talking about what had happened. His stepmum helped him to think about how difficult it had been for Callum and Mike to adjust to living in the same house and encouraged him to talk it over with his mum next time they spoke. They thought about what he wanted her to know, including that he was hurt and felt let down by her but that he also missed her. Callum didn't feel confident enough to start this conversation with his mum because he didn't know how she would react, so they agreed that his stepmum would speak to her first and arrange a time when Callum could meet her without Mike being around. His mum immediately agreed and over a few weeks they started to meet and talk more regularly and Callum explained how he had felt and began to understand how difficult his mum had found the fights he had had with Mike and how frightened she was that he wouldn't want to see her again after he moved out.

Who supported you during this change?

Alongside the practical detail of the change it is important to think about the support you had around you at that time and since. This is important for understanding why you might have found this change difficult to go through. Having close friends or family who you can confide in and talk to about how you are feeling is an effective defence against depression. Depression is more likely to develop if you don't have an opportunity to do that in stressful situations.

Callum

Callum had very little support when his life at home changed and this made it much harder to cope and adjust to the change. He withdrew from his friends and family when the fights with Mike were getting worse and he had no one to help him make sense of what was happening or how he might try to cope with it. He resented Mike for coming into his home and felt like he had lost his mum – who had always been the person he spoke to most – when she didn't stand up for him. When he moved to his dad's house he was much further away from his friends and found it very difficult to make new friends at college because he was feeling so low. His dad did what he was best at when he offered to give him practical help by driving him to see his friends and offering to let them use his garage. This was important because it meant Callum could start enjoying friendly company again, which he hadn't done for a long time. That company lifted his mood enough to allow him to start talking to his stepmum when she asked him about what had been troubling him so much. Callum hadn't thought of talking to her because they had never done that in the past as he didn't see her very much before moving into her house. Starting to talk about how he felt and having her support to start talking to his mum again lifted a weight off Callum's shoulders and left him feeling much less alone and frightened.

Exercise 9.4: Support when change was happening

- How well supported did you feel around the time of the change?
- How well have you been supported since then?
- Has anything made it difficult for you to use the support that is available to you? Describe any difficulties you have experienced.

- How has the support you have received, or perhaps haven't received, contributed to your difficulties with this change?
- Add these details to your storyboard and discuss with your IPT-A team.

And so to the present . . .

> Inside every toilet roll a ship's funnel is waiting to get out.
>
> **(Ian Hamilton Finlay, writer and artist)**

Earlier in this chapter you looked back over your old role and thought about what you liked most and least about it. Now it is time to do the same for your new role. This can be more difficult to describe because the new role isn't always as clearly defined or understood as your old role was. You might feel unsure and confused about what is expected of you or what you should do next. This can be even more difficult for adolescents because you will potentially be facing a number of big life changes for the first time and won't have the benefit of past experience to give you an idea about how things are likely to work out. For example, breaking up with your first love feels absolutely devastating and it is very difficult to imagine that you will ever recover. Adults might tell you that it will get better, and even though they are right, it doesn't help at the time because you have lost someone who you cared about more deeply than you have cared for anyone before. Your emotional brain feels under great threat in the face of this kind of loss and it will overwhelm your reasoning brain, making it very difficult for you to think or consider different points of view. The intensity of these feelings is why most people remember breaking up from their first love for the rest of their lives. With time the intensity does lessen but it remains a very significant memory of a genuinely painful time.

During adolescence you also have much less say about how your life is organised than you will have when you are an adult, so decisions may be taken on your behalf that can have very significant implications for many areas of your life, e.g. if your parents separate and your home life completely changes or if your parent moves to a new job in a new city and again everything is uprooted in your life without you being able to influence the decision in any meaningful way. Having change imposed on you in this way can be a major obstacle to making it work because you may feel resentful and angry with some of the people you might normally turn to for help when you have a problem.

Exercise 9.5: Thinking over your new role

- **How do you feel about your new role?**

    ◊ Include any good feelings like curiosity or excitement and more difficult feelings like anxiety or resentment

- What do you enjoy most about your new role?

    ◊ Include examples of the things you do, who you spend time with, how you feel about the new opportunities available to you

- What is difficult for you in this role?

    ◊ Include examples of frustrations, practical problems, disagreements or difficult relationships that feature in your new role

- How serious are these problems?

  ◊ Can you mostly sort out the difficulties or are any of them more serious? How is depression contributing to this difficulty?

- Can anyone help you to manage these problems? If so, who?

  ◊ Look at your interpersonal inventory and think about the people who will listen to you or do things with you. Have you asked for their help?

- Are there any advantages or opportunities for you in your new role?

  ◊ Does this role offer opportunities that weren't part of your old role or release you from any burdens that weighed you down in your old role?

- Discuss your answers with your IPT-A team

Now let's try to put those feelings into context and think about how your new role works in practice. Most roles – with your friends or family or around activities – involve some kind of day-to-day routine and company. Each role will account for part of your day and will influence:

- where you are, e.g. at school, at home, at training etc.
- what you are doing, e.g. homework, relaxing, working
- who you are doing it with, e.g. family, friends, teammates

Callum

When Callum's friends came to see him they started going out more and they discovered places they could listen to music and see local bands that Callum hadn't known anything about. Sometimes students from his college were there too and this helped him to get to know them, which made going to college much easier and more social. When his mood improved Callum found his new courses much more interesting and he started taking advantage of all the extra activities that college had to offer. This helped Callum to have more of a local friendship group as well as staying in touch with the good friends who had stood by him when he was so low. He arranged to see his mum every couple of weeks and they arranged to do things for just the two of them each time he visited. After a few of these visits he sometimes stayed at his mum's house for the weekend and this meant he would see Mike. Callum found it much easier to manage these visits because he didn't have to live with Mike and his mum was much better at stepping in if Mike started to criticise or if Callum tried to wind him up, which he still liked to do sometimes. Callum was doing well at college and had applied to go to university at the end of the year, which would mean moving again but he was excited about that change and was ready to make the most of it.

Exercise 9.6 Looking at new routines

- What is the day-to-day routine in your new role?
- How does this differ from your old role?
- Who are you in contact with in your new role?
- How does this differ from the old role?
- Could the mix of things you do or people you see be better in your new role? How could you do that? Who could help you?
- Discuss you answers with your IPT-A team

The new role is by definition new, so you might still be unclear about what is expected of you. You might need new skills or relationships to manage the situation you now find yourself in, e.g. making friends at a new school or planning ahead when you see one of your parents less often or negotiating new rules with a step-parent who is around more often. You might find that you already have a lot of the skills you need but have to use them in new ways. This can be a great boost to your confidence when a hazy picture starts to refocus and you regain a sense of direction and competence. You have dealt with lots of other changes successfully in your life and with time you will start to see the similarities between aspects of those changes and the adjustment you are working on now.

Exercise 9.7 Looking at new skills

- How well do you understand your new role and what is expected of you?
- Are there things about this role you don't understand or know how to do?
- Who could help you to understand what is expected more clearly?
- Which of your existing skills will be useful to you in this role?
- What new skills will you need?
- Who do you already know who can help you in this new role?
- Do you need to develop new relationships? What opportunities can you see to do that?

Try to be open to possibilities you had not previously considered. At first it is very difficult to have anything but a limited perspective. The old role obscures your view, and the possibilities that the new role has to offer might be quite well hidden. Initially you might see the new role in terms defined by the old one, e.g. single is no longer dating, and separated family is no longer living together. As the depression lifts, which it will do, you can start to consider what possibilities there are for defining the role less negatively e.g. 'single' might mean free to pursue the friendships you had little time for, in a separated family you might not have to be the peacemaker between arguing parents and you can start to build healthier relationships with both parents individually. Depression is very effective in undermining this kind of problem-solving approach, and as a consequence genuine possibilities tend to be swamped by the overwhelming impact of change.

Change as a process, not an event

As you have been adding layers to your story of change, one by one, you have been tracing a journey from your past through your present and into your future. This journey doesn't stop. You set some personal goals when you first decided to look at this change, and these can be helpful signposts to keep you moving in the right direction. You have been challenged by an event that created an opportunity for depression to take hold. Your ability to make decisions and to motivate yourself was affected and you became stuck. Understanding what you have lost and what is expected of you now will have given you a clearer measure of the challenge and helped you to get moving again. Acting on that understanding and being open to the opportunities that will be revealed or created is the process through which you will turn depression into health and continue your journey.

Remember to rate your symptoms of depression every week (using the table in Appendix 3). Think about how working through this change influences your symptoms, and each week identify two or three points where symptoms and difficulties related to the change overlap to think about in more detail. Talk to your IPT-A team about these difficulties, and use the suggestions in this chapter to help you to manage them more effectively.

Summary

- Role change involves giving up an old role, tolerating a period of change and adjusting to a new role.
- Poorly matched expectations can make a role change more difficult to manage.
- Having and using good social support is a key strategy in successfully managing a role change.
- It is important to distinguish between necessary and unnecessary losses following a role change.
- Many relationships and skills can be usefully transferred from the old to the new role.
- Monitoring how feelings change can clarify the ways a role change has stalled and how to move it on.
- Alongside the losses come new opportunities, which become clearer and more accessible as depression lifts.

Chapter 10

Grief and loss

In this chapter you will learn about:

- Common and less common reactions to losing someone close to you
- The difference between bereavement, grief and mourning
- The typical course of grief and how depression can interfere and interrupt
- Remembering all aspects of your lost relationship
- Finding ways to reconnect with the people who are in your life now

In this chapter you will be asked to:

- Think about your reaction to your bereavement and discuss it with your team
- Notice which memories you think about most
- Create a timeline of your relationship with the person who died that covers the best times, any difficult times and the time around the person's death
- Invite other people into your routines and take up new opportunities that are now open to you

Understanding how we respond when someone dies

Losing a close relationship when someone like a member of your family or a close friend dies is a very painful experience. This kind of loss has been described as one of the most difficult experiences human beings face. We are made to be in relationships of various kinds and losing a close bond can force you to make a very difficult adjustment. This can be especially hard to do if it's the first time you've been through this kind of loss and aren't sure what to expect or if what you are feeling is normal. Sometimes the impact is quite sudden and you know what is making you feel sad or angry or impatient, but for some young people the effect isn't evident until weeks, months or even years after someone dies and this can make it very difficult to understand your own story and get the help you need.

During the days and weeks after someone close to you dies it is perfectly normal to feel sad, lose interest in what's going on around you, find it hard to sleep or eat properly, and to think about death more than usual. When you look at that list you might notice that it looks quite like a description of depression. However, for most people the pain of bereavement is not an illness, but rather the typical pain of loss expressed through your body, thoughts and feelings. It is not uncommon for these feelings to come in waves, which can be surprising and confusing. At first it might feel as though the waves are continually crashing over you, while later you might notice moments of calm before the waves reappear again. It can feel frightening when intense grief sweeps over you, as if you have gone right back to the beginning again. With time you learn to predict when more difficult times are coming, e.g. birthdays or anniversaries, and you can plan around them, have support close by, allowing you to remember without being knocked over by the strength of the wave.

Loss, bereavement, grief and mourning – what do they mean?

It is useful to take a moment to think about the different words people use when we talk about loss. Feeling a sense of loss is at the heart of being depressed. It is very likely that you will feel a sense of loss when you go through important changes, when a relationship isn't as close as it used to be or if you don't feel that you belong. When we use 'Loss' as a focus in IPT-A we are referring to a specific kind of loss – the loss that comes when someone close dies. The experience of losing someone through death is called *bereavement*. We typically use *grief* and *mourning* to describe ways of responding to this kind of event, with *grief* mainly focusing on the feelings, e.g. loss, sadness, emptiness or anger, and *mourning* capturing more of the behaviour surrounding these feelings, e.g. attending a funeral service, sharing memories with other people. Therapy cannot change the fact of the bereavement, but it can help you to re-engage with the mourning process and in so doing gradually reduce the pain of your grief.

Over the weeks and months following bereavement, with the help of family and friends, most people gradually pick up their routines again. They begin to eat regularly, sleep and rest, take some pleasure in doing things and in the people around them, even if this is accompanied by sadness or irritation that the person they have lost is not there to share it. Sometimes people feel guilty when they start to pick up life again, as if it is disloyal or disrespectful in some way, but it is actually a very normal, healthy and human

215

thing to do. It is an important way to guard against grief being replaced by depression. Waves of sadness and distress can come back but these gradually become less and less frequent over time. The change will be gradual for most people and painful for many, but the slow process of adjusting to a new life slowly moves on.

Less common reactions when someone dies

For some young people grief might look quite different to the picture I have described and it might be more difficult to understand how feelings and behaviour are linked.

- For some young people feelings close down and instead of sadness they feel numb or not very much at all. They might not have the support or opportunity to make sense of their loss with someone else so they bury their feelings deep inside. They might not even be aware they are doing it and an instinct to protect themselves against painful feelings takes over. It might appear at first as though they have coped well and have not been badly affected by their loss, so it can be difficult to understand months, sometimes even years, later when sad or angry feelings surface. These feelings may seem out of sync with what is going on in their life at the time and they can feel very alone when other people seem to have moved on following a loss that happened in the past.
- Some young people express their feelings through their bodies rather than in words. They might start to experience aches and pains that are difficult to explain or tiredness that they can't shake off even when they sleep a lot. Some young people imagine that they have, or worry that they will develop, symptoms that are similar to those that the person who died experienced. The worry and confusion can feel so

real and so strong that it tricks their body into believing it is happening to them. This will often stop them doing the things they normally do, like seeing friends and going to school, and might result in the young person having medical tests that overlook the emotional impact of their loss.

- When a young person loses an important adult it can cause a lot of disruption in their life over which they have very little control. It might change where they live, who they live with, who they see or the financial strain that their family experiences. These practical changes can create distraction and extra problems that can interfere with the young person's ability to focus on their feelings and the very personal nature of their loss.
- Some adolescent girls try to find closeness and comfort in other relationships and might start sexual relationships more quickly than they would do at other times, which can make them vulnerable to being overwhelmed, hurt or taken advantage of.
- Some adolescent boys show how they feel through the way they behave and become more destructive and get into fights more often than they would usually do, which distracts the people around them from the pain they feel.

In each of these examples, the young person might find that they get stuck in situations they didn't expect or don't feel that they can cope with and the things that were an attempt to feel better end up making the problem worse. Each of these additional problems can increase a young person's vulnerability to becoming depressed in addition to grieving.

Kanye

Kanye was fourteen when his mum died. She had been ill for a year and he found it really difficult to watch her in pain without being able to do anything to help. He misses her a lot but he also feels really angry that she had to go through all that and that the doctors didn't do more to help. He doesn't really know what to do with all the feelings churning around inside him. He knows he can't change what has happened and bring her back, even though he wishes he could every day, but that doesn't make it any better. He used to be a quiet and shy boy but he has been getting into more fights at school and he doesn't really understand why. The teachers were sympathetic at first, just after his mum died, but they seem to have forgotten about that now and they are angry with him a lot of the time. This just makes Kanye even angrier because they get bothered about such silly little things that he doesn't care about any more. It seems like no one understands what is important any more and no one remembers the most important thing that has happened in his life. Sometimes smashing things up feels like the only way he can show how broken up he feels inside but he doesn't think anyone understands what he is trying to say.

Exercise 10.1: Understanding your reaction to bereavement

- Have you experienced any of the less common reactions to someone dying?
- Has that made it more difficult for you or the people around you to understand the role depression has played in your reaction to bereavement?
- Talk to someone on your team about how these additional problems have interfered with or distracted your attempts to grieve after your loss.

Bereavement, depression and IPT-A

The gradual recovery initially described can be delayed or knocked off track if you become depressed around the same time you are bereaved. Depression makes the pain harder to bear and it is more difficult to tolerate the ebb and flow of your feelings. Although grief and depression look similar there are ways that depression goes beyond the typical experience of grief. Depression is more likely to involve:

- Strong feelings of guilt, which aren't to do with the person who died
- Thoughts about dying, which aren't only about wanting to be with the person who died
- Feeling worthless
- Slowing down and doing less for a long time after bereavement
- Not being able to enjoy people or the things that used to be fun

If you are depressed as well as sad or angry after someone dies, it interrupts the healing process of mourning and is likely to distance you from people who are still in your life. When a relationship with someone who has died continues to be the most important relationship in your life, it inevitably restricts how fully you live with the people who are still in your life now. Getting enthusiastically involved in the relationships around you might feel disloyal or simply have lost its appeal. When life gets smaller and smaller after bereavement it's a sign that you will need some help to learn to live with your loss.

It is important to remember that IPT-A will help you to disentangle the depression that has wrapped itself around your grief but it can't, and won't try, to ignore the reality that someone very important has left your life. IPT-A helps you use the support of the people around you to look at the parts of your loss that upset you the most and helps you to reconnect with the people around you. In many cultures mourning is a very social thing – people meet up, they spend more time together and share memories and feelings. This isn't only because sharing the experience of a loss with other people means you get more support, but also because the very act of turning to other people to help you when you miss someone is part of the process of learning to live with that loss – it connects you to the present while supporting you in gently letting go of the past.

How will IPT-A help?

IPT-A will help you to separate depression from your grief by guiding you through talking with your team about:

- What was important about the relationship you have lost
- What happened when the person died
- What support you had then and what support you have now
- What opportunities there are with the people in your life now

As you work through this chapter you might find it more useful to start by reading the sections and exercises that relate to what is most important to you at the moment. There is no need to force yourself to work through the chapter in the order it is written. For example, if you mostly think about the last days you had with the person who died consider starting with the exercises that help you to think and talk about that time (Exercise 10.5 on pages 237–8) If, on the other hand, thinking about good memories comforts you, you could start with Exercise 10.3 (see pages 225–6) and gradually add more memories from there. If you aren't sure, talk through

Grief and loss

the questions in Exercise 10.2 (see below) with someone on your team and that will help to guide you through this chapter.

When you remember someone you cared about you don't typically think back to the first time you met and remember your relationship step by step in the order it happened. You probably think a lot about some of the times you had together and not very much about other times. You might have to rely on other people to tell you about parts of the relationship that go back further than your memory, e.g. if you are thinking about your relationship with one of your parents and don't know what it was like when you were a little baby. Depression can make it more difficult to move between memories, as you would normally do, and it is not uncommon to dwell on some memories at the expense of others. Use the next exercise to think about which memories come up most often for you.

Exercise 10.2: Thinking about your memories

Think about the last couple of weeks and notice which part of the relationship you think about most often. Do you:

- Remember the good times when you were happy together?
- Remember the days around the person dying?
- Remember difficult times when you weren't getting on, perhaps thinking about things you wish hadn't happened or hadn't been said?
- Remember unfinished arguments or unspoken thoughts that you can't change now?

- Remember a mix of happy and sad memories, running between recent and more distant times?

Talk to someone in your IPT-A team about the parts of the relationship you think about most often. Think together about which part of the relationship it will be easiest for you to start thinking about in more detail

Try to notice what happens to your symptoms of depression when you go over the memories that most often come to mind – do they soothe and comfort you or leave you feeling upset and perhaps keep you awake at night?

Kanye

When Kanye thinks about his mum he remembers her being unwell and in hospital. She didn't seem like herself then and she slept a lot because of the medication they gave her. Kanye remembers feeling awkward and embarrassed and not knowing what to say. There were always people around and they would listen in if he tried to talk to her. She couldn't hear him very well because she was so sleepy and he was embarrassed when he had to talk loudly and slowly so she could understand, so he just didn't say anything at all after a while. He didn't have any time on his own with his mum for a couple of months before she died and he didn't like having to sit for hours listening to the adults talking on and on. It was boring and he just wanted them to go away. Now he feels guilty that he felt bored, as if he should have made more of the time he had with her. Kanye finds it hard to remember other times with his mum, when she was well. It is as if all of those memories died with her and all he is left with are the memories of her illness that he doesn't want.

Remembering your relationship

Thinking and talking about the person who has died is an important part of you feeling better. For mourning to happen, first you have to remember. It is likely you are already thinking about that person, and you might notice that some memories come to mind easily, while others are more difficult to remember. An important part of mourning is being able to think about the many different experiences that will have made up the relationship. This includes remembering the happy and fond memories that can be a comfort, and also the more difficult times that crop up in every relationship. This means you will be remembering the whole relationship, balancing the easy memories with the more difficult.

Focusing much more on some parts of a relationship than others after someone dies is very common, and may be even more likely to happen if you are depressed, but selecting memories in that way can hide the mix of experiences that make up most relationships and may fuel depressive symptoms like guilt or hopelessness. Sometimes memories can be comforting, but only focusing on what was good in the relationship might also mean you avoid thinking about things you found more difficult. You may feel you have little control over the memories that fill your mind, and some may be so painful or powerful that it is as if they have wiped out everything else. Focusing on a limited range of memories or a particular period in the relationship makes it more difficult to remember the relationship in the balanced way that is most helpful to grieving and mourning. If you notice that you have become focused on one part of the relationship only, it will be helpful to involve someone else who can gently encourage and help you to add other memories by asking simple questions and perhaps sharing memories of their own.

Building up a balanced picture takes time and will use your memories from across the whole relationship. Try not to rush when you are building up this picture. Sometimes you will have to take it slowly or come back to it a few times because there may be some difficult things to think about. Trying to piece the picture together too quickly may leave you feeling overwhelmed or troubled by the feelings it stirs up and this could have the opposite effect to the one you intend if it triggers symptoms of depression. Taking it slowly and having support close by can help you to understand:

- It is safe to remember
- You can remember and still get on with day-to-day life now
- You can cope with remembering all of the relationship

Sometimes depression keeps you stuck in a repeating loop, and finding ways to break out of the loop can make the symptoms less intense. When you notice that what you are remembering changes how you are feeling talk with your IPT-A team about how the memory and your symptoms are connected, e.g. feeling sad or as though you don't want to see other people when you remember what it was like when the person you have lost was still around. It can be difficult to think of ways out of these loops, and another point of view can very helpful.

How other people's memories can help you

Talking to other people who knew the person who died can be helpful in opening up your memories. Each person will have his/her own store of memories – some that will overlap with yours and some that will be new to you. This kind of thing happens when people gather together at a funeral and share their stories, although young people are often not included in this kind of memory swap so might miss out on the ways this can help. It may be that the people around you have stopped telling these stories, especially if some time has passed since the person died. Sometimes this is done with good intentions – to avoid upsetting you, or to try and help you to move on. Sometimes other people find it difficult to go over the same memories repeatedly and are reluctant to listen again. By involving your team and asking them to complete the exercises in this chapter with you, you can start to use trusted people to help you to remember. As your confidence grows you can also use other people in your life, who aren't on your team, but who have memories they can share with you.

Exercise 10.3: Sketching out the story of your relationship

- Describe what you can of the relationship you have lost to someone in your team. Start with the memories that come to mind most often and most easily
- Help the person in your team to understand what the person who died meant to you and what you meant to them
- Describe the way the relationship changed over time and talk about how and why that happened
- When you feel that the person in your team has understood the parts of the relationship you are describing try gradually to introduce more details about the relationship. Use this opportunity to expand your story backwards and forwards in time to cover the whole history of the relationship. This isn't

something you can do in a single conversation, so try to come back to this a few times, adding a little more each time

- If your team member knew the person who died ask them to share some of their memories of him or her with you

Kanye

After another letter arrives home from school to say that Kanye has smashed a window and shouted at a teacher, his dad sits him down and asks him to tell him what is going on. He says that he doesn't recognise Kanye because he is so unlike his ordinary self these days and he doesn't know how to help. At first Kanye feels angry and gets ready to defend himself against yet another telling-off but his dad stays very calm and repeats that he really wants to help. He says he is sorry that he isn't as good at this stuff as Kanye's mum used to be and they have to try to help each other to get through. This takes Kanye completely by surprise and he doesn't know what to say at first. His dad starts to talk about how his mum always knew how to sort out problems and Kanye likes being reminded of how gentle and funny she could be and how she was good at making him laugh when they were arguing so that they soon forgot what they were fighting about. He hadn't thought about that for ages. Suddenly he stops feeling so angry and starts to feel sad and he tells his dad how much he misses his mum and for the first time they start to talk about her. Kanye tells his dad that he can't remember anything before mum got sick and his dad says he has lots of memories Kanye can borrow until he can remember his own again.

If you find it easier, draw out a timeline of the relationship, running from beginning to end and covering good and difficult times. Fill in the details as they come to you and over the course of reading this chapter try to add as much detail as you can to the description you build up. Feel free to be creative when you add details using words, stories, pictures, drawings, songs or anything else that helps you to describe the relationship.

James

James remembers his dad being a great guy. He was kind and liked football and used to take James to watch Saturday morning games when he was younger. James remembers that his dad would do anything for anyone and always tried to help when he could. At first James' memories are quite general but very fond and focus on what was good about his dad. James is certain his dad tried his best and he doesn't like to think about the difficulties he had. Many of his memories are from when James was quite a few years younger, before his mum and dad split up. His dad hadn't worked for a few years before he died and didn't have much money so they couldn't see each other as often as James would have liked but he knew his dad still loved him and he thinks he just hit a difficult patch and it wasn't his fault. When his dad died in an accident it came as a big shock to James and he doesn't like to think about that; he prefers to go back to all the times he helped people and was kind. James knows his mum is angry with his dad about lots of things and so he doesn't like to talk to her about him. He doesn't recognise the person his mum talks about so they avoid talking about him at all and this has pushed them apart since his dad died.

Young people are often left out of the discussions about someone who has died that the adults around them have. Parents and families sometimes hold back details to try to protect younger family members' feelings. The story might be complicated or involve upsetting information and adults often worry that this might make upset feelings even worse. Although this is often done with very good intentions it can sometimes make it more difficult to make sense of a confusing time in your life. This is even more difficult when family and friends provide different fragments of the story, sometimes contradicting each other and making it difficult for you to know what to believe. Holding back information in this way overlooks the fact that death is quite difficult to understand anyway and especially when you lose someone close to you for the first time or in difficult circumstances. When important pieces of information are missing or if you don't go through some of the rituals that we use to mark someone's death, e.g. going to the funeral or going to the graveside, it may be more difficult for you to piece the whole story together. You, in turn, might worry about the impact of talking about how you remember the person or asking questions to help you to understand a difficult situation when other people are also grieving. This can result in you and the adults around you backing away from the subject and not talking to each other at a time when having gentle and consistent support to think about difficult aspects can be the most useful thing the people around you can offer. If you recognise that this is happening in your own situation, ask the people who you would like to talk to more to read this chapter and discuss the questions in each of the exercises together to help you to fill in the gaps that interfere with you feeling better. Talking about death can be difficult and it is helped by simple and honest discussions with people you love and trust.

Élise

Élise often thinks about her younger sister at night when she goes to bed in the room they shared before her sister died. This sometimes makes it difficult for her to sleep and she lies awake looking through pictures and videos of her sister that she has on her phone. She likes being reminded of times she had forgotten, but it also upsets her and keeps her awake into the middle of the night. When she wakes up in the morning she feels very tired and finds it hard to cope when the painful reality of her loss hits her again when she looks at her sister's empty bed. Élise often feels sad and irritable in the mornings and gets into arguments with her mum, who doesn't understand why she is in such a mood. At first Élise doesn't tell her mum why she feels so bad in the mornings because she is afraid she will tell her to stop looking at the pictures and videos because they upset her. Then one morning when she feels especially sad she explains how much she misses her sister. She is relieved when her mum immediately calms down and says she misses her too. She gently encourages Élise to tell her about what she remembers and asks her if they can look at the pictures and videos together. This helped them to start talking about many different memories they both have, some captured on Élise's phone and some triggered when they talked about her together.

Remembering difficult times

We have already said that in order to mourn you have to remember but because remembering might involve thinking about difficult times that leave you feeling sad or angry, helpless or frightened you might understandably want to avoid that. However, when grieving is overtaken by depression it is often because it is hard to remember the whole person and the whole relationship. Thinking about the good times means you only miss that part even though the rest of the relationship still exists in your memory and may creep into your thoughts alongside the memories you welcome. This can create a battle inside you as you try not to think about difficult or painful times because they leave you feeling sad, angry, helpless and frightened all over again. As a result, you can get stuck in idealising part of who you have lost or feel overwhelmed by regret over unresolved difficulties.

There are many difficulties that happen in relationships that can be painful to think about after someone dies. The ones you find upsetting will be specific to your own relationship but some common examples include:

- Important things you didn't say or the person didn't say to you

    ◊ e.g. goodbye, I love you, I am sorry, I forgive you

- No longer having the opportunity to sort out differences, or remembering disagreements over things that don't seem important to you now

    ◊ e.g. everyday arguments like what time you have to be home

- Remembering important differences that you couldn't sort out and that created a distance between you

    ◊ e.g. a parent who didn't accept your sexuality, or feeling angry that you were betrayed in a friendship

- Feeling angry that you have been left behind and have to deal with lots of unexpected problems

    ◊ e.g. a parent who didn't provide security for your future

Some of these examples might have passed almost unnoticed or been sorted out if you had had more time together. Others might have been more serious but may not have made you feel depressed. No longer having the opportunity to change the way things were left between you can make it seem much more important in your mind, especially when you are depressed, and it may be more difficult to gain perspective on unfinished business, e.g. you may have made up after every other argument but you don't think about that because you didn't make up after the last one before the person died. Only thinking about the last example doesn't create a very accurate memory of the relationship and can maintain guilty and self-critical feelings for much longer than if you could think about the whole relationship.

Take some time to think about the moments that were difficult in your relationship with the person who died. These might include typical day-to-day arguments, times when you weren't getting on or times when pressure was coming from outside the relationship, e.g. getting caught up in your parents fighting with each other or if your parent found it difficult to give you the freedom you wanted or if you have lost a friend and had times when you didn't talk to each other. Remember it is far more typical to have some problems in close relationships than to have none. However, depression makes it easier to feel guilty or ashamed about past problems when the opportunity to sort them out between you or say sorry has passed.

Exercise 10.4: Remembering difficult times

- What kind of difficulties did you face in this relationship?
- Were the difficulties something you could talk about and try to sort out?
- How well did you manage to sort them out?
- How do you think the other person felt about the difficulties between you?

- Were there difficulties that you couldn't talk about or sort out between you?
- How do you think the other person felt about not being able to sort out those problems?
- Were any of these difficulties happening between you when the person died?
- How do you feel about the difficult times between you now?
- Do any of your feelings now remind you of feelings you had in the relationship when the person was still alive?
- Do memories of any of these difficulties contribute to you feeling depressed now?

Talk over the examples that come to mind with someone in your team and add notes and what this reveals to you to your relationship timeline

This exercise can be difficult to complete and you may have to come back a few times to capture everything that happened between you. It's traditional to frown on 'speaking ill of the dead', but this rule fails to acknowledge how complicated many of our relationships are in life. Many of them fall short of what we hope for or expect, and disappointing or painful relationships can be much more difficult to mourn than happy and satisfying ones because the opportunity to make them better has finally gone. It can be very frustrating when your attempts to sort out problems or to have your hurts acknowledged come to nothing, and the resulting resentment and disappointment can feel even stronger when you have depression. The difficult feelings you may have had about the relationship don't simply disappear after death, and trying to banish them out of mind can take up a lot of energy, which is often in short supply when you are depressed.

This underlines the importance of building a balanced story, in which you acknowledge the difficulties as well as the pleasures, to reflect the relationship you have lost. The aim is not to repeatedly rake over painful memories for the sake of it, like reopening a wound over and over, but rather to clear away the debris, examine the wound carefully and attend to the injury to let it heal. It may be helpful to reread the chapter on emotions (Chapter 8, page 133) to help you to think more closely about this painful emotional part of your experience.

James

James liked to remember his dad as being kind and didn't like to think about the many times when he was taken advantage of and pushed around by other people. His dad found it difficult to stand up for himself or his family and tried to avoid conflict whenever he could. This was one of the reasons James' mum and dad split up and why James' dad lost his job. He found it very difficult to pick himself up after that happened and he didn't work again. This meant James' dad had very little money so on the one or two occasions when James went to stay with him he had to sleep on the floor in his single room. James' mum wouldn't let him stay again until his dad sorted something out but he never did. James' dad drank more after he moved out of their family home and he would sometimes forget that he was meant to meet James if he was drinking with his friends. He was always very sorry afterwards and said it would never happen again but it did; the last time was three weeks before he died. James tried to help his dad by working as much as he could at weekends and evenings. Sometimes he gave him money, which his dad said he would repay but never did. James didn't tell his mum about the money because he was sure she would be angry with both of them.

When James looked at the questions about the difficulties he had with his dad he decided to try talking to his granddad, his dad's dad. James and his dad had often visited his granddad together and he had tried to help his son too. James trusted his granddad to listen to him without getting angry at James' dad, and that made it easier for him to think about what had been more difficult to cope with when his dad was alive. James' granddad already knew about most of the problems he told him about and James was comforted when he discovered that his dad had talked about him and how proud he was of him and how hard he worked. His granddad also told him about his dad when he was younger and how he had been bullied and how that had made it difficult for him to learn to stand up for himself. James hadn't known about that before and it made it easier for him to understand why his dad had behaved the way he had. His granddad was sympathetic but also told James very clearly that it hadn't been his responsibility to turn his dad's life around and helped him to understand that some problems were bigger than he could solve. It helped James to know that his dad had had more support than he had known about and that there was someone he could talk to about all of the different memories of his dad that he had.

Remembering when the person died

The way in which someone dies can have a significant impact on how you grieve, how you recover, the difficulties you face afterwards, and the likelihood of developing depression. There are no simple rules that tell you which bereavement you will manage to cope with and which will be more difficult, but depression is more likely to feature if the way the person died adds its own challenge to your ability to grieve and mourn. For some people the absence of a clear story, because details are missing or memories are avoided, keeps them trapped in a repeating loop of painful feelings and depression because they can't fill the gaps and make sense of their loss. The list below offers some examples of how the way someone dies influences mourning. You might recognise parts of your own story in these examples but, as with previous suggestions, the details will be personal to your own story.

- An anticipated death, perhaps after an illness, might provoke a mix of sadness about losing the person and relief that his or her suffering is over. This may be easier to talk to other people about and so support may be easier to find.
- If you or the person were reluctant to accept the possibility that he or she was going to die it could prevent you from preparing yourself for it and you may have experienced their death as if there had been no warning. There may have been less talking and support before the person died and so you may feel that you have to catch up when you feel least able to make extra effort and this can slow down your mourning.
- An unexpected death, e.g. because of a sudden illness or an accident, can leave a deep sense of shock and confusion because there was so little warning or time to prepare and say goodbye. It may be difficult for you or the people around you to find words to talk about this shock or to make sense of it and this can also interfere with your grief.
- Death following an accident can also trigger anxious feelings about how fragile life is or anger that the accident wasn't some-how avoided. These feelings might keep you feeling preoccupied with the way the person died or on the lookout for something like this happening again, which can be very tiring and will make it difficult to be part of life in the way you were before.
- Death in violent circumstances is shocking and is likely to provoke fear and anger against the person or people who were responsible. This may also be very difficult to talk about and you may not be told all of the details of what happened

and so may struggle to make sense of such an important event in your life. In trying to protect you sometimes the people around you might unintentionally contribute to you feeling confused and frightened.

• When the person is responsible for his or her own death through suicide, it can be very painful and complicated for the people who are left behind. Conflicting feelings of sadness, anger, blaming yourself, shame and abandonment along with a search for unattainable answers are very difficult to cope with. There is still stigma around talking about suicide and there may be a worry that other people will react badly or in an unhelpful way. This can create secrecy and confusion that will increase the risk of depression and make it harder for you to mourn.

James

James didn't like thinking about when he found out that his dad had died. He came home from school and found his mum sitting in the kitchen crying. She couldn't speak at first and he remembers feeling frightened but not knowing what it was he had to be frightened about. When his mum told him that his dad had been knocked down and killed he didn't know how to make sense of the words because she sounded angry when he thought she should have been sounding sad. He felt so shocked and confused that he rushed out of the room and sat alone in his room for the rest of the night. He said he didn't want to talk about it and his mum went along with that so he didn't hear anything more about what happened until the funeral. None of his friends were there because he didn't tell them his dad had died until weeks later. On the day of the funeral he overheard people talking about his dad and saying the accident had been his own fault because he had been drinking and had stumbled out into the street into the path of an oncoming car. James felt so angry that he wanted to hit the people who were talking about his dad that way but instead he kept quiet and refused to speak to anyone.

When James started talking to his granddad he was able to talk to him about the way his dad died too. He discovered that his dad hadn't been drinking when he died and that what happened had been a genuine accident. This helped James to feel less ashamed and after that he started to mention his dad in front of his friends again and was pleased by how many funny and positive stories they had about him because his friends remembered his dad from the football matches and the many ways he had been generous with his time and willing to help them.

Think back to the time leading up to and around the person dying in as much detail as you can. This might have been very quick, if the person died suddenly, or it might stretch over weeks or months, if there was a long illness. Try to describe the time around the funeral and the days that followed when formal ceremonies were replaced by daily life. This may have been a particularly distressing time for you, and so it is important to use the support you have from your IPT-A team as you piece together the memories in detail.

Exercise 10.5: Thinking about what happened when the person died

- How did the person die?
- Were you with him or her when they died? If not, how did you hear of their death?

- How did you react to news of their death?
- What happened in the days after they died?
- Was there a funeral service and did you go to it?
- Is there somewhere you can go to remember the person, e.g. a grave or memorial? Have you gone there?
- Does the way the person died make it more difficult for you to think and talk about it now?

Gradually build up the detail of this part of your story by considering the events from different angles. The set of questions above prompted you to think about the events as they happened. Now think back over the same events, but this time focus on how you were feeling.

Exercise 10.6: Thinking about how you felt when the person died

- How did you feel when you first heard the person had died?
- How did you feel on the day of the funeral?
- How did you feel in the days and weeks after that?
- Have any feelings surprised or upset you, e.g. anger, blame or something else?
- When were you first aware of feeling depressed?

The story around the person's death may involve a number of people, including you, the person who died, the other people who are affected by this death and the network of people who might help. As you work through the steps of your own story, pay attention to who else features in the story and what contribution they made to how you feel.

Exercise 10.7: Thinking about how other people responded

- Do you know how the person who died felt about dying?
- How did other people respond when the person died?
- Did you have support around the time of the death?
- Did you support other people?
- What has happened to the support you give and receive as time has passed?
- Did disagreements develop among family or friends after the death?
- Were you involved in any disagreements?
- How do you feel about the people around you now?

Being close to someone who dies raises questions about 'what happens next' for many people, i.e. is death the end or is there a form of afterlife? You might not know what to think and may never have really had to decide what your view is before now. Facing a significant bereavement can focus belief in a faith system or cause a loss of faith. You might find yourself caught between different belief systems at the same time, such as when parents offer an explanation of heaven and eternal life to their children that they do not believe themselves. The rituals surrounding death may have brought you into contact with religious organisations or belief systems that were unfamiliar to you, or perhaps that are central to how you understand what this event means.

Think about how your own beliefs about death, and those of the person who died, have shaped your experience. Discuss this with your IPT-A team.

Exercise 10.8: Beliefs about death

- How have your beliefs about what happens after death influenced your experience of bereavement?
- Have your beliefs been changed by this bereavement?
- Do the people close to you share your beliefs or have there been disagreements?
- Do you hold similar beliefs to the person who died?
- Was the funeral a religious ceremony?
- Have you sought support from a faith group?
- Who can you talk to about what you believe happens next?

Use your IPT-A team to gradually develop a more detailed description of the time when the person died. Ask them about their own memories of that time. Developing this story will help you to grieve by integrating a very painful time into your bigger story. Try to continue to trace the story beyond the time of the death into the weeks and months that followed, bringing you up to the present. Pay particular attention to how other people have been involved and any opportunities to involve people who are in your life now.

How can other people help to fill the gap created in your life?

As you have been thinking and talking about your lost relationship you may have started to understand more clearly what the relationship brought to your life and how the person helped you. In your interpersonal inventory (see Chapter 5) you described the kinds of support you get from your current relationships, e.g. someone to talk to, someone to hang out with, someone to help you out when you need an extra pair of hands. Now ask the same questions that you used while putting together your inventory about the relationship you have lost.

Exercise 10.9: Understanding what you brought to each other's lives

- What kind of support did you get from the relationship you have been thinking about, e.g. could you talk about how you are feeling, get practical help to get things done etc.?
- What support did you offer, e.g. did you offer company or advice when they needed it?
- How did you spend your time together, e.g. family time, in a group of friends, time spent on interests you shared?
- What do you miss most about this person?
- Was there anything about this relationship you would have liked to change?

Part of adjusting after a loss involves reorganising some of the routines you used to share to include the people around you now. The person you have lost cannot be replaced, but some of the ways you behaved around each other and supported each other might be possible to recreate in other relationships. This is not an easy process and may feel unfamiliar and unsatisfactory for a while. It can be frustrating to have to rely on several people for the things one person used to do but your inventory reminds you that for nearly all of us life is made up of more than one relationship, and these relationships often overlap in what they offer you. By noticing how they overlap, you start to distinguish between necessary and unnecessary losses following your bereavement. There will be some things that can't be replaced, even in other relationships. These are the losses it is necessary to mourn. However, there will be other things that you will, in time, be able to get from current and future relationships. Depression can sometime blind you to these possibilities. These are the unnecessary losses that many depressed and bereaved people suffer.

Can you think of things that are similar, or could be given the chance, in your lost relationship and your relationships with the people around you now, e.g. someone to talk to, to spend time with, to share interests with? It is unlikely that all of the routines you developed with one person can simply be transferred on to a single other person, but many of them might fit across a number of relationships. Sometimes you might even notice new opportunities that have opened up following this loss. Quite often we have to make compromises in our relationships, sometimes willingly and sometimes because it is the only way to keep the relationship going (we will look at this in more detail in the next chapter). Some of the constraints that were part of the lost relationship might no longer be necessary and your existing relationships can develop in new ways, e.g. getting to know an absent parent who you were discouraged from seeing or spending time with friends who your boyfriend or girlfriend didn't like. Look over your inter-personal inventory again with your IPT-A team and try to identify the opportunities for support and company that are still available with the people around you and which may help to limit the unnecessary losses you endure as you learn to live with your loss.

Exercise 10.10: Beginning to develop other relationships

- Who can you share your time and interests with now?
- Who would welcome the support you used to offer in the lost relationship?
- What changes will be necessary to develop the potential in these other relationships?

Joe

Joe has been feeling depressed since his best friend died. They used to do everything together – they shared a flat when they went to college, worked together in a local bar at weekends and hung out together most of the time. At first Joe felt like his whole life had been taken away and he was surrounded by reminders every day that his friend was gone. Joe couldn't imagine how anyone would offer as much to his life as his friend had done. However, when he looked at each area of his life he found people who could offer some of the things he missed, e.g. friends Joe and his best mate used to go out with from work and his girlfriend, who now spent more time at home with him. He didn't used to pay too much attention to these relationships, because he didn't feel that he needed them so much, but he has been comforted by how helpful it has been as these relationships have slowly developed and started to offer some of the things he used to rely on his mate for exclusively.

Exercise 10.11: Thinking about new opportunities

- What opportunities are available to you now that were not available during the relationship?
- Discuss this question with your IPT-A team to help you to consider options that hadn't occurred to you before
- Would taking up any of these opportunities help in your recovery?

Developing existing and new relationships

One consequence of focusing most of your emotional energy on thinking about the person who has died is that it can be more difficult to give your attention to the people who are still in your life. Your friends and family might be understanding at first and accept seeing less of you as part of adjusting after someone dies. However, as other people start to pick up their routines again, you might start to feel more alone and out of sync with the people around you. Other people might appear to adjust more quickly than you, and it may be difficult to imagine that they would still understand or be sympathetic to your distress. Or you may feel reluctant to lean on other people who are also mourning, and your guilty feelings may get in the way of your receiving the support you need.

Sometimes bereavement leads to knock-on effects in lots of other areas of your life too, e.g. you may have had to move house or make new friends if you changed school. It can feel very unsettling when a series of unwanted changes follow one after the other. Using the support that is available in your existing relationships can help you to bridge the gap between old and new routines and to explore the possibilities in the life you now find yourself in. If you have faced lots of additional changes you might find it useful to read the chapter on change (see Chapter 9) as well.

Withdrawing from many of the people around you is common after bereavement and if this isn't interrupted relationships can start to appear increasingly out of reach, especially when depression means you have little interest in once enjoyable activities or company. Many depressed people describe feeling irritable with other people because their presence reminds them of the person who isn't there, and they resent other people for carrying on with life when the person they have lost can't.

You spent some time thinking about the people who are still in your life when you created your interpersonal inventory (Chapter 5). Recovering from depression involves making the most of the opportunities these relationships provide for you. Your pleasure in friends and family might only come in brief flashes at the moment, but it is important to notice those flashes: however fleeting they seem, those brief periods of enjoyment and pleasure are the building blocks of your recovery.

Often, re-establishing your routines with other people involves doing the things you used to do *before* you feel like doing them. The people around you probably haven't changed as much as it might seem to you; it's just that it's harder for you to enjoy them when you are depressed. Picking up simple and familiar routines with other people creates small opportunities to start enjoying those activities and people again. It is often easier to start with familiar routines, such as hobbies you used to enjoy or regular time with friends, and to build up gradually from there. Sometimes young people feel guilty when they start to miss their friends and wonder if it is OK to do the things they normally would. The answer is yes – this is a great sign and good instinct.

Recovery from depression is not about feeling happy all of the time. That is not the way we live life, and it would be exhausting to try. Happiness and pleasure are passing feelings, just as sadness usually is. A healthy life involves a whole range of feelings and being able to move between one feeling and another without getting stuck. In depression, your emotional experience is limited and it is more difficult to change how you feel. Looking out for potentially pleasurable activities and company will help you to rediscover lost experiences and put you back in control of how you feel.

Exercise 10.12: Doing things and seeing people again

- What interests could you pick up again?
- Who could do that with you?
- Plan to do one thing each week that you used to enjoy. Gradually add one extra thing each week to build up to a pleasurable activity each day

- Ask your IPT-A team to help you to think of things you might enjoy doing again and invite them to do them with you

Each of these possibilities highlights the importance of thinking about the people around you. You started this chapter by paying very close attention to the relationship you have lost. That person remains with you in your memories and in the memories of the people around you. As time moves on it becomes important to make new memories with the people who are still in your life and will stay with you beyond depression and into your future.

Summary

- **Mourning is a process, not an event. The process can be restarted if it has been delayed or stalled.**
- **Remembering the relationship you have lost is an important part of mourning and recovery.**
- **A balanced memory of someone does not idealise or criticise the relationship but remembers it as a whole.**
- **Our responses to our relationships are as complex and contradictory in death as they are in life.**
- **Start with the memories you are drawn to and work out from there.**
- **Recalling the difficulties and uncertainties in relationships is as important as remembering the good and certain things.**
- **Tapping into other people's stores of memories will open up your own and build a bridge between past and present.**
- **The person you have lost cannot be replaced, but you may be able to recreate some of the ways you related to each other and supported each other in other relationships.**

Chapter 11

Conflict

 In this chapter you will learn about:

- Disagreement as part of normal and healthy relationships
- The important difference between responding and reacting
- How to approach important conversations and increase their chances of success

 In this chapter you will be asked to:

- Involve the person you are in conflict with in finding a way out of your difficulties together
- Take time to learn about the relationship that is in difficulty and consider different points of view when your time together doesn't go as well as you hoped
- Think about how well you have been understood and how well you understand what the other person thinks and feels
- Plan how to cool things down or warm things up in order to start negotiating a way out of your difficulties together

Having disagreements in your relationships is virtually inevitable, healthy and normal. We all do it. The strongest relationships are the ones in which it is OK to disagree and still be confident you are on the same side. However, it's important to distinguish between an occasional disagreement that gets forgotten about and a cycle of conflict that rolls on and on without ever really being resolved. When conflict becomes a habit that is hard to break it is more difficult to understand misunderstandings and depression takes hold more easily.

It is not unusual for your relationships to change when you feel depressed. You might enjoy being with other people less and feel irritable and wound up a lot of the time. You probably don't feel very motivated to tackle problems that come up and you might not feel very confident that you could do much about them even if you tried. When you get stuck in a cycle of conflict – big, loud arguments or quiet simmering resentment – the impact on your mood and other symptoms of depression is often obvious. Fighting with someone over and over or not talking to someone you used to be close to can keep you awake at night, distract you and make it difficult to concentrate on anything else and leave you feeling sad, frustrated, anxious and hopeless.

Roisin

Roisin is sixteen and has recently moved back home to live with her mum. She isn't happy about it and wants to stay with her aunt and cousins, where she has been living for the last month. She moved to her aunt's house when the arguments with her mum got too bad for either of them to cope. Last week her mum and her aunt had a big argument and stopped talking and her mum insisted that Roisin move back home to live with her. Roisin felt sad, very angry with her mum and as if she had no control over her life.

Responding rather than reacting

When you are trying to sort out conflict in one of your relationships it is important to understand the difference between *responding* and *reacting*.

A *reaction,* sometimes called a gut reaction, is driven by your emotional brain. We know you can make perfectly good decisions a lot of the time but, like a lot of adolescents, you might notice that you are more likely to react when your friends are around, other people are watching you or when the situation is emotionally charged. It isn't surprising then that those are the situations when conflict often flares up. Look back at Chapter 3 (see pages 46–8) for a reminder on why adolescents typically behave differently to children and adults in these situations. This isn't your fault and it is something that changes as connections between your planning, reasoning brain and the emotional centre of your brain become more efficient, helping you to regulate your feelings and pause before reacting.

- Reactions aren't easy to control and are influenced by the wiring in your brain, past experiences, instincts and habits rather than thought and planning. Flying off the handle when you think you are being treated unfairly usually isn't planned and might be hard to resist.
- A reaction is likely to be impulsive with only limited, if any, attention given to the context and longer-term consequences.
- It is much more difficult to hold the other person in mind when you react because they drop out of focus when you are overwhelmed by your own intense feelings.

A *response*, in contrast, is deliberate, takes time to develop and reflects a choice you have made. It involves:

250

- **Seeing the big picture as well as the detail.** When you get caught up in a difficult incident, like an argument, it can be distracting and it is easy to lose sight of the bigger picture, which could help to put an individual incident in context. Being able to step back and think about how typical or unusual an individual example is puts you in a better position to decide how to respond.

- **Remembering your objective.** In the heat of the moment it is tempting to score quick points, e.g. by throwing in a sarcastic comment or trying to have the last word. Unfortunately, the last word in one argument can often turn into the first word in a new one. If your main objective is to break a pattern of conflict you typically need to build in a pause when you can plan how to say what you need to and leave unsaid the wrong thing despite the temptation to keep going. Your long-term objective will win out over short-term gain rather than the other way round.

- **Making good decisions.** Even though it may not always feel like it or be easy, you do have a choice about how to respond to the situations you find yourself in. Slowing down to consider all the options open to you before you decide about how to respond means you will be more likely to take context and your long-term plans into account (see pages 180–3 in Chapter 8 on making good decisions).

If you *react* to an argument you are more likely to repeat unhelpful habits whereas if you *respond,* you open up the possibility of changing unhelpful patterns of behaviour and creating a new healthier pattern. Responding involves a degree of choice that is missing in a reaction. This chapter will look at ways you can prepare your responses and limit your reactions.

Roisin

When Roisin and her mum used to live together they reacted rather than responded a lot. Neither of them felt understood and they were in a constant battle to be heard despite the fact that neither of them was really listening. When Roisin got really frustrated she used to throw things or take it out on herself by scratching her arms until they started to bleed. She couldn't remember how that started but doing something gave her a few moments of relief when she felt like her brain was going to explode and it soon became a habit. Mum shouted more when she threw things and didn't even notice, or if she did she didn't say anything, when Roisin scratched herself. It came as a complete surprise to Roisin when her aunt seemed upset when she saw the scratches. She sat Roisin down and asked her to tell her why she did it and to help her to understand how it helped because she couldn't imagine that on her own. It was hard to put it into words but Roisin tried and they agreed that if she felt like hurting herself she would try talking to her aunt first to see if they could come up with any other options. She didn't always manage to stop herself but sometimes she did and knowing her aunt would give her a hug, even if she didn't have anything else to say, helped Roisin to calm down. She hadn't talked to her mum that way for a long time and talking to her aunt made her realise how much she missed that with her mum.

Selecting a relationship to focus on

The ideas in this chapter are generally more useful if you can identify an individual relationship to focus on. There is a good practical reason for this. You will be asked to think about what happens in that relationship in detail, and that is much more difficult to do if you are trying to think about several relationships at the same time. The skills you develop can of course be used in all of your relationships, but it is easier to learn how to use them by focusing on just one relationship at first. Think back to untying the knot in the cables in Chapter 4 (see pages 67–8) – disentangling one helps you to straighten out most of the cables.

Even when it is obvious to you which relationship you need to work on, it can be difficult to know where to start. Reaching this chapter is already an achievement but one that might fill you with a mixture of apprehension and hope. You might worry about looking at the relationship too closely because you can't imagine how to change it and that might leave you feeling hopeless, but you have come this far and that suggests at least part of you hopes it can be different. That isn't unusual. Your problem-solving ability and creativity get switched off when you get stuck in repeating patterns – a bit like being on automatic pilot – and even quite simple solutions won't occur to you in the way they would in other situations. The exercises you will use in this chapter are designed to help you to imagine and in imagining take a step towards making it happen.

Right now you are probably still in a number of relationships where power is not equally shared, for example with your parents or carers or at school with your teachers. This might also be true with other young people your own age if you are being bullied. Adults might still treat you like a child and not take you seriously, which could be one of the reasons why the relationship is in trouble. Bullies might try to make themselves look bigger by making you look small. You are a young adult with views, ideas and opinions of your own and sometimes the people around you don't keep up very well or get alarmed by all of the changes they see happening in you and try to hold you back. Sometimes the opposite might be true and too much is expected of you before you feel ready to take on all of the responsibilities of the adult world, and the option to learn at your own pace is taken away. Adults and peers have to work at keeping up with all the changes that happen during adolescence too and some of them do it better than others. IPT-A will help you to negotiate differences that can stop you and the people you are close to feeling like you are on the same side.

Involving the other person

You already know that IPT-A is not a private therapy. It works best when other people know what you are trying to do and get involved to help. This is especially true when you are trying to sort out a dispute with someone you are close to. IPT-A can help you both to understand the problems you are having and to negotiate a better solution. The exercises described in this chapter are most effective if you both do them, but that won't always be possible and you can still start by going through them with your IPT-A team. However, do try to involve the other person as soon as possible. If you are being bullied or threatened in any way it will be important to involve people who can support and, if necessary, protect you before you try to tackle the problem.

Relationship difficulties start for many reasons but when they get stuck it suggests that both people are playing a part in keeping them going. It really is almost impossible to keep an argument going on your own. You might try to start an argument but if the other person doesn't react it grinds to a halt. You might try very hard to end an argument but if the other person won't let it go it springs back into life again. Anyone with a little brother or sister who just won't let it go will know what I mean! When you are in a dispute with someone, you often feel unhappy about how the other person behaves towards you. It can be tempting to accuse or blame them for how bad you feel. When you are feeling depressed, you are also much more likely to feel guilty, and perhaps assume responsibility and blame yourself too often. Whether the problem lies in blaming or being made to feel to blame too much it rarely gets you very far. Rather than blaming yourself or the other person it is better to *understand* what is keeping the dispute going and break the pattern down step by step to bring about change.

* Have you told the person you are in dispute with that you are depressed and that you would like to work on making changes in your relationship to help you to feel better?
* Read on for ideas on how to approach this conversation

This is an important conversation to have. Let's think about why. Depression and relationship difficulties keep each other going. It is not your fault that you are depressed, but you and the people you have relationships with will feel the impact of this illness, and knowing about depression is going to be one of your weapons in fighting it. As you become expert in understanding the way depression affects you, you will get better at targeting your efforts to make effective changes in the relationship that is in trouble. The same is true of the people you have relationships with, especially the person you are going to focus on. If they understand the nature of depression, they can see more clearly where the battle lies – with the illness, not with you – and they can become one of the team working towards your recovery rather than one of the obstacles in your way. Improving your depression and your relationships will be of benefit to both you and the people you have relationships with.

Tips for important conversations

- **Timing:** Try to find a time that is convenient for both of you when you won't be interrupted. This might take a little planning with both of you making time to talk about things that are important to you rather than springing an important discussion on the other person without warning.
- **Content:** Take some time to think about what you want to say and what you want the other person to understand before you get started. You are more likely to get mixed up or forget things if you just hope for the best and say the first thing you think of.
- **Take a break when either one of you needs it:** It's possible that one or both of you might feel upset or worked up about what you are discussing. If that happens agree to postpone the rest of the discussion until you are both calm and can express yourselves clearly and listen carefully. Be sure this means *postpone* and not *cancel*. Agree when you are going to come back to the discussion – that might be after a few minutes or the following day – and stick to the plan.
- **Follow up:** Expect to follow up on the discussion after you have both had time to think. Remember that *good communication is a process, not a one-off event*.

If you and the person you are having problems with haven't watched the short film about how other people can help you with your depression, think about watching it together now. (see page 12 for the link.)

Alternatively ask him or her to read the information in Appendices 1 and 2 to about depression and how IPT-A can help.

This could help you to think about what depression has done to your relationship and how your relationship is keeping the symptoms of depression going.

Taking time to observe

We are going to start by taking time to look carefully at the way you and the person you are in conflict with behave around each other. Understanding how the relationship works now will help to give you ideas about how to improve it. This sounds simple, but taking time to just watch can be tricky to do when you are feeling worked up and ready to react. The ultimate goal is for you to be able to make informed and well-thought-out decisions about your relationship, rather than getting caught up in unhelpful repeating patterns. To make the best decisions, start by collecting as much information as you can on how the relationship is working now.

By now, you should be familiar with being curious and gathering more information in IPT-A. You practised this in Chapter 8 (see pages 175–80) when you watched examples of arguments on TV and identified what did and didn't work and then thought about those ideas in relation to your own communication style. By building up additional layers of the story, you start to see what is happening from a number of different perspectives. This time you are going to imagine yourself being an actor/director making a documentary about your chosen relationship. Your job is to observe and record, but not – just yet – to try to influence the course of the events you see. Your role is more complex this time because you are both one of the people in the relationship and the observer. It is tempting to try to rush and change things, but that will risk misdirecting your energy in unproductive ways. The first step is to research your subject.

Exercise 11.1: Observing the relationship

- Think of one or two occasions when you have spent time together in the last week, especially if you noticed a change in your symptoms of depression around then, e.g. a drop in your mood or a sleepless night afterwards.

- To help you to stand outside the scene, try describing each example from more than one perspective to someone in your IPT-A team. For example, start with your own point of view, the one you know most about. Next, tell the story from the point of view of the other person. This is how the other person *would* tell it, if asked – not how you think they *should* tell it. You don't have to agree with this version, simply try to imagine the scene from another point of view. Then tell the same story from the point of view of a neutral observer – perhaps someone who was there, or if no one else was around, a fly on the wall.

- Try to include details about where you were, when it happened, what was said, how it was said, how each person felt, how they looked, moved and sounded, as you learnt to do in Chapter 8.

- Were you talking about what you wanted or needed to talk about?

- Were you talking about the same thing?

- **Discuss what this reveals that wasn't so obvious from your original point of view with the person on your team.**

- **Repeat this exercise each week to identify examples to work on and use it to track changes in the relationship:**

  ◊ **Celebrate your successes**

◊ **Use the ideas in the rest of this chapter to target areas that need more work**

When you start to look at examples in detail like this you might discover how much of the story you normally forget or edit out. You will probably find there are quite a few gaps in your descriptions at first, bits of information you have forgotten or perhaps never knew, e.g. what the other person was thinking. You might also notice the things you tend to remember, e.g. your own contribution, the things that made sense or seemed important to you. Communication routinely relies on you filling in these gaps and working with your best guesses when you don't know all the details, for example about another person's feelings, intentions or understanding. This usually works well enough for ordinary communication, but it is less reliable when you are arguing or have strong feelings about something. That is when mentalising – your ability to hold your own and another person's mind in mind – is most vulnerable and your ability to understand misunderstandings breaks down. The diagram below will help to remind you of the gaps you might be filling in without realising or checking with the other person.

It is just as important to notice what has **not** been said as what **has.** When you think back over recent exchanges, do you realise that there are important things that you wanted to say that you didn't say directly? Try to be honest with yourself here and be clear about what you *actually said* – not what you meant to say, not what you implied, and not what you think any reasonable person would understand (all of these can open the misunderstandings flood-gates in disputes). Ask yourself the same questions about what you heard. Did you understand the other person's main point or is it a bit fuzzy in your memory? If the most important messages are getting buried or sidestepped, it is easy for them to be missed and forgotten.

Exercise 11.2: Key questions to ask

- Have you said what you want the other person to know and understand?
- How well do you think he or she understood you?

And, on the flip side:

- Have you heard what the other person is saying?
- How well did you understand his or her message?
- Ask the member of your IPT-A team who has been helping you with these exercises if they understood the same messages from all they have heard so far and discuss any differences in what you understood. These differences might give you great clues about why the misunderstandings happen.

- It is a great idea at the end of important conversations to summarise in one or two sentences what you think the other person was saying and check if you have understood correctly, and to ask them to do the same for you. It is one of the quickest ways to prevent misunderstandings rolling on and on.

Where will I begin?

We often start our stories in the middle – at a point of crisis or dramatic change. This is especially true when you are depressed or anxious, because your perspective tends to narrow. You are less likely to focus on the events leading up to or following a problem, and instead become fixed on the actual crisis or argument. This is unhelpful because it keeps you focused on the worst part of the story and doesn't develop your awareness of triggers or how it worked out in the end. It's a bit like trying to find what you are looking for with a small pocket torch rather than floodlights.

Exercise 11.3: Filling out the scene

Expand your description of each recent incident by adding the following details:

- What happened in the lead-up to the incident, e.g. another argument earlier in the day, a bad day at school, feeling exhausted after a poor night's sleep. Rewind back to the point when you last remember feeling OK before this incident and tell the story from there. Try to identify all of the things that contributed directly or indirectly to the incident going badly.
- What happened after the incident, e.g. sat alone in my room and cried, called a friend and took my mind off it, hurt myself, forgot about it as soon as it was over. Now fast forward to the point when you think the incident was no longer the main thing on your mind and tell the story until you reach that point. Take note of who or what changed, how you were feeling and what you were doing.
- Does this give you any idea about how you could reduce the chances of something similar happening again or how you could limit its impact on you if it does happen?
- Discuss this with your IPT-A team and the other person (or people) involved.

Roisin

When Roisin thinks about the last fight she had with her mother before she moved out she immediately remembers them screaming at each other and Roisin smashing a plate on the floor in the kitchen. She drops straight into the middle of the fight, with little sense of how it started or what happened next. When she uses the questions in the exercises to prompt her she remembers that the fight actually started the night before when her mum had been getting ready to go out. Roisin told her she didn't want to go to her dad's and she wanted to stay at home on her own. Her mum refused and said either Roisin went to her dad's house or her mum would have to stay in and her boyfriend would come round. Roisin didn't want to do either of them because she didn't like mum's new boyfriend and dad's house was boring and she didn't have all of her things there. What she really wanted was her mum to stay in with her, as she hadn't seen her all week because her mum had been working night shifts at the hospital, where she was a nurse. Roisin wanted them to watch a film and eat popcorn on the sofa like they used to do but she didn't tell her that. Looking back Roisin doesn't think her mum had any idea what Roisin wanted. Instead Roisin told her she hated her life and ran upstairs and locked herself in her bedroom. Her mum looked angry but Roisin doesn't know if she felt anything else or what she was thinking. When Roisin was in her room she turned her music up loud and ignored her mum when she knocked on the door and tried to talk to her. She kept knocking on the door for ages but when Roisin wouldn't reply she eventually gave up and Roisin stayed in her room for the rest of the night. She scratched herself badly that night but didn't want to leave her room to clean up in case her mum heard her and started again.

When they saw each other early the next morning they were both very tired and it looked like neither of them had slept. Her mum immediately told Roisin that she had ruined her night and Roisin said she cared more about her boyfriend than her. That is when her mum said she was going to have to get used to him being around and Roisin felt like her worst fear was true and mum didn't care about her anymore. Roisin felt so many things all at once that she pushed her plate off the table and smashed it on the floor as she rushed out. She ignored her mum shouting after her as she ran out of the front door and called her aunt and asked her if she could come and stay at her house for a few days. Rosin is surprised how many details she had forgotten until she really took time to try to remember how it all started in the first place.

How is it between us?

The questions in the next exercise are designed to help you to pull together all of the things you have noticed when you have been studying your subject, that is the relationship you are focusing on. By looking at what is happening between you at the moment, you will be better informed when you make a plan about what to do next. Do you notice any patterns when you think about recent examples of spending time together? Are you trying to sort things out but finding it difficult or have you backed off from each other and are trying to keep your distance? Often we move back and forth between these two approaches.

Exercise 11.4: Summarising

- How would you describe the majority of your time together – tense, enjoyable, distant, close, confusing?
- Do you argue? If so, how often?
- If there are arguments do you work them out or are they left up in the air?

Conflict

- Do you feel as though an argument is just under the surface even if it doesn't blow up?
- Do you actively avoid spending time with each other?
- Have there been any enjoyable times together, free from tension and disagreement? How much of your time together is like that?
- Discuss this with your team and the person you have been thinking about. Do they agree with your summary? Have they noticed anything that you didn't?
- Discuss whether it would be useful to start to set limits on the arguments you have, or to try to talk a little more to break into the silence

These questions will help you to think about whether your relationship is best described as **fired up** or **frozen**. **Fired up** suggests arguments, unfinished business and feeling tense with each other – it is too hot and needs cooling down. **Frozen** suggests fewer flare-ups but a sense that there is something to be sorted out lingering in the background – it is too cold and needs to be heated up a little. It is quite likely that you will recognise features of both patterns.

Fired up

If you are both aware there is a problem but still end up having the same arguments over and over it's likely that the strategies being used to tackle the dispute are not working, or are falling short of what is needed in some way. The challenge is to make the strategies that are being used more effective. If you are arguing over and over again, particularly if you are covering the same ground without moving on, it will be useful to stop this pattern repeating by identifying when the pattern starts and interrupting it early. This tips the balance in favour of healthy communication, and limits repetitive and unhelpful exchanges.

Lin

Lin chose to live with her boyfriend against her parents' wishes. She thought they were being boring and old-fashioned, and she kicked back against their control by throwing herself into the relationship. She was very surprised when her parents refused to speak to her while she was still with her boyfriend, but it made her all the more determined to stick to her guns. When Lin and her partner started to have arguments and the relationship started to feel a bit shaky, Lin wondered if she had made a mistake when she chose him over her family. She blamed him for her unhappiness and felt guilty that she did not feel as loyal to him as he was to her. Her resentment and anxiety fuelled their disagreements, but she couldn't say that so instead they had lots of arguments over trivial things. Lin found it difficult to understand all of the petty niggling and criticism, even though they were her indirect way of saying she was unhappy and unsure about her decision. Chipping away at the relationship by trying to correct unimportant differences didn't help them to get on and got in the way of talking about the important differences between them.

Frozen

When relationships go back and forth over the same old ground it can be exhausting, especially when you are depressed and your energy and motivation are already low. Under these circumstances you might find that you back off from each other. You might not have decided to end the relationship – it might be difficult to imagine how you would do that, e.g. if your conflict is with your parents and you still live together, or that might not be what either of you wants, but nonetheless you find yourself living on the outside of a relationship while still being part of it. You might feel on your own and disconnected rather than part of a team. If this describes what is happening for you one option will be to find ways to become more involved in the relationship again to open up options to improve it. In the scenario with Lin, things needed to be cooled and contained, while with Roisin they needed to warm up and bring some life back into the relationship.

Roisin

Roisin had been nervous and unsure about moving back to her mum's house. Although they hadn't been fighting as much since she left she was sure that was just because they hadn't seen each other so often and their phone calls and text messages were brief. When she first moved back in there was an uncomfortable atmosphere and they had quickly fallen into the habit of sitting in different rooms and could spend several hours without seeing each other despite being the only people in the house. After thinking through the last exercise and talking about it with her aunt, Roisin wonders if suggesting watching a film together might be a good way for her to start spending time with her mum again. They used to have a film night every week and until recently nothing was allowed to get in the way of that plan. Roisin talks to her aunt about it and her aunt thinks that it is a great idea and offers to help by suggesting a film that they both might like to watch. Her aunt was keen to make up with Roisin's mum too so this gives her an excuse to get in touch. Roisin's mum is relieved to hear from her sister because she didn't like it when they weren't talking to each other and she agreed that reinstating film night is a good idea. This simple change helps them to be more relaxed with each other than they had been for months and the calmer atmosphere offers an opportunity to approach the more difficult discussions they still have to tackle, although they don't try to do that right away. Just being around each other again is an important first step and they don't try to rush it.

In the relationship you are focusing on are you still able to enjoy each other's company, even for short periods of time? It is encouraging if this hasn't disappeared entirely. If you don't have any enjoyable or calm time together, finding ways to build it back in needs to be an early target. The plan doesn't need to be elaborate. It might be something simple like going for a coffee together or watching a film or something funny on TV – anything that you used to enjoy that you haven't done recently. These plans don't have to start with talking openly about your relationship difficulties; just get used to being in each other's company again, as a first step.

Ending the relationship

A third option, alongside fired up and frozen, emerges when the differences between you are important enough for you to seriously consider ending the relationship. Before you act on that though it is a good idea to take time to look at the relationship carefully and try to use the ideas in this chapter and Chapter 8 (see pages 157–80) on improving your communication and clarifying what you both expect from the relationship. Sometimes the problem is not that change is impossible but that neither of you knows how to make changes. If the relationship does end, the suggestions below and in Chapters 8 and 9 can be helpful in talking through this difficult kind of change.

Renegotiation

Whatever your starting point, our goal will be to help you to move towards ***negotiating a way forward together***: that is, constructively talking about your differences and identifying ways to change that both of you find acceptable. It is important that the plan is acceptable to everyone involved if it is to have a chance of working. That means talking to the other person in the dispute, so that he or she knows what you are trying to do and knows what he or she can do to help, is crucial.

Repeating patterns across relationships

So far you have been working hard to understand more about what gets in the way of sorting out differences in one of your important relationships. It is also helpful to think about whether the problems you are noticing are only typical of that relationship or if the same kinds of problems crop up with other people too. It isn't unusual to have similar difficulties with more than one person, but you might notice that the way you deal with disagreements depends on who the other person is and what situation you find yourself in, e.g. compare how you deal with disagreements with your best friend, with your teacher and with your parents. You probably approach those disagreements quite differently and perhaps with quite different results.

If you manage similar difficulties in other relationships more easily, it means you already have useful and relevant skills that you could use in sorting out the problems you have been focusing on in this chapter. For example, you might be good at sorting out problems with friends because, when you aren't feeling low, you like spending time with them and so it is important to you to try to clear up differences as quickly as you can. If you and your friend both try to patch things up after a disagreement it might feel quite easy and so you overlook the helpful things you do to work it out. It is also easy to overlook the things you do well when you feel depressed and you might be tempted to dismiss successes as irrelevant or more to do with the other person than you. The problem with not giving yourself enough credit for your own successes is that it can stop you from using the ideas and skills you already have in a relationship that is proving more difficult to sort out. Take some time to think about the questions below and consider whether there are any ideas and skills you could transfer from one area of your life to help with the relationship problems that have become stuck.

Exercise 11.5: Learning from other relationships

- Have you noticed similar difficulties to those you picked up on in earlier exercises in any other relationships?
- If so, have you found any ways that are useful in sorting out problems in those other relationships? What are they?
- If you aren't sure what makes the difference describe how you approach similar problems in other relationships to someone on your team and ask them to help you to work out what contributes to your success.
- Have you been using your own top tips to try to sort out the problems in the relationship you have been focusing on?
- How could you transfer some of the good ideas that you

already use to the relationship that needs a little extra help
to sort out?

• Ask someone on your team to help you to think through how
to switch approach to make room for your own good ideas.

You may also notice that you have difficulties in other relationships similar to those in the relationship you have been focusing
on and you haven't been sure how to sort them out. Possibly some
of those relationships feel less threatening to focus on initially
because they are less significant in your life or because the other
person is more willing to try to find a solution with you. For example, it might feel easier to talk to your best friend about a comment
that upset you than to tackle this kind of discussion for the first
time with your critical teacher. These relationships could offer
you great opportunities to practise new skills and build up your
confidence before approaching the relationship that has become
quite stuck. Success with one relationship can give you the confidence to try with another.

The big picture

The relationship you are in has its own history and its own timeline, which started before the disagreements and, if you want it
to, will hopefully continue after the conflict has been resolved.
You might have come through similar difficulties in the past, or
perhaps this is the first time the relationship has faced this kind
of challenge.

Exercise 11.6: Your relationship timeline

Sketch out a timeline of the relationship, as you did with your depression, and describe how the relationship has developed over time. Ideally, do this with the other person in the relationship, to help you to think about the bigger picture together. If this is still too difficult, start to think about this with one of your IPT-A team and share your thoughts with the person involved in the conflict when you feel ready.

Go back to how the relationship started and try to remember what has been good about it in the past and how you have managed difficult times previously. Use the questions below to guide you through the timeline.

- When has the relationship worked well? What are your best memories of it? Try to describe them in detail.
- Who and what contributed to the good times?
- When have been the most difficult times in this relationship?
- What or who has helped you to get through difficult times before now?
- Talk to the people who have known you while you have been in this relationship and ask for their memories too.
- Most importantly talk to the other person in the relationship and try to create a timeline together that captures your shared and your different memories about how your relationship has worked.
- Have you tried to use the ideas that have helped in the past recently? Try to reintroduce one or two things that have been good in this relationship in the past.

272

The timeline will remind you of the big picture, and it might also suggest what will be helpful in sorting out the problems. The best solutions are not always new ideas. Sometimes it is a matter of reminding yourself of your own good ideas and skills – things that you may have quickly forgotten when you became depressed. If you have come through similar difficulties in the past, think carefully about how you did it and whether any of the things you did then could be useful to you now.

Roisin

Roisin remembers being very close to her mum when she was growing up. Dad was away with work a lot so her mum was the main person in her life. Her mum didn't work when she and dad were still together and she was always around for Roisin. Roisin remembers feeling like the most important person in mum's life. Dad left when Roisin was twelve and she adjusted quite easily. She hadn't been used to seeing him very much and still saw him every two or three weeks. Mum used to ask her if she was OK a lot and Roisin never doubted that mum held her in mind. The big change came for Roisin when mum went back to work and so wasn't at home as much as she used to be. Even that was OK at first because Roisin was spending a bit more time with her friends and mum always insisted that they made time to be together, like film night once a week. As time passed mum worked more because dad didn't always send the money he said he would. Mum started to get stressed about money and missed film nights if she was working. Roisin didn't like this and they started to argue more. Her mum started saying that Roisin should see her dad more because he wasn't helping as much as he should but Roisin didn't like it there because it took two buses to get to where dad lived, so she couldn't see her friends, and she had to sleep on a sofa bed in the living room because he didn't have a spare room. She didn't have her things around her and always felt like a visitor in dad's house. She started to feel as though mum was trying to push her away and Roisin didn't know how to deal with it. She and mum were talking less and it was around then that Roisin started to scratch her arms and spend more time alone in her bedroom. When mum started dating Roisin felt less important than ever and scared that everything was falling apart.

Issues and key difficulties

As you have been thinking about recent examples, you might have noticed that the same issues tend to come up time and time again, sometimes directly and sometimes indirectly. You might already have had a good idea about what the big issues are between you but others might have been more of a surprise, especially if the important issues aren't the same for each of you.

Exercise 11.7: Identifying the main issues

- What are the top two or three issues you would like to be sorted out in this relationship? For example, agreeing rules with your parents about staying out with your friends.
- Do you think the other person knows they are the important issues for you? Have you told him or her?
- What do you think the other person's top two or three issues are?

- Have you asked? Remember it is important to check you understand each other's concerns accurately.
- Do the people on your IPT-A team recognise the issues you have identified? Did they identify any other issues you hadn't thought about?

Roisin

Main issues for Roisin:

- How much time mum and I spend together

  ◊ Don't think mum wants to spend time with me, she's only interested in her boyfriend
  ◊ I haven't told her I miss her – I think she should know. If she cared about me she would miss me too

- How much time I have to spend with mum's boyfriend

  ◊ Mum wants me to do this more than I do. She is trying to force us to be a family so she can spend more time with him

- I am not important to mum anymore

  ◊ I don't think she is interested. Everything else seems more important to her than I am

Roisin struggled to imagine what the main issues were for her mum. She didn't feel as though her mum held her in mind and that made it difficult for Roisin to imagine what was going on in her mum's mind. When she showed her mum the questions in Exercise 10.5 and her answers she was very surprised to discover:

- Her mum had no idea how much Roisin missed her or that she felt forced to be part of a new family. She thought Roisin was angry with her and missed being in a family
- Mum's main concern is how to cope when Roisin gets so upset and breaks things at home. It makes her sad and frightened to see Roisin so upset and she feels like she is letting her down by not being able to help
- Roisin's mum feels worried about the financial pressure of being, effectively, a single parent. She can't rely on Roisin's dad and so works as much as she can to make sure their home is secure. Sometimes she is so worried that she forgets that her being around is one of the important things that make home feel safe for Roisin
- Roisin's mum does worry that she misses being part of a family and having her dad around. She hopes that if Roisin gets to know mum's boyfriend it would feel more like a family again and she wouldn't be so upset

By thinking about these questions and sharing their answers Roisin and her mum started to have a much better idea about how each other felt and how they were each trying to make sense of the difficulties between them. They could understand how misunderstandings led them to pull in opposite directions at times and created unnecessary arguments that made them both feel sad and worried.

In the next section we will look at things that can help if you discover differences like that when you and the person you have been having difficulties with answer the questions in Exercise 10.5 about your relationship.

Give and take: negotiating expectations

When a relationship is working well it is usually a good sign that you are getting what you need and the relationship is working in the way you expect it to. The match doesn't need to be exact for a relationship to work; we can often manage well with 'good enough'. This is relatively straightforward if you both know what you want and that is what you get. It is more difficult if either one of you isn't sure what to expect from the relationship or if you definitely want different things, which is more common when there is conflict, e.g. if your parents want you to be an obedient child and you want to be an independent young adult, making your own decisions.

Let's think about what it means to have expectations. Lots of people find it quite difficult to say what they expect from their relationships, either because they aren't sure what they want, or because they have difficulty putting expectations into words. Having expectations is not the same as telling the other person what they have to do or how they have to be. Expectations are more useful if you think about them as ways of saying what you need and want from the relationship. If your expected relationship and actual relationship are similar, you are likely to be satisfied; if they are different, you are likely to feel dissatisfied or frustrated. Understanding the differences between what you expect and what you get is helpful in sorting out conflict.

Some expectations describe basic building blocks of any decent relationship, e.g. respect, fairness, honesty, being reliable. Others are more specific to the individual relationship, that is, what you can rely on this relationship to give you, e.g. a certain amount of time together, being the person you can talk to about difficulties, being the person who will go with you when you try something new no matter what it is, being a priority over other things. It is reasonable to expect the things on the first list – the building blocks – from everyone, but you won't expect exactly the same specific things from everyone.

If you feel let down and the relationship doesn't live up to what you expect in terms of the basic building blocks, it can create a serious problem. You might learn not to expect these basic things – fairness, honesty etc. – from the people around you. The intention is usually to protect you against more disappointment but that is achieved at a very high price and denies you the things that are most valuable about having people in your life. Depression is very good at creeping in through the gaps this kind of arrangement creates.

There is often more room for negotiation on the specific expectations in individual relationships, e.g. how much time you spend together. Sometimes the expectation might have been too high, something that you or the other person couldn't offer or couldn't continue to offer or perhaps something that you always had slightly different ideas about but didn't say. Realising that can be disappointing or hurtful for a while. You might realise that having that expectation met was really important to you and without that the relationship falls short of what you need. You then have a choice to live with something that isn't as good as you hoped it would be or to let go of the relationship and find others ways, or other relationships, that will meet your needs. On other occasions you will notice that letting go of the expectation doesn't matter so much or perhaps even helps. Those expectations might not matter to you so much or are easy to meet elsewhere. The relationship might be easier because your expectations of each other can be adjusted and fall more closely in line with each other.

Tanya

Tanya is very bright and loves throwing herself into heated debates about challenging subjects. She enjoys the thrill of being around people who have inquisitive and questioning minds. When Tanya started seeing her boyfriend she hoped he would enjoy the same things and expected to be able to debate and discuss a wide range of subjects with him. Tanya's boyfriend has little interest in the subjects Tanya likes to talk about. He is much quieter and feels uncomfortable in the heated debates that Tanya tries to draw him into. He is much more emotionally insightful and aware than Tanya and is often good at calming her down when she gets worked up in a debate that then turns into an argument. Tanya doesn't always notice when he gently calms her down because he does it in a quiet and understated way. Many of their initial arguments were fuelled by Tanya's disappointment that her expectations were not being met. She only noticed what was missing and overlooked the helpful things he did. As they started to talk about what they each wanted from their relationship they slowly began to appreciate which expectations they shared, e.g. loyalty and making time for each other, and also the ways in which their expectations differed, e.g. having heated debates. When this became clearer to Tanya she began to rely more on her university friends for intellectual stimulation and on her partner for emotional support and companionship. By talking clearly about their expectations, she found a way to use the best of what each relationship offered and focused less on the inevitable gaps.

As Tanya's example shows, differences in expectations can be sorted out in a number of ways:

- Find common ground

    ◊ Look for ways in which your expectations overlap and agree a compromise that focuses on where you agree rather than disagree, e.g. Tanya and her boyfriend both wanted to spend time together.

- Give up expectations that aren't essential to you

  ◊ One person in the relationship might give up something that they had previously expected or hoped for when it becomes clear that there is little scope for a particular expectation to be met, e.g. Tanya wants her boyfriend to love debating as much as she does. Not all expectations are equally important, and in good relationships it isn't unusual to set some expectations aside when it becomes clear they are not going to be met. Sometimes giving up one small thing, e.g. regular political debates, can help a bigger thing, a happy relationship, to flourish.

  ◊ It is important to check that it isn't always the same person who gives up their needs and expectations. It is particularly important to remember when you are feeling depressed and might feel guilty and less worthy. If too many compromises leave you feeling ignored or resentful, it is a shaky plan for the future.

- **Match expectations to the strengths in the relationship**

  ◊ No single relationship can meet all your needs or expectations. You will achieve this best by having different people in your life for different reasons. Sometimes when you don't get what you want from one relationship you don't have to give up the expectation entirely and it is possible to look to someone else who will do a better job of meeting that need. Tanya's story is a good example of calling on the strengths of each of her relationships to meet her needs.

- **Help each other to get what you each want**

  ◊ In really good teamwork each member of the team doesn't just make an effort for him or herself but instead it is for the team. Helping the members of your team to be happy and them doing the same for you makes it more likely that the team will work well. Offering someone something they want or need when it is easy for you to do it is a very powerful way of getting on the same side.

- **Be flexible**

  ◊ All of this might involve accepting that one or the other or perhaps even both of you have expectations that might not be entirely fulfilled in the relationship. Continuing the relationship becomes more important than meeting every expectation you had when the relationship started. If your goal is to keep the relationship going, both of you will need to be flexible in order to find a solution. Rigidly holding out for what you want, exactly as you want it, or being faced by the same from the other person, will simply flip you back into the dispute. It is important to be prepared to compromise when you can and ask the other person to do the same.

Exercise 11.8

- Go back to the list you created in Exercise 11.7 and go through it item by item.

- What do you expect from this relationship when you think about each issue on your list?
- Does the other person know that? How do they know it?
- Does the other person agree with this expectation?
- What does the other person expect when s/he thinks about the first issue on your list?
- Have you asked him/her or are you filling in a gap? Make sure you check that you understand his/her expectations accurately before making a plan.
- Is this a difference in expectations where you could:

    ◊ Compromise and find common ground?
    ◊ Agree that one of you will give up an unimportant expectation or help each other to get what you want or need?
    ◊ Meet that expectation in a different relationship?

Repeat this for each of the issues you identified on your own list and on the other person's list

Roisin

When Rosin and her mum looked at her list they realised that they both wanted Roisin's expectation of regularly spending time with her mum to be fulfilled. Roisin understood that her mum couldn't be around as much as she used to because she had to go to work and Roisin's mum understood that she was enough for Roisin and she didn't need to create a replacement family to make her happy. Roisin was able to give up her idea that they would have film night every Tuesday night like they used to but they agreed that they would do something together, just the two of them, at least once every two weeks. This was flexible enough to allow them to work around mum's shifts and the fact that Roisin spent more time with her friends than she didn't when she was younger but it was a firm enough plan to make sure they did drift apart in the way they had been doing. Each time Roisin's mum brought her new work timetable home they sat down together and wrote a date on the kitchen calendar that was going to be their time no matter what.

You might feel anxious about the idea of trying something new in a relationship that is tense or where you expect a strong reaction. If it is difficult, keep talking to your team about how you feel and what you are starting to understand by using the questions in this chapter. You could try to build up your confidence by using some of the communication skills you have been developing with other members of your network as a first step. This doesn't have to be about a disagreement. It is simply a way of practising communicating more clearly in general. Ask the people you trust for feedback about how easy they find it to understand what you were saying. As you get more comfortable talking about your feelings and what you want or need, you can start to introduce these communication skills into discussions in the relationship you are trying to sort out. By practising in this way, you will have the confidence to use your new skills when you tackle more difficult conversations.

Summary

- **Disagreements are inevitable in relationships and can be healthy, as long as they do not become established as a pattern.**
- *Reacting* **is impulsive and doesn't hold the other person in mind.**
- *Responding* **slows things down, keeps your main objective in mind and gives you an opportunity to make better choices.**

- Conflict becomes unstuck through *renegotiation*, which involves making expectations clear and working together to find acceptable common ground.
- IPT-A is not a private therapy and it works most effectively if you let other people know what you are trying to do and ask them to help.
- When you have learned to stand back and observe your disagreements from a distance, you can invite someone else to look through the director's lens with you and work out your differences together.

Chapter 12

Isolation

In this chapter you will learn about:

- Reasons why it might be difficult to make friends and to keep them
- Using what has gone well and what has been difficult in relationships to plan for the future

In this chapter you will be asked to:

- Describe the good times you have had with other people
- Notice what your good relationships have in common
- Compare your current relationships with your best relationships
- Imagine what other people like about knowing you
- Describe difficult times you have had with other people
- Notice what your difficult relationships have had in common
- Compare your current relationships with the difficult relationships you have had

> • Plan how to do more of what your good relationships and less of what your difficult relationships have in common

When therapists use IPT-A with young people and they talk about the four focal areas for the first time, isolation is almost always a problem young people recognise. It doesn't always turn out to be the difficulty they focus on, but it is something most people feel sometimes and many young people feel a lot of the time. Being alone isn't good or bad, and might be necessary sometimes, but when you don't know how to stop it, being alone can turn into being lonely, which is a painful feeling for anyone. After all, we are made to be in relationships and feeling on the outside feels uncomfortable and sometimes frightening. As with all of the other feelings you have, loneliness generally comes and goes, fading into the background when new opportunities or people appear. However, if you find it difficult to make the most of those people or opportunities, feeling isolated can become an unwelcome back-drop to your life.

Young people are often especially sensitive to feeling isolated because adolescence is a time when you are stepping away from mainly being with your family to spending more time with friends. For most young people family provides some form of company, whether they want it or not, but there aren't the same guarantees with friends and you might worry that you will get left behind or overlooked. Adolescence is a time when you will have lots of questions about yourself, who you are, how you fit in, or who will be around for you. These are important questions and having other people around to think about them with you can be a great help.

The exercises in IPT-A might seem quite daunting if you don't feel very sure of many people around you. Remember you don't have to transform lots of relationships to start to feel better. Making progress with just one relationship is a great start. Lots of the ideas in this chapter as well as in Chapters 8, 9, 10, 11 and 13 can help you to understand what gets in the way of relationships being more fun and reliable for you and to help you to make the kinds of changes that can really help. Just like the other chapters this one is broken up into several different sections so you can take it one step at a time.

 You might find it easier to imagine how involving other people can work for you if you watch this video of a young person talking about how talking to other people helped him when he felt isolated and was being bullied. The video can be found here:

www.bbc.co.uk/education/clips/zyxkq6f

Repeating problems

'Isolation' is a helpful focus if you find it difficult to get to know people or if it is difficult to get on with the people around you in the way you want. You might always have felt somewhat this way, but the pressure to make new friends and try new things that comes with adolescence may have made this a bit more obvious to you. Depression typically makes young people feel less interested in other people but this will be even more difficult to overcome if you don't feel close to many people or your relationships felt a little shaky even before you became depressed.

Not feeling close to many people will probably have shown up when you were drawing your inventory of relationships in Chapter 5 (see pages 92–99). It might have been difficult to think of people to include or talk about for a variety of reasons:

- You feel awkward when you meet new people so avoid them
- You feel shy around other people and anxious in social situations so try to stay in the background
- You aren't sure how to take the leap from knowing someone to say 'Hi' to making them your friend
- You worry about getting close to people in case they hurt you because that has happened before
- You have been bullied and other people have made it difficult for you to have friends
- You do what other people want so that they will be friends with you and what you want gets overlooked or ignored
- You just don't really 'get' relationships and you find other people confusing
- You quite often find yourself in disagreements or arguments with several people at the same time
- You can make friends but it is hard to keep them

Most young people will recognise some of the experiences described in this list. Feeling awkward and unsure of yourself is a very normal part of growing up and we usually get through it because we also have some friends or people in our family who we get on with and can have fun with. They can help us to feel OK about the times when we feel a bit wobbly around people we don't know so well or don't get on with. However, if some of the examples on this list describe how you feel with most people most of the time, it is likely that being around other people is hard work for you and could add to how depressed you are feeling. When that happens, isolation and loneliness keep depression going, as well as being among its effects. That will make things like finding your IPT-A team more difficult to do and that might seem more like a goal to work towards rather than somewhere to start. Given that, it is really impressive that you have kept reading and stayed curious about what IPT-A can offer. You should be really proud of yourself for that, it can't have been easy. The good news is that, even if it has been difficult to recruit as many people to your IPT-A team as you would like, there are lots of ways you can still use this book, and this chapter in particular, including:

- To feel better about the relationships you have
- To work on specific difficulties that crop up with several people
- To give you ideas that will help you when you meet new people
- To help you when you use IPT-A with a therapist, who can provide regular support
- To use these ideas to get you ready to join a group to help you learn new skills or to meet young people who live with the same kinds of difficulties as your own and who can offer you support and understanding

Jasmine

Jasmine is nineteen years old and had been depressed for over three years. She finds it very difficult to go out and spends most of her time alone in her bedroom in her parents' house. She hasn't had a job since she left school at sixteen and the only people she sees are her family. Jasmine feels bored and lonely a lot of the time and she comfort eats to distract herself. As a result she has gained a lot of weight, which makes it even harder for her to go out because she feels ashamed of how she looks and she doesn't want to bump into someone she used to know and have to explain why she has been doing nothing for so long.

One of the few people Jasmine sees, other than her parents, is her cousin, who drops in and chats with Jasmine every couple of weeks. When her cousin announces that she has been offered a new job and will be moving away, Jasmine gets really upset and panics because she will have even less contact with the world beyond her bedroom walls. Although Jasmine can't find the words to say how she feels to her cousin, her distress is easy to see, and her cousin suggests this might be a good time for Jasmine to ask for some help so that she could visit her after her move. With this goal in mind, and with her cousin and mum's support and encouragement she goes to speak to her GP about her low mood and difficulty going out. Jasmine's GP recommends that she speaks to a therapist about how she is feeling. Jasmine feels anxious about talking to someone she doesn't know and worries that the therapist will judge her, just like she has imagined everyone else will, but she also sees that there is little prospect of her life improving unless she takes a risk and tries to understand and change the day-to-day difficulties that limit her life so much. She talks this decision through with her mum and her cousin and decides to try.

Over the weeks of meetings with an IPT-A therapist, Jasmine talks about her difficulties and starts to understand the patterns that are repeating in her life and how they block almost all opportunities for satisfying relationships, even those with her family. As a result of these conversations and feeling that someone understands rather than judges her, Jasmine gradually starts to spend more time with her family by moving from her bedroom to the sitting room they all use. She stops eating alone in her bedroom and starts eating with her family, which helps her to get back into the routine of regular meals rather than constant snacking. With her cousin's encouragement and support she even starts going out for a short walk around the block each day and sometimes she even walks to the local shop and back. This is tough but she has never felt more proud of herself than the first time she managed to stay out long enough to have a coffee and a chat with her cousin before heading back home. By the end of therapy Jasmine has a much clearer idea of the kinds of problems that continually trip her up and the things she can start to do to change them. Her depression has lifted enough for her to take another big step and join a support group for young people who have had mental health problems, which gives her ideas and helps to continue building up her self-confidence and to start to make plans for the future. Before her final IPT-A session she buys a train ticket to go and visit her cousin for the weekend and for the first time in a long time enjoys having something to look forward to.

Looking back over your relationships

Now and in the past you have had all kinds of relationships. These might have been with your family, friends, romantic partners, classmates, teachers etc. and you might have found some of them easier and some of them more difficult than others. Each of these relationships has its own story – how it began, how it developed and perhaps how it ended. Remembering these stories will help you to work out what goes well when you are with other people and how difficulties creep in. Focusing on isolation doesn't mean that all of your relationships are difficult all of the time, and it is good to remind yourself what has worked as well as thinking about what is more difficult for you. Depression will try to tell you that nothing goes well for you, but the fact that you have been really brave and determined and kept reading to find new ideas tells me depression has got it wrong about you.

It will be really useful to ask someone to work through the exercises in this chapter with you. This might be one of your family, a friend or your IPT-A therapist. Thinking about relationships that have been confusing or hurtful is difficult for everyone, and it will be very helpful to talk to someone else about what that has been like for you. The other person can help you to think about what has happened from different points of view and that might help you to notice things you weren't aware of before. This is not meant to make you feel bad about yourself or to create a long list of failings, but rather to help you to step back and start to see things from a different perspective, and to think about the ways in which you can help relationships to get started and to last.

When it has gone well

Let's start with the relationships that have gone well for you, at least in part. They don't have to have been perfect – few relationships are – and they may not even have lasted very long. These might be relationships that you are still in or relationships from your past. It is probably easiest to think about the people who are still in your life first and then add people who aren't around any more afterwards. The relationships from the past can be very helpful because each of those stories will help you to understand the beginning, middle and end. This list will include, among other things, people you:

- Felt close to
- Had fun with
- Worked with well on a team or a project
- Felt 'got' you or who you 'got'
- Shared a common interest with

You might include the classmates you speak to now, your first friend at school, a teacher or coach who helped you or members of your family. People come into our lives in all kinds of ways so try to think as widely as you can about moments when this has worked for you.

It is possible that you are so used to relationships being a problem or disappointing that this task will seem a little difficult. Depression will try hard to persuade you how few good relationships you have had and will make you want to give up before you get started. Try not to listen. Even if you can't think of anyone at first, come back to this a few more times and let memories gently bubble to the surface. Remember you don't need to produce a long list and you might just be thinking about bits of relationships that have been good. Most relationships are a mixture of good bits and difficult bits. Starting with just one or two people who have been good to know will be a great start. If more people come to mind later, you can always come back and add them to your list. If you have asked someone to help you with this exercise you could start by thinking about the story of that relationship. Perhaps the person who is helping you can remember people that you have forgotten.

Exercise 12.1: Reviewing your good relationships

- Try to think about your favourite times with other people. These might be quite recent and include people who you still see now or they might be memories from a while ago with people you don't see anymore. Make sure you try to think back to before you started feeling depressed and think about who was in your life then.
- Write down the names of the people who come to mind – the people you have shared some nice times with, even if they didn't last for very long.
- When you have a list of people to think about, however short, start to create a simple timeline for each relationship, using the questions and diagram below to guide you. You already did something similar to this when you drew a picture of your relationships in Chapter 5. This time, however, you will include people from your past as well as people who are in your life now.
- Don't worry if you can't answer all of the questions in the list below – that's fine. The questions are just meant to give you ideas about some of the things that are useful to know about your relationships. You might have other details that you want to add – that's great. Describe whatever you think is most important about the good relationships and experiences with other people that you have had.

Isolation

How did it start?

How did you meet?

Did you choose
this relationship?

↓

**How did it
develop?**

What did you do
together?

How did you keep
in touch?

↓

**What was best
about it?**

What did you
like most?

What did the other
person like?

↓

**What was most
difficult?**

What didn't
you like?

What didn't the
other person like?

↓

**How did it
end?**

Did you leave?

Did the other
person leave?

- **How did you meet?**

  ◊ How did you get to know each other? When was that?
  ◊ Was getting to know each other your idea or the other person's?
  ◊ Did you choose to be in the relationship?

- **How did the relationship develop over time?**

  ◊ What did you do together? How much time did you spend together? Did you have fun together?
  ◊ How did you feel about the time you spent together?
  ◊ Did you mainly spend time with each other or in a group with other people? How did you feel about that?
  ◊ How did you keep in touch with each other?
  ◊ Did it change over time? In what ways?

- **What was best about the relationship?**

  ◊ What did you like most about it?
  ◊ What did the other person like most about it?
  ◊ Could you talk to each other about how you were feeling?
  ◊ Could you ask each other for help to get things done or for advice?
  ◊ What do you think was successful about that relationship?
  ◊ What did you do that contributed to the success of the relationship?
  ◊ What did the other person do that contributed to the success of the relationship?

- **What wasn't so good about the relationship?**

  ◊ What didn't you like?

- **Did you have symptoms of depression when you were in that relationship?**

  ◊ If you did, did the relationship change when you became depressed?
  ◊ In what way did it change?
  ◊ Did the relationship make your symptoms of depression easier or more difficult to manage?
  ◊ Did the other person know about your depression?

- **Are you still in that relationship?**

  ◊ If not, why did it end and how did that happen?

Talk these questions over with someone on your IPT-A team. They may help to highlight good things in your relationships that are hard for you to see when you are feeling depressed.

Switching perspective

After you have thought about these good relationships from your own point of view, switch the focus – imagine yourself as a film director, turning the camera around to capture the other person's point of view. How would each of the people you have been thinking about describe their relationship with you?

Exercise 12.2: Describing the other person's point of view

- What do you imagine the other person liked about his/her relationship with you?

- What do you think s/he thought went well in this relationship?
- What would s/he say you contributed to the relationship?
- Could you ask him/her?
- If the relationship ended, why would s/he say it did?

This is, of course, more difficult to do. The other people might have told you the things they like about you – try not to let depression close your ears to that, because it will try, but sometimes you have to imagine what other people think. Ask your IPT-A team or therapist about the ideas they have after hearing you describe your good relationships. They might be able to help you think about why other people would be lucky to know you and why they might be just as likely to enjoy knowing you as you enjoyed knowing them.

Judith

In Judith's school older pupils are asked to buddy new students for the first few weeks after they move from primary school to high school. Judith likes doing that because she understands how frightened and lost they feel a lot of the time. Some of the teachers and other students are impatient with the new pupils when they get lost or overwhelmed by how much they have to learn and how big the school building is, but Judith is always kind and patient because she knows just how they feel. She regularly feels like an outsider and this helps her to be understanding and respectful of other people who feel the same. When Judith got feedback from her buddy she got top marks because her gentle approach really helped the new pupil to fit in and not feel so afraid. Judith pinned the report to her bedroom wall so that next time she felt bad about being shy and awkward with other people she would also remember that being gentle and patient is helpful and can make difficult situations much easier for another person.

Helpful patterns

Now that you have considered both perspectives try to find things that are similar across the relationships that you have described. Think about how each of these relationships got started, how they developed and changed over time and how they ended, if they have. These are important clues for you to use in understanding the things that help your relationships to be more enjoyable and stable, e.g.

* You chose to be in these relationships
* You got to know each other gradually before you got close
* You had something in common
* You showed an interest in each other
* You saw each other regularly
* You talked to each other about how you felt
* You did things together and didn't have to talk too much
* You didn't let disagreements drag on
* You didn't hold grudges
* You had friends in common
* You were in a team or a group together

Exercise 12.3: Patterns in good relationships

Add your own examples to the list above. Try to identify at least three things that some of your good relationships had in common.

Leon

When Leon looked at his list he noticed that lots of the

relationships he had enjoyed most had been in teams or groups. Leon felt shy around other people and often didn't know what to say when he first met someone. He wanted to be friendly but when it was just him and one other person he worried he would say the wrong thing and when that happened his mind would go blank and he wouldn't be able to think of a single thing to say. When he was on the football team and in the Cadets he didn't feel that way. It was always a lot easier to talk about the game or what they were learning or doing together as a group. He didn't feel like he was 'on show' when there was something that everyone was doing at the same time. He was surprised to discover when he looked back over his relationships that he was a really good teammate and his teammates knew they could rely on him. Realising how important this had been in the past helped Leon to keep going to his football practice and Cadets each week even when depression left him feeling tired and less interested than he used to be. This made sure he made the most of his strength as a team player while he worked on being more confident in one-to-one situations.

You might already have described some of the people you have been thinking about when you drew a picture of your relationships in Chapter 5. If you have added any new people who were not included in your original interpersonal inventory compare the two sets of descriptions.

**Exercise 12.4: Comparing your current relationships
and your good relationships**

- How are the relationships you have now similar to the good relationships you have been describing?
- How are the relationships you have now different from the good relationships you have described?
- How could you make your current relationships more like your good relationships? Do any of the items on the list of things your good relationships had in common give you ideas? How could you bring those things into your current relationships to make them better?
- Pick one example from your list that you will try to bring into one of your current relationships. Remember you have done it before so you can do it again.
- How could the people you see now help you to make the changes you have identified?
- Do you think it would help your depression if your current relationships were more like the good relationships you have described?
- It can be difficult to imagine how to change a relationship on your own. Ask the people on your IPT-A team if they can think of any ways that your current relationships could be more like the ones you have most enjoyed.

Learning from what has been difficult

The next step in breaking unhelpful patterns is to repeat the same exercises for the relationships that have been more difficult. This list might include relationships that ended more quickly than you wanted or where disagreements were difficult to work out, or relationships that did really get going in the way you hoped they would. Depression will make it easier to remember times when relationships haven't gone well. Don't worry that you are going to have to go through every example you think of. Instead try focusing on three or four relationships that are typical in some way of the kinds of problems you notice happening with other people. You might have been hurt or disappointed by some of these relationships. If that is the case, be gentle with yourself as you go through these exercises. Take a break after you think through a significant relationship and don't force yourself to complete the whole list at once if you start to feel sad or upset. Remember that there is a positive reason for looking at past difficulties, and that is to learn more about the patterns that have caused you difficulties so that you will have new ideas about how to avoid them in the future.

Again, it will be really useful to involve your IPT-A team or therapist when you go through these questions. This will help you to stand back and look carefully at what happened in those relationships rather than getting caught up in the feelings that may come with these memories and could make it more difficult for you to think about them. Once again, try to see yourself as if you were making a documentary on your past experience, standing back to observe the whole scene and understand how it works.

Exercise 12.5: Reviewing less successful relationships

When you have made your list of people you are going to think about in detail, build a timeline for each of those relationships. Use the questions and diagram below to help you to understand more about the problems that have been difficult with other people.

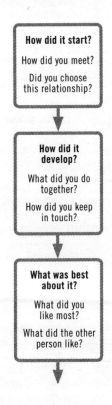

How did it start?

How did you meet?

Did you choose this relationship?

How did it develop?

What did you do together?

How did you keep in touch?

What was best about it?

What did you like most?

What did the other person like?

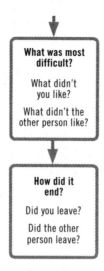

What was most difficult?

What didn't you like?

What didn't the other person like?

How did it end?

Did you leave?

Did the other person leave?

- **How did you meet?**

    ◊ How did you get to know each other? When was that?
    ◊ Was it your idea or the other person's?
    ◊ Did you choose to be in this relationship?

- **How did the relationship develop over time?**

    ◊ What did you do together? How much time did you spend together? Did you have any fun together?
    ◊ How did you feel about the time you spent together?
    ◊ Was there anything you didn't like about it?
    ◊ Did you mainly spend time with each other or in a group with other people? How did you feel about that?
    ◊ Was there anything you didn't like about it?
    ◊ How did you keep in touch with each other?
    ◊ Did it change over time? In what ways?

- **What was best about the relationship?**

  ◊ Was there anything you liked about it, even for some of the time?

  ◊ Were any parts of the relationships successful, even for some of the time?

  ◊ What did you do that contributed to what was successful in the relationship?

  ◊ What did the other person do that contributed to what was successful in the relationship?

- **What wasn't so good about the relationship?**

  ◊ What didn't you like about it?

  ◊ What were the difficulties in that relationship?

  ◊ How did the difficulties develop over the time you knew each other?

  ◊ Can you think of any ways that you contributed to the difficulties in the relationship? What were they?

  ◊ Can you think of any ways that the other person contributed to what you didn't like about the relationship? What were they?

- **Did you have symptoms of depression when you were in that relationship?**

  ◊ If you did, did the relationship change when you became depressed?

  ◊ Did the relationship make your symptoms of depression easier or more difficult to manage?

  ◊ Did the other person know about your depression?

- **Are you still in that relationship?**

  ◊ If not, why did it end and how did that happen?

◊ What impact did ending the relationship have on your depressive symptoms?
◊ What are the things about the relationship that you are glad to have given up?

Talk these questions over with someone on your IPT-A team. This may help you to understand how and why the relationships didn't work out the way you wanted.

Switching perspective

Exercise 12.6: Describing the other person's point of view on problems

Now, just as you did before, try to think about each relationship from the other person's point of view. Does this different point of view reveal anything new?

• What do you imagine the other person didn't like in your relationship?
• What do you imagine they found difficult in your relationship?
• What would they say you contributed to difficulties in the relationship?
• What would they say they contributed to the difficulties in the relationship?
• If the relationship ended, why would they say it did?

A word of caution here. When you are feeling depressed, it can be tempting to rush to blame yourself for difficulties. While it is important to understand how you contribute to problems, because it will guide you in making changes, it is just as important to recognise the contribution other people make. Talk this over with your IPT-A team to help you to think about different points of view.

When you look over your answers can you see anything that is similar across the relationships that you have felt disappointed or hurt by? Common patterns that make isolation harder to break out of include:

- Feeling shy and not being able to approach people and get to know them
- Not being able to ask for what you want and being taken for granted or ignored
- Being critical or intolerant of other people and having disagreements across many of your relationships
- Not being able to tolerate any kind of conflict and leaving the relationship rather than sorting out difficulties
- Not being able to get close to other people and keeping them at a distance
- Rushing into relationships quickly and making a big emotional investment before you are sure the person can meet your expectations
- Choosing vulnerable people to be friends with and feeling overwhelmed by someone else's problems
- Trying to fit in at any cost
- Being bullied

Let's consider a few examples:

Shamila has two close friends that she has known for a long time. They used to do everything together and Shamila didn't feel like she needed anyone else. She doesn't see them so much since she changed schools and she misses them. She worries they will forget her, but she hasn't told them that. Sometimes she is a bit quiet and snappy with them when they are talking about things they have done without her. They don't understand why she is being that way when they are trying to keep her up to date with the news. She hasn't found it easy to make friends at her new school. She doesn't know what to say or how to join in when everyone else already seems to have friends. When she is stressed she finds it really hard to talk to anyone about how she is feeling, even her two friends, and she has started to cut her arms as a way of calming herself down. This helps for a little while but usually ends up with her feeling lonely and worse than she did before.

- Which good relationship skills does Shamila have?
- Which new skills and ideas would help her with the problems she is finding difficult?

Cory seems to know lots of people and he works hard to stay in touch and to keep them happy and entertained all the time. He plays the joker a lot and will do just about anything to keep everyone amused. It takes a lot of effort but somehow no matter what he does it never seems to be enough to stop him feeling lonely. He often worries that if he isn't funny and making people laugh they won't be interested in him but he doesn't know how else to be. If he feels down or annoyed, he can't risk showing it because he worries that then people won't like him.

- Which good relationship skills does Cory have?
- Which new skills and ideas would help him with the problems he is finding difficult?

Lena makes the relationships she needs when she needs them. She is good at making friends and usually has a few people around who she spends time with. If nothing changes things seem to go OK, at least on the surface. She doesn't ever let anyone get too close because she likes to be able to walk away whenever she needs to. If her situation changes, so do the people she has around her. Sometimes it only takes a small change so her relationships don't tend to last long and can seem quite superficial. She doesn't ever feel like she really knows anyone or that they know her.

- Which good relationship skills does Lena have?
- Which new skills and ideas would help her with the problems she is finding difficult?

Alison has always been shy. She is small for her age and everyone always thinks she is younger than she is. This often means that people don't seem to notice her and she sometimes feels like she is invisible. Over time she has grown used to being overlooked and left out and now she doesn't expect to be included. She minds her own business, gets on with her work and studies hard and hopes that when she leaves school and goes to university to study to be a vet it will be better. Her best friend is her pet dog. She loves him very much and takes great care of him. Alison thinks he is a better friend than any of the boys or girls at school could ever be. When girls in the year above her start picking on her for no reason she doesn't know what to do. At first they call her names but then they start to push her around and send her horrible text messages and emails. They tell her it will only get worse if she tells anyone so she doesn't say a word. She has never felt so alone.

- Which good relationship skills does Alison have?
- Which new skills and ideas would help her with the problems she finds difficult?

Exercise 12.7: Recognising repeating patterns of difficulty in your relationships

What are the main difficulties or patterns you have noticed in your current and past relationships? Try to find two or three difficulties that you notice repeating in your more difficult relationships. These will become targets for your IPT-A – something you are going to look out for in your current relationships and use your good relationship skills (look back at the list of things your good relationships had in common) and the skills you have developed in communicating more clearly and talking about your feelings to avoid them in the future. Write them down to help you remember what you are going to work on changing.

Exercise 12.8: Comparing your current relationships and your difficult relationships

- How are the relationships you have now similar to the difficult relationships you have been describing?
- How are the relationships you have now different from the difficult relationships you have described?
- What effect do these problems have on your depression?
- How could you stop the problems you have noticed repeating in the past from happening in your current relationships?

- Do any of the strengths you noticed in your good relationships give you ideas about how to manage or avoid the problems that come up with other people?
- Look again at Chapters 8 and 13 and think about how the ideas described there could help you to change some of these patterns, e.g. communicating clearly, talking about your feelings in a safe way or negotiating expectation.
- It can be difficult to imagine how to change a relationship on your own. Ask the people on your IPT-A team if they can think of any ways that your current relationships could be less like the ones you have found difficult.

Shamila, Cory, Lena and Alison all have relationships that are limited in different ways:

Shamila has some close friends but finds it difficult to get to know new people and backs away from the people she is close to when she has a problem.

- Shamila has lots of good relationships skills that kept her two close friendships going for a long time. She has started to forget these skills since she has been depressed and seeing them less. When her relationships were good she was in a friendship group where they all knew each other, she was seeing her friends regularly, they showed an interest in each other and enjoyed the things they had in common.
- It would help Shamila, and her depression, if she arranged to see her long-standing friends every week, even though this means they have to plan more than they used to. They have lots in common that they could still enjoy together. They haven't fallen out but could do if the unspoken grudges are allowed to build up.
- One of the problem patterns for Shamila is not talking about

her feelings when she is unhappy. This is making her feel very isolated and learning to talk about how she feels and asking for help from the people who care about her could make a big difference to Shamila's depression. (See Understanding your feelings, Chapter 8, page 140)

- Another difficulty for Shamila is not feeling confident to approach new people. She hasn't had to do this for a long time so hasn't had a chance to practise. This is another way her long-standing friends could help her – they could practise ways for her to approach new people before she tries it in real life. She might discover that she isn't looking very welcoming and changing the way she approaches people could encourage other people to be more welcoming (See Non-verbal communication, Chapter 8, page 163). They could also go with her to give her encouragement when she tries to join in on social things with pupils at her new school, e.g. a party or a school social event. (See Chapter 9)

Cory keeps other people happy but doesn't do the same for himself. He tries to fit in at any cost.

- Cory also has lots of good communication skills but he is exhausted when he uses one or two skills over and over and doesn't develop his range. He is very good at being interested in people, tuning in to how they feel and what makes them happy. He is enthusiastic as a friend and people like him but take him for granted because he always does all of the work and doesn't ask for anything in return.
- One problem that shows up for Cory is that he spends so much energy trying to keep lots of people happy that he doesn't have time to focus more on a smaller number of relationships that would allow him to get closer to some of the people in his group of friends. This would help Cory to see that real

friendships aren't always about having fun and laughing, although it is great when you can do that with someone else, and that it is interesting to do a whole range of things with other people.

- Cory, and his depression, would be helped if he used his skill of being interested in what other people like, to find out what interests his friends have, and then find things that they could do together where Cory doesn't have to be the centre of attention and provide the entertainment.

- Much like Shamila, Cory finds it difficult to talk about his feelings and learning how to do that might help Cory to see that people are interested in more than just being entertained all the time. He might even find that some people find it a relief just to be able to chat and get to know him without having to laugh and joke about everything all the time (See Understanding your feelings, Chapter 8, page 140).

Lena generally holds people at a distance, even when they are her friends, and she leaves relationships behind as soon as something changes.

- Lena is good at making friends. She can work out what people are good at and how they can be useful in her life. She is good at making relationship opportunities.

- Despite these good relationship skills she still doesn't really know people because she hasn't developed her skills to deepen the friendships she starts. She doesn't yet make the most of the opportunities that she is so good at creating.

- Lena, and her depression, would be helped if she could develop her communication skills, which could help her to show more of an interest in the people she gathers around her. (See Listening and checking, Chapter 8, page 172) This might reveal that the people in her life can stay with her even when things change and many friendships can adapt to new circumstances just as Lena does herself (See Chapter 9).

• One of the problems that is clear for Lena is that she finds it difficult to manage the feelings of getting close to someone and perhaps relying on them and she protects herself against the risk of being hurt by leaving relationships before someone leaves her or lets her down. If Lena was able to talk through her worries and learn to compromise so that her relationships didn't have to be exactly the way she wants them or nothing at all she would have much more chance of feeling close to and understood by the people she invites into her life (See Give and take: negotiating expectations, Chapter 13, page 277).

Alison is very isolated and has no one to help her when bullies take advantage of that and start to pick on her.

• Alison has become so used to not having friends at school she has focused all of her energies into her studies and her pet dog. She has made the very best she can of the skills she has and has done well at school and has poured all the love she has into her most devoted friend. It is very impressive that with so little help she has managed to create two success stories.

• Being so isolated made Alison vulnerable to being picked on by bullies. Bullies make themselves feel bigger by picking on young people who will find it difficult to fight back. Alison is small, shy and has no friends to stand up for her so she was vulnerable to this kind of horrible treatment.

• One of the problem patterns that shows up for Alison is that she finds it hard to be noticed and to speak up and contribute to what is going on around her. She feels invisible and it seems that she has learnt to behave as if she is invisible as well. Learning to make herself taller than she is in her head

314

and say all the things that are in her bright and inquisitive mind could make a big difference to how isolated she typically feels and help Alison to make the friends that might be right beside her if they just noticed each other (See non-verbal communication and body language in Chapter 8).

• Another big problem for Alison is that she doesn't have anyone she feels she can turn to when she is frightened and under threat. Bullying creates a different type of isolation to many other situations because people are trying to deliberately keep Alison away from the people who can help her. Talking to the people who can take action and make sure she is safe, like her parents and teachers, will do a lot to help Alison. This will help to reassure her that the horrible things the bullies say are not true and with other people's help the unacceptable treatment she has faced can be stopped.

Opportunities for change

Now that you understand more about the strengths that you bring to your relationships (see Exercise 12.3) and the difficulties that will be helpful to target (see Exercise 12.7), start to look out for examples of those strengths and difficulties in your life each day. Your aim is to practise using your good relationship skills as often as you can – try to find an opportunity, however small, every day – and to notice as quickly as you can when unhelpful patterns are creeping in. Don't worry if, at first, you don't notice the patterns until after they have happened. That is very normal. It is new for you to have such clearly thought-out targets and it will take a while for you to catch the repeating patterns as they happen because they will often be linked to strong feelings and you know that when your feelings get stronger your problem solving and planning slow down temporarily.

This is another time when your team or IPT-A therapist can really help. At least initially, it is often easier for other people to notice repeating patterns more quickly than we can do for ourselves. Their perspective allows them to see the bigger picture that depression and strong feelings can sometimes block from our sight when we are looking at ourselves.

Exercise 12.9: Noticing patterns and changing patterns

Take some time each day to think about how you feel when you are around other people. Sometimes you might find yourself thinking about times when you aren't with other people but would have liked to be. Those are good examples to think about too.

- When did you notice yourself using your good relationship skills today?
- How did you feel when you used those skills?
- How did the people you were with respond when you used those skills?
- Which unhelpful patterns did you notice today? Describe what happened.
- Did you notice the pattern before it started, when it was happening or after it was over?
- Which of the skills that you have been learning could have helped to interrupt the repeating pattern? Look back at the exercises throughout this chapter and in previous chapters to help you.
- Discuss each example with someone on your IPT-A team and use them to help you to think of ways that the problem patterns you are targeting could be interrupted or avoided. Patterns often repeat because they are difficult to resist and you feel pressure to behave in certain ways. This can be

difficult to stop on your own, but with your team's help you will be able to see and take up opportunities for change that you may not have been able to see on your own, and to continue to take risks and step out of your isolation and into the spaces between people where relationships happen.

You have been working incredibly hard to understand your relationships and to make changes in order to feel better. Let's look at how you got on and what will be useful for the future in the final chapter.

Summary

- Feeling lonely can happen both when you have too few relationships and when you are in relationships that don't meet your needs.
- Feeling isolated does not mean that all of your relationships are a problem. It is just as important to remember when things go well as it is to work on the problems that trip you up.
- Using your good relationship skills that have worked in the past can be one of the simplest ways to make small changes now.
- Understanding how problems have developed in the past can help you to change those patterns in the future.
- Change involves crossing stepping stones rather than making a single great leap.

Chapter 13

Reviewing your progress and planning for the future

 In this chapter you will learn about:

• Reviewing progress and planning for the future

 In this chapter you will be asked to:

• Describe what IPT-A has been like for you
• Compare your depression when you started with now
• Review your progress towards your goals
• Understand and plan how to manage setbacks
• Plan how other people will contribute to you staying well

Counter Argument: Yes it can.

Ian Hamilton Finlay, writer and artist

Over the last few weeks you have been working hard to make a change: a change in your symptoms of depression and a change in your relationships with the people around you.

Depression is a painful and difficult illness to live with and so it has been important to turn it around as quickly as possible. You are on the brink of lots of exciting new opportunities in life and we don't want you to miss out on them for a moment longer than you have to.

Over recent weeks you have been becoming an expert on what depression is doing in your life and how to change its course. You now know that this isn't a job for you alone, so by sharing what you have been learning with the people in your life you have been giving yourself the best chance of feeling better.

Exercise 13.1: What has IPT-A been like for you?

- How has IPT-A worked for you and your team?
- What are the most important things you have learnt about depression?
- Who has it been useful to tell about your depression?
- What impact has sharing this information had on you and on the people around you?

Talk these questions over with your team and use the table below to remind yourself what has been helpful and what would be useful to continue to do in the future.

What has worked?	How has this helped defeat depression?
1. Using the feeling and symptom charts every week	It made it easier to tell people how I feel and that makes it easier for them to know how to help
2. Spending time with my friends every week, even if I don't feel like it	At first this was really hard because I didn't want to see anyone but it got easier. Sometimes I only enjoyed some of my time with friends but I did always enjoy some of it and that made it easier to see them again. Gradually I started enjoying more of the things we do again.
3. Allowing myself to make mistakes	Quite often I had to try a few times before I could do the things that are suggested in the book. Instead of beating myself up about not managing first time, I gave myself credit for trying and that made it easier to get a little further each time.

Over the weeks that you have been reading this book you have been regularly rating your symptoms and goals, so let's look at how IPT-A has been able to help and make a plan to keep any gains you have made in place for the future. Look at your individual weekly responses on the symptom chart to review your journey though IPT-A.

When you learnt about depression in Chapter 2 you thought about lots of the typical signs and symptoms and the impact they can have on your life. Before you go through the next exercise, it's worth recapping the main symptoms we are talking about.

Feeling sad or irritable Nothing is interesting or fun			
Problems sleeping	Can't remember things	Feeling guilty or to blame all the time	Problems at home
Eating too much or not enough	Can't concentrate	Feeling bad about myself	Problems at school
Feeling restless or wound up	Can't make up my mind	Feeling hopeless	Problems with friends and family
Feeling tired		Want to die	

Back in Exercise 2.2, I suggested that you could use red, yellow and green highlighter pens or circles and lines on the symptom wall to describe the symptoms that trouble you most or all of the time (red or circled), those that bother you a bit some of the time (yellow or underlined), and those that don't bother often or at all (green or not marked). Let's compare then and now. If you have been filling in the symptom wall every week, compare the first wall and the one you filled in most recently. If you haven't filled in the wall recently take a few minutes to rate your experience of the symptoms now to allow you to compare.

Exercise 13.2: Comparing your depression symptoms before and after IPT-A

- How does your experience of depression when you started IPT-A compare to how it feels now?
- Which symptoms have improved and which are still troublesome for you?
- Are any of your symptoms worse? Which?
- What differences have you noticed in the different areas of your life: home, school and with friends?
- Have any areas of your life improved more than others?
- What changes have other people noticed in you? Ask your IPT-A team what they have noticed.
- What difference have these changes made to how you get on with the people around you?

Martin

When Martin filled in the symptom wall for the first time it looked like this:

Feeling sad	Feel tired a lot	Can't get to sleep	Not eating
Nothing is fun anymore	Wish I was dead	Feel guilty and blame myself for things	Problems with friends
Can't think clearly	Don't want to see people	Wake up early and can't get back to sleep	Feel bored
Problems at home	Sleep too much	Feel irritable	Feel restless and on edge
Feeling bad about myself	Can't get going	Eat too much	Difficulties at school
Wake up during the night	Feel hopeless	Forgetful	Feel I have let other people down

His sleep had been a big problem and it made it hard for him to concentrate at school, and when he was tired he was grumpy with his friends and didn't want to see them or hang out the way they usually did. Reading the information about sleep problems in Chapter 3 and Appendix 4 gave him some ideas about how to change this and he asked his mum to help him because he found it really hard to switch off his phone and computer at night because they were the only things that he was still interested in. He was surprised how quickly it made a difference and when he could concentrate, school felt easier and when he had energy to see his friends he didn't feel so bored all the time. There were still problems with one friend he had to work hard to change but overall he felt better after using some of the ideas he had read about. Everything wasn't perfect and there were things Martin was working on but he felt hopeful that things would continue to improve and this showed on his last symptom grid, which looked like this:

Feeling sad	Feel tired a lot	Can't get to sleep	Not eating
Nothing is fun anymore	Wish I was dead	Feel guilty and blame myself for things	Problems with friends
Can't think clearly	Don't want to see people	Wake up early and can't get back to sleep	Feel bored
Problems at home	Sleep too much	Feel irritable	Feel restless and on edge
Feeling bad about myself	Can't get going	Eat too much	Difficulties at school
Wake up during the night	Feel hopeless	Forgetful	Feel I have let other people down

It was especially helpful to use the wall to draw a picture of how he was feeling because this made it easier for him to compare his symptom wall with the one his mum filled in about how she thought Martin was feeling. She was so pleased to see that he was feeling better but realised that she missed some of the sad and guilty feelings he still has sometimes. Noticing the differences in the way they filled in their walls helped Martin and his mum to talk about some of the more invisible problems he still struggled with at times.

If there are fewer red and yellow (or circled and underlined) and more green (or unmarked) items on your last symptom wall that is very good news because it means that at least some of your symptoms have improved. Well done! You have been working really hard and that's a great result. When you are in the midst of depression you can feel very stuck and as if nothing can change. But the change in how you have marked up your charts shows at a glance that your efforts with your IPT-A team have helped you to become unstuck and to nudge your life towards the way you want it to be. This is a fantastic achievement and something to be really proud of.

As much as I hope that this book has helped you it's possible that, for some of you, many or even all of your symptoms will still be difficult despite all of the effort you have been making. If that's true for you, remember: ***it is not your fault*** and it is so impressive that you are still reading to try to find a way to get out of depression. That alone is something to be very proud of. There are several reasons why your symptom ratings might not have changed and taking some time to think about that might give you and your team some new ideas.

- Self-help approaches are most useful for treating mild depression, where you only have a few symptoms. If you have more than a few symptoms this approach might not be enough on its own to help to move things on. It is the treatment that hasn't been strong enough, not you.
- Self-help approaches are also most useful when you use them with other people – even though that sounds like a bit of a contradiction. If you have been using this approach on your own and your symptoms are still troublesome, it might mean you need a little more help to make the most of it. You have been encouraged throughout to involve an IPT-A team but

you might have found this very difficult to do, or perhaps your team has only been available for some of the time you needed them. If this approach has seemed to match your problems but you need more support to make the most of it ask your parents or carers to go with you to speak to your GP or local specialist service for children and young people (CAMHS) and ask to see an IPT-A therapist in your area who can help you. You can find information about going to specialist services for children and young people here: www.youthwellbeingdirectory.com and here www.mycamhschoices.org

- If IPT-A has seemed relevant to you and despite having support it hasn't been enough to help you with all of your difficulties, using IPT-A in combination with anti-depressant medication might work for you. This is another reason to talk to your GP or CAMHS about this treatment option. You can find more information about medication here: www.headmeds.org.uk
- Self-help approaches can be very effective, but for some people this may be a useful first step towards recovery, but more assistance is required. That is why there are several different treatments for depression, of various degrees of intensity depending on your particular needs. You can find information about all of the well-researched treatments for depression here: www.nice.org.uk/guidance/CG28/ifp/chapter/What-treatments-are-best-for-me.
- If self-help has not provided everything you need to overcome your depression don't give up hope. It definitely doesn't mean that you have failed. Looking at what has helped and what remains to be done can be really useful in helping you and your team to plan your next steps in this journey.

Patterns of change

Now let's look at what has happened to your symptoms in a little more detail. Change can happen in lots of different ways and understanding what has changed – and how – is useful as you start planning what to do next.

- It might be that all or most of your symptoms have improved. Great!
- You might have noticed that some symptoms aren't so troublesome while others remain difficult. Let's keep the good stuff going and think about what else is needed for the bits that are still stuck
- Some of the central symptoms that make lots of things difficult might have improved, e.g. being able to sleep at night, or no longer feeling life is not worth living. This might be a great relief and open the way for other changes to follow. Don't forget there are suggestions that can help with sleep in Appendix 4
- You might have noticed that you manage better in some areas of your life, such as at home, even if you still need some extra help to achieve the same in other areas, for example at school. Breaking down depression from whichever direction is a great start and puts you in a stronger position to sort out remaining difficulties
- **What do you notice about the way your symptoms have changed?**

Your goals

Looking at your symptoms is only one way to measure what IPT-A has helped you to do. You also set some goals that were personal to you and described how you wanted your life to be different.

These might have described skills you wanted to improve, relationships you wanted to be closer, interests you wanted to develop or a whole lot of other things. Many young people find that even when some of their symptoms haven't improved as much as they hoped they still find them easier to live with because other parts of their lives have changed and become easier. You might find that your goals capture what you have achieved over the last few weeks better than symptom ratings because each goal was chosen especially for you. Remember not every goal needs to be rated at 10 to be a success.

Exercise 13.3: Working towards your goals

- What progress have you made towards each of your goals?
- Have you achieved as much as you wanted in each of your goals?
- Have you achieved more than you expected in any of your goals?
- What effect has achieving this progress had on you?
- What effect has it had on the people around you?

Emily

Emily used a chart to track her progress towards her goals. When she picked her goals she made a note of the top score she hoped to achieve for each goal (6, 8, 10). She didn't expect to get to 10 on all of her goals so this helped make sure she gave herself credit when she achieved what she hoped to. At first she wasn't going to school at all and she hoped she would get there just over half the time. She did much better than she expected and was going to school almost every day at the end of IPT-A. She didn't talk to her friend Sarah very often when she was sad when she started IPT-A, although she did do it sometimes. She hoped she would be able to talk to her most times when she was feeling sad and she did really well and achieved her goal of 8, which meant she talked to Sarah a lot more than she had done. Emily also wanted to change her bedtime routine to help her to sleep and she hoped to do this every night. This proved to be more difficult than she had expected, especially when she was back at school and in contact with her friends more often. She was halfway to achieving her goal when she made her last rating. She was still pleased with how much she had achieved because that made it easier for her to go to school, which was her first goal. She planned to keep working on having a better bedtime routine. Her final goal chart looked like this:

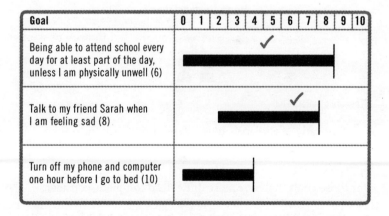

So far, you have focused on one main difficulty with another person or people. However, you might be facing several problems in your life at the same time. It's worth pausing now to consider whether the work you have done has had a positive effect on any other areas of your life, even though that wasn't your main aim. Remember the tangled cables in Chapter 4 (see pages 67–8)? By gently unravelling one cable from the knot, several other cables started to fall loose as well.

However, you may also have found that some of your goals changed along the way or were more difficult to achieve than you originally anticipated. This is not unusual and doesn't take away from the success you have achieved. Depression can make you focus on problems and overlook your successes. This may still be happening now. Give yourself the credit you are due and allow for the setbacks, which are a normal part of the process.

Exercise 13.4: Looking at goals that have been hard to reach

First ask yourself:

- Have any of the goals been more difficult to reach than you anticipated? Which ones?

For those goals that *were* more difficult to complete, consider:

- Would a more clearly defined goal have been a better guide?
- Was the goal realistic in the time you gave yourself?
- Might you get closer to achieving your goal if you had more time or support?

- Have new obstacles come up that you couldn't have predicted?
- Were any of the individual steps particularly difficult and, if so, in what way?
- Is this something you still want to achieve or is it no longer relevant?
- Have you achieved something else you did not expect?

Understanding the obstacles that are in your way more clearly is an important achievement in itself. All of the experience you have built up using IPT-A might help you to revisit some of your goals to make plans that will suit you better now. Discuss your options for adjusting your goals with your IPT-A team or therapist, and think about how you could continue to work towards the goals that are still meaningful for you. You have started a process of change, and that doesn't stop just because you have reached the final chapter of this book. All of the ideas you have read about and skills you have developed are still there for you to use as you continue with the task of recovering and remaining well. You have done the really tough bit of getting the ball rolling, now you want to keep it rolling in whichever direction you'd like.

Understanding Setbacks

Recovery is often not a simple and straightforward process. It doesn't simply follow a straight line from illness to wellness. Instead, it typically follows a more changeable course, with progress sometimes being interrupted by setbacks before getting back on course towards recovery again.

Over the past weeks, as you have worked through this book, you may have noticed progress towards your goals wobble from time to time. This is totally normal and sometimes it is the foundation for some of the most important lessons you will learn. Understanding setbacks when they happen and working out ways to pick yourself up again and carry on can be among the most valuable skills you can learn. The trick isn't to avoid the setback, the trick is to learn from it and carry on despite temporary delays along the way.

Take some time to think through any setbacks you faced while you have been using this book and try to remember what and who helped you to overcome the obstacles life has thrown in your path. These might have been times when your symptoms got worse or your goals seemed to move out of reach.

Exercise 13.5: Dealing with setbacks in progress

- What setbacks have your faced over recent weeks?
- How did you recover from those setbacks that didn't manage to stop you in your tracks?
- Who helped you to pick up after a setback and carry on?
- What did you learn from your setback and recovery?
- Which setbacks proved more difficult to manage?
- Did you learn anything from that?
- What or who did you need to get past that obstacle?
- Talk your ideas over with your IPT-A team so that they know what helped as well
- Ask if they have noticed ways in which you have been resilient – 'bounced back' – that you might have overlooked

If you find a visual reminder more helpful, write your strengths in the balloons that lift you up and your difficulties in the weight that drags you down. Use the diagram in the online folder.

Involving other people

You might have noticed that I am quite keen on you involving other people, like your IPT-A team or your IPT-A therapist, in helping you to feel better! Involving other people doesn't do anything to take away from your achievement. The fact that you could take the risk to let other people in to help you is a huge achievement in itself. Depression will do everything it can to stop you doing that and if you managed not to listen to its bad advice even some of the time you have reason to be very proud. That really isn't an easy thing to do. By working together you tapped into the potential to achieve real progress.

Exercise 13.6: The role of involving other people in your recovery

These are particularly important questions to talk over with your IPT-A team, who can continue to offer you support in the future. Write your answers down in your notebook or online journal to remind you to go on involving other people in the future.

- How has involving other people contributed to you feeling better?

- What difference has joining forces with your IPT-A team made to how you manage your depression and work on relationship problems?
- How will involving people in the future help to keep you well?
- Which positive routines do you and your team need to keep going?
- How have the members of your team felt about being involved?
- What do the people in your life need to know about your goals and the things that help you to be of as much help to you as they can?
- What do they need to know about the possibility of depression returning in the future to help you most effectively? See Appendix 2 for information about depression for friends and family.
- Do new people need to be added to your original IPT-A team to help you now and into the future? Who are they? How can they help? Can existing team members help you to recruit them?

Will depression come back?

If you are feeling better you probably don't want to think much more about depression. The idea that depression could come back into your life again in the future, if you face extra stress or difficult times, is probably quite frightening. This might mean you try to avoid feelings that remind you of being depressed, like feeling sad or irritable. However, as we saw in Chapter 8 (see pages 140–156) being able to think and talk about your feelings is an important part of being well. It is also very important to be able to distinguish feelings that come up from time to time, like sadness or disappointment, from depression. In Chapter 2 we looked at all of the symptoms of depression – in your body, your feelings, how you think and how you are with other people. You now understand that these symptoms are different to a passing low mood and they last for much longer. In Chapter 8 we also looked at the many different feelings that are part of life and you have worked hard on becoming more aware of how you feel, which helps you to understand how to respond and to tell other people about what you are going through. As you look to the future, it will be very useful for you to be able to tolerate and talk about your feelings as well as pinpointing early signals that depression may be coming back.

One of the things we know about depression is that it is an illness many people experience more than once. Unfortunately this is especially true if it first appeared in your life during adolescence. If you have ever had a sports injury you might notice that, even though you can play or run again, you have to be a little more careful with the part that was injured because it remains vulnerable to flaring up again, which will make the problems come back. It is similar with depression. It isn't something that is guaranteed to come back but it will be important for you and your team to know what to do if you pick up on the early warning signs that depression is on its way back because then you can get the help you need quickly to stop depression gathering momentum. It is very understandable, that just as you are, hopefully, starting to feel better you won't want to think about the possibility of becoming depressed again but while you may not be able to control whether or not depression comes back into your life again, you *can* influence the impact it will have.

As you plan for your future, it is very important that you and the people close to you are tuned in to the early warning signs that depression is coming back. What do you remember about

335

depression starting this time? As you look back, you might notice changes and signs that you didn't realise at the time were hints that depression was on its way, e.g. your sleep getting messed up or not being able to throw off a bad mood. If your understanding of the early warning signs forewarns you and your team you can put up a defence much more quickly.

Over and over again in this book we have used different perspectives to understand more about the situations you find yourself in. Watching out for depression is no different. It is really useful to ask the people close to you to tell you what they noticed when you started to become depressed. It's possible they will notice a subtle change that you might be less aware of, e.g. it takes you longer to answer text messages. Writing your early warning list together gives you a much better chance of covering all the angles.

Exercise 13.7: Early warning signs of depression

You have been using the symptom wall each week to help you to track your journey out of depression, now use it to describe the early warning signs that depression might be coming back. Use a blank copy of the wall to highlight the symptoms you would notice first if depression started coming back – I have used an exclamation mark for your signs in the example below, but you can use anything that will grab your attention.

Show your team members this picture of early warning signs of depression and ask them to highlight any symptoms they would notice if depression starts coming back for you. I have used a star to show the different signs that your team might notice. Don't forget you can both use the empty boxes at the bottom to add any signs that aren't on the grid.

Discuss what you can do to interrupt these symptoms as quickly as possible with your team, e.g. go back over the sleep advice in Appendix 4, reread Chapter 8 on recognising and talking about your feelings, let someone know when you are feeling sad and ask them to help you to do the things you normally enjoy, be kind to yourself etc.

Feeling sad /	Feel tired a lot	Can't get to sleep	Not eating
Nothing is fun anymore	Wish I was dead	Feel guilty and blame myself for things	Problems with friends
Can't think clearly /	Don't want to see people	Wake up early and can't get back to sleep	Feel bored
Problems at home	Sleep too much	Feel irritable	Feel restless and on edge
Feeling bad about myself	Can't get going ✳	Eat too much	Difficulties at school ✳
Wake up during the night /	Feel hopeless	Forgetful	Feel I have let other people down
Scratch my arms	*Cry a lot*		

Making a plan

Throughout IPT-A you haven't just been thinking about symptoms of depression, you have also been thinking about the stresses and problems with other people that can trigger symptoms or make them worse. Try to think ahead for the next six months or so – can you think of any stresses or changes that are coming up that might be difficult for you? These might include problems that you are already working on, e.g. arguments with parents or friends or new stresses that are coming up, e.g. moving out of home, going to college or university, exams. Ask your team if they can think of any stresses that you might not have thought of and add them to the list of things to look out for. A copy of a form you could use to gather this information is available online. Use this to remind yourself and your team of the times and situations when you might need some extra support and help to keep good routines going, e.g. sleeping well, eating well, seeing your friends, taking regular breaks.

What to do

Use the table below to make a plan for what you and your team can do when you hit predictable or unpredictable stresses. Think about who can help to reduce the stress you are facing or help you to manage stress that you can't avoid, e.g. by helping you to make difficult decisions, listening to you to help you understand why you are feeling the way you do, giving you practical support or simply being around so you don't feel alone in facing problems.

A copy of this table is available in the online resources folder.

Exercise 13.8

Who can help?	What can they do?	How would this help?
	1. 2. 3.	
	1. 2. 3.	
	1. 2. 3.	
	1. 2. 3.	

Professional help

There may be times when it will be important to ask for more help than your team alone can offer. Many different professionals are trained to provide expert advice and help with exactly the kinds of problems we have been talking about in this book. How will you know if you need to ask for professional help, such as from your GP or CAMHS? Signs that professional help would be useful are:

- Your symptoms have lasted for more than two weeks
- You can't go to school
- You feel like hurting yourself
- You are taking anti-depressant medication
- You don't feel you have all the support you need from your team
- Your team don't feel they can give you all the support you need

Take time now to discuss these signs with your team. It can be difficult to make plans when you feel stressed or low. Making a plan with your team now means that the help you may need in the future will be available to you as quickly as possible and depression will be shown the door before it gets a chance to settle in. Add contact details for your GP and local CAMHS service to the team contact list you created when we got started with IPT-A and you can be reassured that it is there for you to use if you ever need to in the future. Add a note to remind yourself who can help you to get in touch with professional services if you need to in the future.

If you have been using anti-depressant medication it is important to continue to take it for a few more months, even if you no longer have symptoms of depression. This helps to protect your recovery and doesn't mean you are dependent on it. Stopping medication too soon can make you vulnerable to depression coming back more quickly and can create a short-term but unpleasant reaction. Any decisions about changing your medication should be discussed with your GP or a psychiatrist at CAMHS first to make sure you have all the information you need to make the best decision for you. Include their details in your contacts list.

Exercise 13.9: Add contact details for the professionals who can help you

As you finish this chapter and move on to the next stage of your story, be sure to take the key messages of this approach with you.

- Depression is a treatable illness. It is not your fault and there are lots of ways you and the people around you can change its impact in your life.
- Talking to other people and telling them how you feel really can transform situations that feel stuck and hopeless.
- Recovery is often punctuated with setbacks. Don't be afraid of them or to ask for help to get going again. Learning that you can bounce back is going to be one of your greatest achievements.
- You have done brilliantly to get here. It is so impressive that you kept going despite everything that has tried to stop you. You have so many reasons to be proud of yourself. Keep going!

Appendix 1:

Useful information about Interpersonal Psychotherapy for Adolescents (IPT-A)

IPT-A is a treatment for young people with depression, which looks at your relationships with the people around you. It is important to pay attention to our relationships because how we feel often has a lot to do with how we are getting on with other people. Sometimes feeling down is a response to what is going on in our relationships and at other times our relationships become more difficult when we are low and have lost interest in the people close to us. IPT-A helps you to make sense of the difficulties you are experiencing and to understand how your relationships with other people contribute to how you feel. By helping you to sort out the main problems that trip you up with other people we expect your mood and interest to improve too.

IPT-A is especially helpful with the kinds of things young people often find difficult when they are depressed:

Not getting on with an important person in your life: No relationship is perfect, but sometimes an important relationship at home or at school can get really stuck in disagreements or

343

arguments and it becomes very upsetting to be part of. You might start to feel hopeless about finding a way to sort it out.

Changes in your life that affect your routines and the people around you: Life changes all the time and you can suddenly find yourself in a situation that is unfamiliar and perhaps frightening, like when you change schools, fall out with friends or families breaking up. When this happens it can feel like a whole new set of challenges comes along and you might not be sure how to cope with it all.

When someone important in your life dies: It is entirely natural to feel sad when someone we care about dies. Sometimes this is so difficult that we struggle to adjust to life without that person and it is as if we put life on hold because we miss them so much, and this makes it really hard to be close to the other people who are around us.

Difficulty in starting or keeping relationships going: Some-times relationships are difficult because of what is missing, for example not having enough people around us or not feeling as close to other people as we would like. Not having someone to spend time with or to turn to when you are feeling sad, or even when you are happy, can make life feel very difficult and lonely and might lead you to feel overwhelmed by having to do every-thing on your own.

What does IPT-A involve?

Everyone's therapy will be a bit different. Sometimes IPT-A is used with a trained therapist. This book will guide you through the main ideas and how to use them with the support of your family and friends. It can help you between sessions if you are working with a therapist too.

How long will it last?

If you are seeing a therapist IPT-A is usually offered over twelve to sixteen sessions. Your parents or carers will also be invited to three additional sessions, which you might also want to join. Your therapy sessions will be weekly and will last for fifty minutes. If you are using this book you can work through it at your own pace but giving yourself three or four months to make the changes that are suggested is a reasonable estimate of how long this might take. You will be involving your IPT-A team at every step.

Getting started

Many young people find it difficult to talk about their problems, and it is important that your IPT-A team show you that they can be trusted, and can help you manage if you talk about things which upset you or about which you feel embarrassed.

Talking openly about yourself, perhaps for the first time, can feel difficult and you may be worried about what your IPT-A team thinks about you. Your IPT-A team will be interested in how you are getting on with using this approach together and will help you to make sense of any worries you may have about getting started. They should give you the feeling that they know that this can be difficult and that they are interested in understanding what life is like for you.

Your team should make it very clear that they are interested in hearing about what is and what isn't working for you and your relationship with them. If difficulties do arise your team should take these seriously and find a way of working them out with you.

Getting a picture of what you need

Your team will need to get as good a picture as they can of what you are finding difficult in your life and how this is affecting you and people close to you. You will be asked to discuss some questions in each chapter, but you only need to give as much information as you feel comfortable with. Many people find that as the process gets going they are able to talk more openly, and in the early stages you shouldn't find yourself under pressure to say more than you want.

In the first chapters of this book you will be asked both about your symptoms and also about the people in your life. This is because IPT-A is interested in understanding how difficulties in your relationships may have contributed to your depression. Your team will be asked to help you to think about what is going well and what isn't going so well in your relationships to help you to decide which relationships it would be most useful to focus on for the next few weeks.

How will you know that it is working?

Each week you will complete a symptom wall and rate how close you feel you are to achieving your personal goals. Your team will be able to do the same every few weeks and you will talk about your responses. These will give you both a better idea of the sorts of problems you have as well as how difficult these are for you. By completing the symptom wall each week it will help you and your team see what progress you are making. By including your teams' thoughts about this you will also see how other people understand what it is like for you right now. This is very useful, because not everyone makes progress at the same rate. If the symptom wall show that IPT-A isn't helping as much as you hoped it gives you and your team a chance to think about why this might be and how you can work together to improve the way IPT-A helps you with your problems.

Once you and your team have gained a clearer picture of the relationship difficulties that are connected with your symptoms, you will agree on the main areas that IPT-A will help you to focus on. Bearing in mind that you want to feel better as soon as possible, your team will also help you to think about what you want out of using IPT-A and to identify realistic goals. You will track your progress towards these goals each week and your team will support you in working towards them at a pace that is right for you and will help you to keep going if you experience any setbacks along the way. You can find more information about using questionniares and goals at www.minded.org.uk (Type 'David Trickey' into the search box to find some very helpful sessions).

How can your team help you?

Your team will help in a variety of ways that will include:

- Being active and helping you to do more enjoyable things
- Thinking through the questions in each chapter with you
- Helping you to keep focused on the relationship problem(s) you agreed to work on
- Helping you to develop new relationships that can provide the support you need
- Supporting you in making positive changes in your life
- Helping you to understand how you are feeling and find ways to tell other people about it so that they can help you or to get back into routines that you used to enjoy but that have been

more difficult to keep up with when you have been feeling low

Not everyone in your team will do all of these things. You will select your team members to make sure you have different kinds of support when you need it.

Medication and IPT-A

It is quite common to use IPT-A alongside medications such as anti-depressants, if you have a lot of symptoms or they have lasted for a long time. For some young people this may be more helpful than receiving either treatment alone. You should discuss this with your parents/carers and a medically trained professional, like your GP or a child and adolescent psychiatrist who will help you to make the best decision for you. You can find more information about mental health medication at www.headmeds.org.uk.

You can find more information about IPT-A at www.iptuk.net and at www.minded.org.uk (Type IPT-A into the search box).

Appendix 2:

Information for family and friends

Adolescence is often a complicated and confusing time for the young person going through it and for friends and family who watch all the changes that come with it. Relationships change, sometimes getting closer and sometimes more distant, and this can be unsettling and challenging for everyone involved. It is not surprising that, in the midst of all of this change, depression can be overlooked or thought of as being 'typical teenage behaviour'.

However, depression is more than being a moody teen, and living with a young person with depression may also leave you feeling frightened, frustrated and confused. It can be difficult to understand what they are going through and so it is important for families and friends of a young person who is depressed to have good, clear information about depression. Knowing about this illness will help you to support the young person and deal with your own feelings, so that you can work towards recovery as a team.

The first step in tackling depression is to know what you are dealing with. Without understanding, you might battle with each other rather than depression.

One simple way to learn more about living with depression is to watch these two short films. The first short animation describes how you can help if someone you know is living with depression and in the second film, three young people who have experienced depression describe what is was like for them. Watching these films with the young person you know who has depression and talking about them afterwards can be a helpful way of understanding the impact this illness is having on your lives:

www.youtube.com/watch?v=2VRRx7Mtep8

www.bbc.co.uk/education/clips/zxqcd2p

What does it feel like to be depressed?

Depression is more than being sad. It changes how young people feel, how they see themselves and other people, how they feel in their changing bodies, how they plan, respond and manage their daily routines.

You may have noticed that the young person you are concerned about:

- is unhappy or irritable most of the time
- has lost interest in things and people they used to enjoy
- talks about feeling guilty, ashamed or worthless
- looks anxious and agitated
- has lost confidence in themselves
- has problems concentrating and making decisions
- isn't looking after themselves as well as usual
- is tearful and easily upset
- talks about life not being worth living or wanting to die
- has lost their appetite, or eats more than usual
- is forgetful

- sleeps more than usual but is still tired all the time
- is not coping with things that used to be manageable

All these symptoms are difficult to live with and can be upsetting to see in someone you care about. These symptoms make it difficult to be around other people, and young people with depression often struggle to keep their normal routines going and to pick up on the new opportunities that are opening up for them at this time in their lives. It is important to try to be patient, and to understand that this kind of change is a common effect of depression and not a deliberate attack on you or your relationship.

Why do people get depressed?

The reasons why some young people get depressed are not always obvious. Some young people are more vulnerable to depression if they have been depressed before or if they are physically unwell, and the illness can run in families. Depression can also be triggered when young people face big changes or losses, such as relationship problems, family break-ups, changing school, becoming a young parent or bereavement. Feeling lonely and on the outside with peers is also strongly linked to depression in young people. Around twice as many teenagers experience depression compared to young children, because during adolescence life and the relationships we have with other people, family and friends, become more complicated. A teenager's brain works differently to an adult's and this means feelings are processed differently and the impact of other people is felt more intensely. The changes in teenagers' brains are fantastic for preparing young people to go out into the world but can also make some young people vulnerable to emotional disorders while these changes are a work in progress. This is one of the reasons why 50 per cent of lifetime mental illness starts by age fourteen and 75 per cent has started by the mid-twenties, when adolescence ends. To understand more about the changes that are happening in teenagers' brains, watch these films:

www.ted.com/talks/sarah_jayne_blakemore_the_mysterious_workings_of_the_adolescent_brain?language=en

www.pbs.org/wgbh/pages/frontline/shows/teenbrain/view/

What is useful to know about depression?

Depression is a very common mental health problem – it affects around 3 per cent of children and 8 per cent of young people over fourteen years old. Depression is identified twice as often in teenage girls as in teenage boys, although we suspect that depression in boys is often missed or overlooked when there are attention-grabbing behaviour problems. Depression is much more unpleasant than the low mood we all experience at times. It lasts longer and interferes with day-to-day life and relationships. As severity increases so do the range of symptoms experienced and the impact depression has on schoolwork, family and social life, all of which become very difficult to manage.

Young people typically become depressed for a period of time – usually about four to six months – and then recover, but an episode of depression can last longer than this. Depression also comes back for about half of the young people who have had it before. With support, and in some cases treatment, recovery from depression can also happen more quickly, and young people can develop skills to prevent or limit the impact of future episodes. It isn't possible to just 'snap out of' depression, but it is possible to help people to recover from this illness. This is important during adolescence because, as you will have seen in the films about adolescent brain development, the patterns developed in adolescence shape future experience so it is important to tackle the patterns depression promotes as quickly as possible.

What treatments are available?

Depression is treatable. Treatments include self-help (which really means a team effort), 'talking therapies' and medication. These different approaches can be used separately or together. Self-help is most useful when a young person has mild depression, but adolescents should not be left to try to sort this out for themselves – having a team of caring family and friends is an invaluable part of helping a young person to help themselves to feel better. If depression is moderate or severe, talking therapy and medication have been shown to be helpful for many young people.

The ideas behind Interpersonal Psychotherapy for adolescents with depression (IPT-A) can be used to guide assisted self-help because most of the ideas involve the young person and the people who are in their lives. That means you really can help the young person you care about to feel better. In IPT-A, depression is treated by tackling the difficulties that often crop up in relationships, focusing on those that are commonly experienced when a young person faces significant change, conflict, loss, or becomes isolated. Understanding and disentangling the connections between depression and what is happening in the young person's relationships makes improvements in both more likely. Family and friends can make a very important contribution in this approach to the young person's recovery.

Anti-depressants can be effective if the depression is moderate or severe or goes on for a long time without change. They can help to reduce symptoms and to make it easier to join in with other people and to cope better, so that the young person can start to enjoy life and deal with their problems effectively again. Anti-depressant medications are not addictive and are designed to be taken over months and sometimes years, and the young person should continue to take them for some time after their symptoms have improved to help protect against future risk. Anti-depressant medications should always be closely monitored by professionals and parents or carers to help young people to use them safely and as prescribed. It can be very helpful for the person to have the support of the people around them to persevere with treatment so that they get as much benefit from it as possible.

Many people will recover from depression without active treatment, but this route to recovery can take much longer and is less likely to end in success if the depression is moderate or severe. It is in everyone's interests for depression to be treated as quickly and effectively as possible.

How can you help someone who is depressed?

Try to be a good listener – even if you hear the same thing several times or not very much at all from a silent young person. Try not to judge or rush to solve problems. It may be too soon to talk about solutions and stay focused on one subject at a time. It may be difficult for them to concentrate.

Encourage them to tell you how they feel and check that you have understood correctly. Being misunderstood is a painful experience for us all and it is better to check when you aren't sure than to try and mind-read. Admitting when you don't understand, and showing that you are interested in learning more, is more helpful than guessing and getting it wrong.

Only give advice if asked for it or if you have checked that they are ready to listen to your ideas. If you think you can see the problem that is behind the depression, you could offer to work with them to find a solution.

Sometimes depressed adolescents will need you to make decisions for them because they don't feel able to do it for themselves. This won't always be true and it is important to be open and clear about what decisions are being made and why and to give the young person an opportunity to be as much a part of the process as they can.

Spend time with them and support them in doing activities they might enjoy. Encourage them to keep going with helpful routines, such as going to school, spending time with friends, taking regular gentle exercise and eating well. This may be achieved slowly so be prepared to be patient and encouraging, noticing small successes as they gradually build up.

Help them to establish a wind-down routine before going to bed that includes switching off phones, computers and tablets an hour before going to sleep. This is a real challenge for most young people and they often need help to manage this important change in their routine.

If the young person with depression you are concerned about is quiet and withdrawn, let them know that you are available when they want to talk but also that you recognise this isn't easy for them. Lots of questions can feel overwhelming, especially when they don't have the answers you are both looking for. Don't underestimate the value of knowing you are there for them, even if nothing is said.

Recognise that your ways of relating to each other might change while the young person is depressed. Spending less time with the whole family and more time with friends or one family member at a time is normal and healthy in adolescence. They are likely to need more from the people around them than they can give back for a while. This will change again when the depression lifts. You can help by being flexible around these changes.

Remind them that depression is treatable and that it's not their fault that they are depressed. Be on their anti-depressant team.

If they are irritable, it is helpful to slow down and try not to react. Listen for opportunities to acknowledge their feelings and comments. At these times, conversations about important decisions or issues are unlikely to be productive. Plan to discuss important issues some other (specific) time, and make sure to return to the discussion at the time you've agreed to. This helps to build trust and encourages the young person to talk when they feel able to.

Take them seriously if they talk about feeling hopeless or harming themselves. Many young people with depression think about dying or harming themselves as a way of coping with difficult feelings. A smaller proportion of young people plan to act on these thoughts, but even if they don't, the thoughts themselves are frightening and can make people feel very isolated. Talking about them does not put ideas into the person's head and it can be reassuring to know that someone will listen and give support, without over-reacting, when it is most needed. Watch this film about a young person with depression who describes how self-harm was part of her experience to learn more about what can help:

www.bbc.co.uk/education/clips/zhjgkqt

IPT-A will provide several opportunities for you to help the young person you know to recover from their depression. They will be developing their own personal story of depression and they will need your help to do that. This will help you both to understand their experience and to talk about it in a way that you will both find useful. They may ask you to help in developing this story, perhaps by providing information or by talking about your relationship. Accept this invitation and join in the exercises described in this book.

Some of the exercises in this book will be about using support more effectively; others can be used to sort out difficulties between you both, if your relationship has suffered while they have been depressed. Neither of you is being blamed. Depression is difficult to live with and puts even the best relationships under strain. Sorting out relationship difficulties can make an important contribution to helping someone recover from depression, and you can make a valuable contribution to this process.

Be ready for a relapse

It is tempting to try to forget depression as soon as it lifts. However, this is an illness many young people will have to face more than once. The best way to handle the risk of it coming back is to know what to do before it happens.

As your friend or relative recovers and is able to think and plan more clearly, the self-help guidance will prompt them to plan what to do if depression returns in the future. They will be asked to create a list of early warning signs. You will both have different points of view, so together you can create a more comprehensive list than either of you could do on your own. This will serve as a safety net for your friend or relative and for your relationship. The list should also include what you will each do in response to these signs to interrupt the depression as quickly as possible next time. Follow this plan if the need arises. Templates that will help you to structure your plan are available online to print out and complete together.

Create a support team that includes family, friends, and others the young person who has been depressed feels confident to include. When depression is kept secret, it is made stronger. Reverse the process by making sure the necessary people are well informed and ready to act when required, and you will help to protect your friend or relative now and in the future.

Appendix 3

Feeling sad	Feel tired a lot	Can't get to sleep	Not eating
Nothing is fun anymore	Wish I was dead	Feel guilty and blame myself for things	Problems with friends
Can't think clearly	Don't want to see people	Wake up early and can't get back to sleep	Feel bored
Problems at home	Sleep too much	Feel irritable	Feel restless and on edge
Feeling bad about myself	Can't get going	Eat too much	Difficulties at school
Wake up during the night	Feel hopeless	Forgetful	Feel I have let other people down

Appendix 4:

Improving your sleep

- Cut out caffeine and stimulants (caffeinated or energy drinks, tea, coffee, chocolate, tobacco) after lunchtime. Generally try to keep these to a minimum or cut them out totally if you are having sleep problems – they make your body clock's job much harder
- Try to work with your body clock rather than against it. This means trying to set a regular bedtime during the week and not sleeping at totally different times over the weekend
- Ask for help from your parent or carer. It's frustrating but going to bed around 10pm rather than midnight, is actually a good idea and adolescents who do have been shown to function better and remember more the next day than adolescents who don't
- Have a warm milky drink and/or a warm bath before going to bed
- Switch off all digital screens (and I really mean all of them) – TV, mobile phones, laptops, tablets, game consoles – one hour before you go to bed. I know that sounds like the worst news, but the light sends your brain a mixed message and makes it think it is time to be awake. Ask your parent or carer to look after them until morning if you find this difficult to do
- Go one step further and leave your phone in another room – even if the light is off late messages can interrupt sleep and it

is tempting to switch on and check if you wake in the middle of the night. Count how many messages you send or receive and how many times you check your mobile phone *after you go to bed*. Every time you are sending a wake-up call to your brain

- If you really can't sleep get up and go to another room – not the one where you left your mobile phone! Do something quiet and relaxing like listening to music until you feel sleepy and tired and then go back to bed and try again
- Try not to sleep into the middle of the day at the weekend – your body clock won't know if it is coming or going

Appendix 5

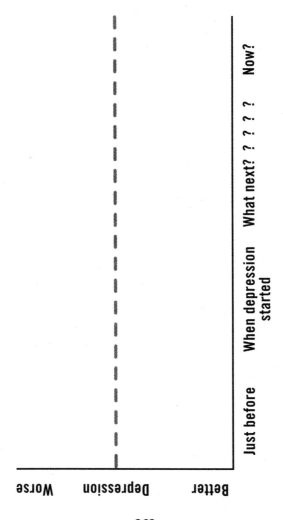

Appendix 6

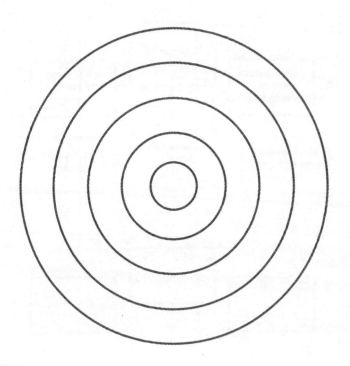

Appendix 7

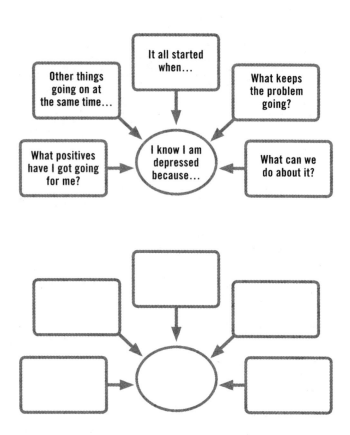

Appendix 8

Index